Impression Manag[ement] in Organizations

MW00472607

Impression management – our ways of controlling what others think of us – is central to our working lives. So central, in fact, that we often use it automatically. *Impression Management in Organizations* is the first integrated study of this often overlooked aspect of organizational life. Among other topics, the authors discuss:

- psychological, organizational and communications-oriented approaches to impression management
- our ways of building, enhancing and protecting our reputation at work
- the influence of impression management on recruitment and selection procedures, and on HRM generally

Covering theory, measurement and current business practice, the authors illustrate the practical effects of impression management on organizational life and companies' performance through research studies and examples drawn from recent business history.

Impression Management in Organizations will make an important addition to the library of any organizational psychologist and human resource manager. It will also appeal to anyone interested in the dynamics of organizational politics and in the exercise of power and influence strategies.

Paul Rosenfeld is Personnel Research Psychologist at the US Navy Personnel Research and Development Center, San Diego, California; **Robert A. Giacalone** is Associate Professor of Management at the University of Richmond, Virginia; and **Catherine A. Riordan** is Professor of Psychology and Director of Management Systems at the University of Missouri–Rolla.

Impression Management in Organizations

Theory, Measurement, Practice

Paul Rosenfeld, Robert A. Giacalone, and
Catherine A. Riordan

London and New York

First published 1995
by Routledge
11 New Fetter Lane, London EC4P 4EE

Simultaneously published in the USA and Canada
by Routledge
29 West 35th Street, New York, NY 10001

© 1995 Paul Rosenfeld, Robert A. Giacalone and Catherine A. Riordan

Typeset in Times by Solidus (Bristol) Limited

Printed and bound in Great Britain by
Biddles Ltd, Guildford and King's Lynn

British Library Cataloguing in Publication Data
A catalogue record for this book is available from the British Library.

Library of Congress Cataloguing in Publication Data
A catalogue record for this book has been requested.

ISBN 0–415–12679–7 (hbk)
ISBN 0–415–10332–0 (pbk)

— Contents

— *Illustrations*

FIGURES

TABLES

BOXES

— Series editor's preface

The rapid, far-reaching, and continuing changes of recent years have brought about a situation where understanding the psychology of individuals and teams is of prime importance in work settings. Organizational structures have shifted radically to the point where individual managers and professionals have far greater autonomy, responsibility, and accountability. Organizations seek to reduce central control and to "empower" individual employees. Those employees combine in teams that are frequently cross-functional and project-based rather than hierarchical in their construction. The traditional notion of careers is changing; increasingly, the expectation is that an individual's career is less likely to be within a single organization, which has implications for how organizations will command loyalty and commitment in the future. The full impact of the information technology revolution is finally being felt, with all the consequences this has for the nature of work and the reactions of those doing it.

The capacity of people to cope with the scale and speed of these changes has become a major issue, and the literature on work stress bears testimony to this. The belief in the importance of individuals' cognitive abilities and personality make-up in determining what they achieve and how they can contribute to team work has been demonstrated in the explosive growth in organizations' use of psychometric tests and related procedures. Perhaps more than ever before, analyzing and understanding the experience of work from a psychological perspective is necessary to achieve the twin goals of effective performance and quality of working life. Unfortunately, it is the latter of these that all too often seems to be overlooked in the concern to create competitive, performance-driven, or customer-focused cultures within companies.

It is no coincidence that the rise in the study of business ethics and increasing concern over issues of fairness paralleled many of the organizational changes of the 1980s and 90s. Ultimately, an imbalance between the aims and needs of the employees and the aims and needs of the organization is self-defeating. One of the widely recognized needs for the years ahead is for a greater emphasis on innovation rather than on simply reacting to pressures, yet psychological research and theory indicate that innovation is much more likely to take place where individuals feel secure enough to take the risks involved, and where organizational reward systems encourage experimentation and exploration – which they have signally failed to do in the past decade. Seeking to help organizations realize the potential of their workforce in a mutually enhancing way is the business challenge psychology has to meet.

The aim of the *Essential Business Psychology* series is to interpret and explain people's work behavior in the context of a continually evolving pattern of change, and to do so from the perspective of occupational and organizational psychology. The books draw together academic research and practitioner experience, relying on empirical studies, practical examples, and case studies to communicate their ideas. Hopefully, the reader will find that they provide a succinct summary of accumulated knowledge and how it can be applied. The themes of some of the books cover traditional areas of occupational psychology, while others will focus on topics that cut across some of these boundaries, tackling subjects that are of growing interest and prominence. The intended readership of the series is quite broad; whilst they are most directly relevant for practitioners, consultants and students in HR and occupational psychology, much of what they deal with is increasingly the concern of managers and students of management more generally. Although the books share common aim and series heading, they have not been forced into a rigid stylistic format. In keeping with the times, the authors have had a good deal of autonomy in deciding how to organize and present their work. I think all of them have done an excellent job; I hope you think so too.

Clive Fletcher

— *Acknowledgments*

The publication of this book renews our commitment to an area of interest that began when we met as graduate students in the late 1970s. It was in those days at the State University of New York at Albany that we first formulated the idea of applying the impression management perspective to organizational life. Although the challenges of the moment (e.g., getting our dissertations done!) initially prevented us from acting upon these ideas, our resolution to develop this area now brings forth this book borne of a notion that the theatrical metaphor is as appropriate to the workplace as it is to daily social interaction.

As with our past works, we wish to thank our families, friends, and colleagues for their love, support, and encouragement. Being good impression managers, we wish to apologize for ignoring them during the working weekends, long nights, and missed meals necessary to get this book done!

In particular, our sincerest thanks to our parents, Abraham and Judes Rosenfeld, Frank and Theresa Giacalone, and Beverly and John Riordan. We are also greatly indebted to Mary Sellen, our favorite librarian; Karen, Andrew, Joshua, and Elizabeth Giacalone who make the work worthwhile; and to Phil Thompson and Amy and Katie Riordan for keeping it all in perspective.

Special thanks are reserved for some people who helped along the way. We thank Clive Fletcher for asking us to do this project and for his very positive feedback throughout it. We also are very pleased to have this book published by Routledge. They have done a great job keeping the book and its authors on schedule. We greatly appreciate Marcy Scott's clerical skills and dedication to her work that helped us to see this project through to completion. Lance Haynes' comments on the entire manuscript and interest in the project were also very helpful.

We owe a special thanks to our colleagues, students, friends, and relatives for their influence on our thinking, careers, lives, and impression management skills: Renatte Adler, David Alderton, Jamie Archer, Jon Beard, Stephanie Booth-Kewley, Steve Butnik, Pat Callahan, Linda Doherty, Jack E. Edwards, Dafna Eylon, John Fulton, Jean Henry, Dave Hoch, Laura Jarvis, John Kantor, Steve Knouser, Farrell Scott Malkis, Carol Newell, Steve Payne, Hinda G. Pollard, Sharon Scott, Richard Sorenson, Jerry Stevens, Jim Tedeschi, Dick Teevan, Marie Thomas, Pat Thomas, Steve Thomas, the 1994 St Louis Leader Sisters, the Shanske family, and the Siglers. Finally, we thank the students who took "Seminar in Impression Management" at the California School of Professional Psychology during the Fall 1994 semester. As a reward for having read many of our past writings, they get a chance to "bask" in the present one: Jeannette Bongiorni, Sari Brody, Lisa Cree, Kerri-Jo Cooper, Judy Heinrich, Ian Rosen, and Angie Schinkel.

Paul Rosenfeld
San Diego, California

Bob Giacalone
Richmond, Virginia

Catherine Riordan
Rolla, Missouri

1 Impression management in organizations An introduction

CHANGING JOBS: IMPRESSION MANAGEMENT IN THE RISE OF APPLE COMPUTERS

One of the better known business figures over the past 20 years has been Steven Jobs, a cofounder of Apple Computers. While producing the first personal computer and the remarkable subsequent success of his company alone might have led to Steven Jobs' notoriety, it was his use of *impression management* that contributed to him being both famous and infamous.

Press accounts of Jobs' life and career have consistently made reference to how his appearance and behavior created a very distinctive public image. As a way of introducing you to organizational impression management, we rely on a biography by Lee Butcher (1989), to analyze Jobs' public identity and give you an idea of what impression management is, and how it is critical to success in the business world, and to understanding behavior in the workplace.

One thing is clear about Steven Jobs: he did not initially use impression management to create an image of someone who would "fit in." In both his early life and with the image of Apple products, he seemed to resist what, as we shall see in Chapters 2 and 3, are often common goals of impression management: to be liked by others and to be seen as normal. Jobs seemed to thrive on being perceived as "strange." Though the son of devoted parents, Jobs "wanted to look and feel like an orphan who had spent a few years bumming around the country, hopping on freight trains or riding in eighteen-wheelers" (Butcher, 1989, p. 41).

Jobs did not change his haggard appearance even when he took his first job at the Atari Computer Company. "While at Atari, Jobs was following Ehret's mucusless diet, eating yogurt and fruit. He believed that the diet eliminated the need for bathing. Others disagreed" (Butcher, 1989, p. 49).

While we don't know exactly why Jobs really did some of these weird things, we do know that he was devoted to and very effective at managing the impression of being an eccentric. Although it is possible that his strange behaviors may have been the result of being oblivious to reality, we think that Jobs, like many up-and-comers in contemporary organizations, was actively trying to create a particular identity. Consider the following example of a Steven Jobs job interview. In recruiting prospective employees, he would take them to lunch at a nearby restaurant. "Often Jobs would throw his dirty bare feet up on a table and attack them mercilessly" (Butcher, 1989, p. 119). Jobs clearly seems to have been using impression management to create an identity of a peculiar nonconformist.

Even when Jobs was desperate for start-up money for Apple Computers, he refused to conform to even the most basic standards for making a positive impression in the business world. "Thin, somewhat grubby, with long hair, he ran around either in sandals, or barefoot. It was not an image likely to instill confidence in money men accustomed to dealing with older people wearing ties, suits and shoes" (Butcher, 1989, p. 68).

As Apple became more successful, Jobs' appearance and brazen self-confidence offended a lot of people on Wall Street. Jobs had two qualities that allowed him to overcome these deficits, at least in part: he was persistent and had a knack for convincing people he was smart and competent. After hounding an advertising representative Jobs wanted to represent Apple, he got him to visit the operation. The representative said that within three minutes he knew that Jobs "was an incredibly smart young man" (Butcher, 1989, p. 82). This ability to manage an impression of great intellect may have been responsible for Jobs' success at persuading others. Later in his career, Jobs is said to have "pulled off an almost impossible deal when he convinced a software supplier to accept a small fee instead of royalties. The supplier said Jobs made it seem that he was providing a service to humanity. 'He made me feel like I should pay him for letting him use my software,' the supplier said" (Butcher, 1989, p. 219).

Jobs' success demonstrates that though physical appearance and other nonverbal cues are important when we present ourselves to others, they can often be overcome by skillful verbal impression management. Jobs used presentations of his products to impress audiences about his own intellect and his products' potentials. He could create a good first impression, and was not shy about claiming credit for success or for accomplishments within the company. Ironically, according to a partner, Jobs lacked engineering know-how. Jobs' identity outside the company was not consistent with his partner's assessment. He successfully used impression management to create a much more positive image of himself as a highly creative engineer.

As we shall see in Chapter 3, *intimidation* is an effective form of impression management. Once in power, Jobs used intimidation as a management style. "He ruled by intimidation, yelling and screaming at people" (Butcher, 1989, p. 96). This type of impression management technique may be why Jobs managed to retain so much power despite the fact he was not as knowledgeable as some and more disliked than most.

In summary, we can see in Steven Jobs someone who appears to strategically select identities he wants to manage and goes about doing so. Some of the identities chosen were effective for himself and his products. He pulled off many good sales jobs by masterfully controlling his public image. However, not all his strategies worked. As we shall see, the indiscriminate, nonjudicious use of impression management can backfire. Jobs' use and abuse of impression management through fabrication and intimidation led to hostility, noncooperation, and doubts about the truthfulness of what he said. Jobs was eventually stripped of his managerial responsibilities at Apple.

Steven Jobs' use of impression management may seem bizarre and excessive. That is because of the identities he chose to create and his inappropriate and inconsistent use of impression management in critical situations. While everyone does not use impression management as indiscriminately as Jobs did, they do use it often to help achieve their own social and organizational goals such as being liked and valued by friends, coworkers, and supervisors. The how, what, why and where of impression management in organizational settings is the topic of this book.

INTRODUCING IMPRESSION MANAGEMENT IN ORGANIZATIONS

Getting along with other people at work, school, or home is often a daily struggle. In many parts of our lives, there are no longer clear guidelines for how we "should" behave. Even the expectations we thought we understood quickly change. To an increasing extent we are interacting with others, not in conversation in an office, business, or living room, but over telephone lines, through satellites and computer networks. Each of these factors make relations with other people harder. Today it is even more important to understand who is playing which role, how we should act, and why other people are doing what they are doing. The focus of this book, *impression management*, is the process whereby people seek to control the image others have of them (Rosenfeld, Giacalone, and Riordan, 1995). We impression manage in many different ways: what we do, how we do it, what we say, how we say it, the furnishings and arrangement of our offices, and our physical appearance – from the clothes and make-up we wear to nonverbal behaviors such as facial expressions or posture. All these behaviors in some way can help define who and what we are. They convey an identity and what we want and expect from other people. These *social identities* constitute how individuals are "defined and regarded in social interaction" (Schlenker, 1980, p. 69).

WHAT IS IMPRESSION MANAGEMENT?

Sociologist Erving Goffman wrote one of the first books devoted specifically to the area of impression management. In *The Presentation of Self in Everyday Life* (1959), Goffman said impression management involves attempts to establish the meaning or purpose of social interactions, and that it guides our actions, and helps us anticipate what to expect from others. Impression management is a sort of mutual ritual that helps to smooth and control social relations and to avoid embarrassment. Goffman contended that even actions which at first glance appeared to be innocuous, might actually be strategically calculated to show the social actor in the best possible light. People are performers, according to Goffman, with their main task being the playing of many different roles to construct their social identities. Some of these impression management behaviors are consciously controlled while others such as eye contact and posture are often unwittingly expressed. We attempt to control our impression management behaviors because they are a primary means of influencing how we are treated by other people. Goffman describes the reasons for, and the consequences of, impression management:

> When an individual enters the presence of others, they commonly seek to acquire information about him or to bring into play information about him already possessed. They will be interested in his general socio-economic status, his conception of self, his attitude toward them, his competence, his trustworthiness, etc. Although some of this information seems to be sought almost as an end in itself, there are usually quite practical reasons for acquiring it. Information about the individual helps to define the situation, enabling others to know in advance what he will expect of them and what they may expect of him. Informed in these ways, the others will know how best to act in order to call forth a desired response from him.
>
> (Goffman, 1959, p. 1)

Let us see how Goffman's vision of impression management would apply to the following performance appraisal example. Assume that Lance is an employee who will be evaluated by his supervisor Wayne. Wayne begins the appraisal interview with a brief greeting and outlines his intent to discuss Lance's performance over the past year. Lance sits stiffly, and acts aloof and uninvolved. Wayne had intended to include a number of criticisms of Lance's tendency to miss project deadlines, but now, noting Lance's defensiveness, he hesistates in order to avoid an unpleasant encounter (and the negative impressions of him as a supervisor that might result). Instead Wayne tries to calm Lance's fears by communicating the positive part of his evaluation but avoiding criticizing him. Lance awkwardly smiles and makes eye contact. Wayne continues the performance appraisal, emphasizing Lance's contributions. He wants Lance to see him more like a helper or coach rather than critic. He suspects as long as he is able to maintain this identity, Lance will listen to what he has to say, believe he is trying to help, and respond positively to his suggestions. Lance, upon hearing his praises, relaxes, realizing that because he has a positive identity in his supervisor's eyes he will probably not be blamed for missing several key deadlines on projects he was responsible for during the past year. Consistent with this positive identity and perceived support from Wayne, Lance acts like the cooperative productive employee his supervisor is describing. He senses Wayne's interest in improvement in certain areas and willingly participates in a problem-solving dialog about how improvements might be gained so that he is able to be an even better employee in the future. Wayne and Lance have successfully negotiated a *working consensus* of their identities and roles in this situation. At some level, they both know that Lance is not really as good as Wayne says he is, but through this process of mutual impression management, both "go along" with the positive evaluation and avoid the negative in order to smooth a potentially rocky, awkward interaction (see Villanova and Bernardin, 1989 and Wayne and Liden, 1995 for further discussion of impression management in the performance appraisal process).

Research on impression management gradually accelerated over the years since Goffman's ground-breaking work. Impression management can be found in the fields of sociology, management, organizational behavior, social psychology, communication, criminology, and political science, to name just a few. In this book we will draw on research from all these areas to focus primarily on applications of impression management to organizational life.

Since Goffman, some authors have defined impression management negatively, as a form of interpersonal manipulation occurring in very confined settings or as applying to a limited set of behaviors. This view supports a common misperception: that impression management is something basically bad, involving actions performed primarily to attain the upper hand over others, or to deceive them. However, most recent perspectives see impression management as a very broad and common phenomenon; a fundamental part of all interpersonal interactions (Rosenfeld, Giacalone, and Riordan, 1994).

Schlenker and Weigold (1992) have labeled this more positive perspective the *expansive view*, while calling the more limited, nefarious, Machiavellian perspective, the *restrictive view* of impression management. It is the broader, more humane and extensive concept of impression management that we adopt in this book. This perspective assumes that people actively carry out impression management in ways that help them achieve their objectives and goals both individually and as part of groups and organizations. Sometimes the impression management is done consciously and deliberately, while other times it may be unconscious, automatic, and habitual. At times, the impression that is managed serves to bolster or protect our own self-image; other times we manage impressions in hopes of pleasing significant audiences. Sometimes impression management is truthful and accurate, other times it involves "false advertising" through the use of exaggeration, fabrication, deception, and outright lying. Sometimes the target of impression management is a stranger, sometimes a former coworker, sometimes a boss, sometimes a jilted lover. There are times when the target audience is real, while on other occasions the audience exists only in our imagination. Thus, there are many facets to impression management. A definition offered within this expansive perspective is that impression management is the regulation of "information about some object or event, including the self" (Schlenker and Weigold, 1992, p. 138). In this context, impression management is a broad phenomenon in which we try to influence the perceptions and behaviors of others by controlling the information they receive. In our opening example, Steven Jobs used impression management to control information about himself so that he would appear eccentric.

The expansive view contends that we not only engage in impression management for other people but that our impression management behaviors may affect what we think about ourselves. Try dressing up at home one day in business attire and then see if you actually start feeling and acting more like the role appropriate to the clothes you are wearing. Similarly, we've seen a shy employee become self-confident after she successfully described the results of an employee opinion survey during her first major corporate presentation. It was almost as if she observed her outstanding performance and concluded, "Hey, I'm pretty good at this!" In impression management terms she had done such a good job persuading the *external audience* of her competence that she also persuaded her *internal audience* as well.

With this broad-brush background about the scope of impression management behaviors, we now provide more details on impression management theory and research that laid the groundwork for the information you will receive in later chapters. Following this brief overview, we address some general questions that students of impression management often ask when they are first introduced to the field.

HISTORICAL BACKGROUND: IMPRESSION MANAGEMENT METAPHORS

A number of different metaphors have been used to describe individuals as they engage in impression management. In his classic *Principles of Psychology*, William James (1890) used the *metaphor of multiple selves* to describe human behavior. Rather than having a single unified self-concept, James argued that people have multiple selves of which they show different sides in various situations. He wrote that a person, "has as many social selves as there are distinct groups of people about whose opinions he cares. He generally shows a different side of himself to each of these different groups" (1890, p. 294). James' notion that we have multiple social selves that are strategically presented to gain favor with different audiences, greatly influenced later theorists, including those known as *postmodern psychologists*. Postmodern psychologists believe "that we have no single, separate, unified self. They maintain that we contain many selves and that the proper response to the suggestion, 'Get in touch with yourself' or 'Be yourself' is 'Which one?'" (Stephens, 1992, p. 40). This very contemporary view was advocated by James over a century ago (1890, pp. 46–47): "We do not show ourselves to our children as to our club-companions, to our customers as to the laborers we employ, to our own masters and employers as to our intimate friends."

Within sociology, beginning in the early part of this century, there has been a perspective referred to as *symbolic interactionism*, that popularized many of the concepts used in contemporary impression management theory. Within this framework, the *dramaturgical metaphor*, life as being like the theater, was elaborated and refined. The dramaturgical metaphor implies that social and organizational life are something akin to a theatrical play, with each of us playing different roles for important audiences. William Shakespeare captured the essence of the dramaturgical metaphor when he wrote in *As You Like It*, "All the world's a stage, and all the men and women merely players. They have their exits and entrances, and one man in his time plays many parts."

Take, for example, Stephanie, a successful bank manager. At work, Stephanie is a cool decision-maker and tough task-master. At home she is a tender mother who becomes highly emotional when her young son Andrew trips and cuts his lip. At the market, Stephanie screams at a clerk who drops her groceries. In the community choir, she is fun-loving and spontaneous. To survive, to succeed, to excel, Stephanie must be different things to different people; a busy actress in the drama of everyday life.

While Goffman felt impression management served as a *social lubricant* greasing the skids for smooth interactions, later work by social psychologists characterized impression management as serving more specific, goal-oriented purposes such as gaining power and influencing others. The *metaphor of the yes-man* emerged in the 1960s largely through the work of Edward E. Jones on the impression management technique of ingratiation (see Chapter 2). The yes-man uses ingratiation tactics such as opinion conformity to get others to like him. Since we tend to reward those we like, the successful yes-man uses liking as a stepping stone to power and influence.

The 1970s saw the impression management perspective become increasingly popular among laboratory-oriented experimental social psychologists. Indeed, during the late 1970s the three authors of this text first became interested in the role played by impression management in social and work settings. The impression management theory we encountered then used the *metaphor of the manipulator*. Impression management was seen as being performed to control other people; to dupe an audience, often for nefarious reasons. Today we see this metaphor as too restrictive because it included only a small subset of impression management behaviors and often assumed that most people had sleazy motives for their impression management actions.

The *organizational politician metaphor* (Mayes and Allen, 1977; Pettigrew, 1973) developed about that time and is still common today. It sees people as having a diverse set of objectives in social interaction, often related to power, and they use impression management in political ways when it will help them accomplish their goals. Just as politicians have good and bad motives, so do impression managers. Just as politicians seem to be ever-conscious of pleasing the voters back home, impression managers are conscious of audiences or potential audiences to much of their behavior. Today, the politician metaphor is still apt, but the focus has broadened to include an ever-increasing range of organizational behaviors that fit under the impression management tent (Giacalone and Rosenfeld, 1989).

Metaphors are frameworks for illustrating basic assumptions – in this case about impression management. They serve as a basis for the development of theory. For behavioral and organizational scientists, which include many of those doing impression management research, those theories must also be "tested" to see if the processes and relationships they describe match with how people really behave. The Appendix (see pp. 186–193) describes the various research methodologies used to test impression management theory.

IMPRESSION MANAGEMENT IN ORGANIZATIONS: A JOURNEY FROM EXTREME TO MAINSTREAM

Even though Goffman emphasized that impression management was a common, very normal feature of most interactions, few theorists in other fields initially adopted this broad perspective. In social psychology, for example, impression management was originally characterized as being an "extreme" form of behavior for several reasons. During the 1960s, impression management was seen as a contaminant or artifact of laboratory research that needed to be eliminated or controlled so that important, "real" relationships among variables could be observed.

During the 1970s it was gradually acknowledged that impression management was not simply an artifact of laboratory research but that it played an important role in behavior. However, as previously mentioned, the consensus, especially among those in social psychology, was that it was a form of deceptive manipulation. To many during the 1970s, impression management was seen as meaning the impression manager was consciously trying to deceive others.

In organizational settings, as mentioned above, a form of impression management research had been carried out under a framework known as *organizational politics*. This earlier work was sporadic and not well-integrated. Although popular management books had long recognized that impression management processes were crucial to organizational success (e.g., Korda, 1975; Molloy, 1978; Ringer, 1976), the academic side of organizational research was slower to accept impression management as a viable theory, again perhaps because it was viewed as too extreme (Rosenfeld and Giacalone, 1991). In the mid-1980s, more organizational studies using the impression management framework began to appear (Giacalone, 1985; Giacalone and Rosenfeld, 1984, 1986, 1987; Ralston, 1985; Zerbe and Paulhus, 1987). In 1989, two of us edited *Impression*

Management in the Organization (Giacalone and Rosenfeld, 1989). It was the first attempt to systematically apply an impression management framework to a wide spectrum of organizational processes. *Impression Management in the Organization* was directed primarily toward scholars and researchers. Two years later, Giacalone and Rosenfeld (1991) edited *Applied Impression Management: How Image-Making Affects Managerial Decisions*, a book focusing on organizational and practitioner applications.

Together, these two volumes served as sourcebooks for what has become a rapidly growing and now distinctive field called *organizational impression management*. These two edited books integrated previous impression management research conducted by leading social psychologists like Edward Jones, Barry Schlenker, Mark Snyder, Roy Baumeister, Robert Cialdini, and Mark Leary, with organizational and business applications of impression management associated with the work of scholars such as Gerarld Ferris, David Ralston, Mark Martinko, Jerald Greenberg, and Robert Bies. In retrospect, it is difficult to see how impression management could have been overlooked in many theoretical discussions of the job interview, employee theft, substance abuse, career strategies, performance appraisals, exit interviews, negotiations, conflict resolution and many others (for discussions of these topics see Giacalone and Rosenfeld, 1989, 1991). Incorporating impression management in today's research and practice is beginning to yield a better understanding of how organizational processes are substantially affected by individuals' concerns over how they are being perceived by others. Box 1.1 describes a good example of how a finding from a laboratory study in psychology is now being used to prescribe how managers can be more effective.

Today, as impression management has become more popular among organizational researchers and practitioners, it has also come to be viewed as more "mainstream" than "extreme." We view impression management, as many others now do, as a commonly occurring and very "normal" part of organizational life. Impression management, in this contemporary perspective, is seen as being essential to effective organizational communications. It is an important aspect both of marketing products and in marketing the self. From understanding what a new company policy is, to letting employees know our expectations for them, being able and willing to engage in the management of impressions is central. Today

BOX 1.1

Impression management and the self-fulfilling prophecy

Out of the closet and into the live arena of management applications

The phrase above comes from a chapter by Dov Eden in *Applied Impression Management* (Eden, 1991, p. 37). He is referring to the emergence of impression management from being studied in highly controlled laboratory experiments in social psychology to use by practitioners trying to improve the exercise of management and make organizations more effective. Eden's focus is the *self-fulfilling prophecy*, the finding that when people expect something to happen, they act in ways that make the event more likely to occur, and thereby increase the likelihood of the event actually happening (Merton, 1948). While the self-fulfilling prophecy was once considered a form of impression management that could harm the validity of laboratory experiments, Eden's work has shown that it can have positive organizational benefits.

Eden's extension of this work into education and organizational training derives from the famous study *Pygmalion in the Classroom* by Rosenthal and Jacobson (1968). It was shown that students' academic performance could be increased by merely leading their teachers to expect that those students were "late bloomers" and would show significant increases in performance during the year. Since the original study, increasing expectations has been shown to have effects in organizational training programs and many classroom settings.

According to Eden, the self-fulfilling prophecy can be a powerful management tool: "The practical implication ... is that anything that raises managers' expectations concerning what subordinates are capable of achieving can lead to improvements in subordinates' performance" (1991, p. 15). Eden also points to ways an employee can use impression management to raise a manager's expectations for her performance. If she suspects, for example, that the manager doubts her ability in certain areas, she could manage a contrary impression by completing some exceptional work in those areas and being

---

Box 1.1 continued

sure the manager hears about it. If the manager changes his expectations to be in line with the new information, the raising expectations make it more likely he will act in ways that aid the employee's higher achievement, making her higher achievement more likely to become a reality. An interesting application of this reasoning occurred in the US Navy when low-performing sailors who were taught to manage more positive identities actually increased their performance and their supervisors' evaluations of them (Crawford, Thomas, and Funk, 1980).

Managers can use impression management to be sure they are conveying high expectations to those who report to them. Eden suggests a number of ways managers can signify expectations they hold: explicitly stating their expectations; setting difficult but realistic goals for their employees; giving employees tasks on which they are likely to succeed so they can build up their own self-confidence; and suggesting interpretations for employees' successes and failures that reinforce employees' motivation. A poignant example of the last strategy is an executive who said to one of his managers who was afraid he would lose his job because he had just made a mistake that would cost the company $100,000, "Why should I fire you when I've just invested $100,000 in your development?" (McCall, Lombardo, and Morrison, 1988, p. 154; cited in Eden, 1991). This statement clearly conveys the executive's confidence in the manager's ability and probably helped the manager to see the mistake as a painful learning experience rather than as a failure revealing his inadequate ability.

we know we have to understand impression management to fully understand organizational life. As we shall see, the range of phenomena it helps to explain include all aspects of organizational behavior from the job interview to leadership, from ethics to organizational surveys, from performance appraisal to issues of diversity.

ORGANIZATIONAL POLITICS AND IMPRESSION MANAGEMENT

As mentioned, the study of organizational politics developed in the business area parallel to the study of impression management in social psychology. Organizational politics is "a social influence process in which behavior is strategically designed to maximize short-term or long-term self-interest, which is either consistent with, or at the expense of, others' interests" (Ferris, Russ, and Fandt, 1989, p. 145). Inasmuch as impression management is considered a social influence process, it is clearly a form of organizational politics. Organizational politics is broader, though, because there are many ways, in addition to impression management, we can attempt to maximize our self-interests.

Because organizations, groups, or individuals can engage in organizational politics, "self-interest" should be thought of as referring to the "entity's interest" (Ferris *et al.*, 1989, p. 145). Impression management has primarily been focused on individuals; however, scholars in business are more likely to focus on organizational politics that go beyond the individual level. Cobb (1986) has noted political action can be at any one of three levels: *individual*, *coalition*, and *network*. Impression management in the service of organizational politics may be used to create impressions by the individual to maximize self-interest. When impression management is used by a group of individuals who are trying to attain an outcome on a single issue (e.g., fairness for minorities, smoking rights at work), the politicizing is said to be at a coalition level. Trying to create the appropriate impression at this level will usually involve a group whose constituency will stay together only as long as the issue needs political tactics. Impression management at the network level politicizes, not for an issue, but for groups of people. Impression management at this level is interested in the individuals who are part of the network (e.g., Hispanics in US corporations), their well-being and career progress, rather than the issues which may underlie the network's membership (e.g., discrimination against Hispanics).

The tactics used by organizational politicians and impression managers are sometimes, but not always, the same. For example, the research on political behavior in organizations reveals some tactics (e.g., ingratiation, association) common to both organizational politics and impression management (Allen *et al.*, 1979). However, some tactics, such as forming power coalitions and developing bases of support, tend to be almost exclusively studied within the organizational politics framework.

Perhaps of most interest are the different "triggers" for organizational politics and impression management. The impression management literature tends to provide an extended consideration of both internal (e.g., personality) and external (e.g., environmental) triggers for impression management behavior, whereas organizational politics has traditionally tended to focus more on the external triggers in the organization. These triggers include the *concept of uncertainty*, such that lack of clear objectives, poorly defined decision processes, strong competition, unclear performance measures (Beeman and Sharkey, 1987), and change (Raia, 1985) will foster higher levels of organizational politics. These triggers are consistent with an overall understanding of what causes impression management behaviors at work. However, impression management, because of its psychological underpinnings, also considers individual differences and interpersonal interactions as potential triggers of impression management behaviors rather than just organizational characteristics. Thus, while the overlap in the organizational politics and impression management literature is considerable, we cannot assume that the fields or tactics are identical.

While researchers have used both the organizational politics and impression management perspectives to help them better understand organizational behavior, the focus in this volume will be on findings from the rapidly growing field of organizational impression management. Before beginning our journey into the specifics of organizational impression management, we first address some common questions that students new to the study of impression management often ask.

WHEN AND WHY DO WE USE IMPRESSION MANAGEMENT?

If you are asked why you chose a particular career or college major, you might list a series of reasons, or motives, for your behavior. Similarly, people impression manage for a number of reasons and one impression management behavior can serve several purposes. Take, for example, Mary, a young engineer at her first staff meeting trying to manage the impression she is a computer expert. While we might initially think that Mary is acting the role of computer expert only to impress others, some theorists (e.g., Baumeister, 1982) have argued that Mary may also be trying to impression manage herself. In Mary's case to be perceived as an expert might boost her own self-confidence and self-esteem concerning her professional abilities. To be an expert may signify for her she is closer to the type of person she ultimately wants to be (her "ideal self").

Mary may be managing the impression of computer expert for another reason – during her job interview she claimed to be a computer expert and two of the interviewers are sitting in this meeting. Thus, she needs to be consistent with her previous statements.

Finally, Mary may be claiming the identity of computer expert as a way of influencing how others will treat her at work in the future. Convincing others that she is a computer expert will increase her chances of being assigned computer-intensive projects that would allow her to get choice job assignments and increase her future promotion opportunities.

For Mary, managing the image of expert could result from trying to accomplish all or any of these goals at the same time. Moreover, her motivation to manage the image of expert could change as might be the case if the people who had interviewed her left the meeting, or as she gains more confidence about her ability and place in the organization.

As Mary's case-study illustrates, people engage in impression management for many reasons that are influenced by social, personal, and situational factors. Some theorists explain how we choose when and what to impression manage by describing people as engaging in a quick *cost–benefit analysis* (Jones and Wortman, 1973; Schlenker, 1980). People are simultaneously assessing the benefits they might achieve from successfully presenting one image rather than another, at the same time they are estimating the costs involved in portraying that image, including not being able to carry off the impression and being perceived as a fake, phony, or charlatan. To return to Mary, she is likely to manage the expert image if she feels she knows enough about computers to carry it off and if she sees more benefits than costs resulting from being perceived as a computer expert. In her case, benefits seem to exceed costs. However, costs might exceed benefits if the computer system was fraught with problems she might not be able to fix, or if she would be viewed as a lowly computer "technician" rather than a multi-talented engineer.

We have defined impression management as the attempts to control the impressions that others form. Therefore, it is not surprising that impression management is more likely to occur in public, when other people are around. There are times, however, when we engage in impression management even when no one is present. Sometimes we rehearse an impression management attempt to fine tune its effectiveness or anticipate its impact on an audience. A nervous employee may anticipate being questioned concerning her knowledge of a prank that caused the office voice-mail system to play the first line of the song "Take this job and shove it" when a caller wanted to leave a message. She may imagine the interaction with her boss, formulate an explanation for why she was working late on the night of the episode, while carefully noting in the mirror her facial expressions in response to certain questions.

A three-component model

Leary and Kowalski (1990) proposed a theoretical model designed to help us better understand when and why we engage in impression management. The three components in the model are *impression monitoring*, *impression motivation*, and *impression construction*. These can be seen in Figure 1.1. Impression monitoring occurs when individuals are conscious of the impressions they are making, either because of the particular situation they are in, or because they are the type of people who often are aware of the impressions they make. If people see impression management as a way they can accomplish important goals or change how they are perceived in a more desired direction, they will be motivated to engage in impression management. The type of impressions people choose to construct depends on their self-concept, the type of identity they have or would like to have, the values they assume the audience has and the setting for impression management.

To see how this model might work, let us take the case of Steven Jobs as he started up a new computer company, Next, after being forced out of Apple in the late 1980s. It is very likely that Jobs did a lot of impression monitoring. The turmoil at Apple had taught him well that his every public action could be grist for the international media. Additionally, during his ouster from Apple, the press portrayed him much more negatively than it had previously. Certainly, Jobs would have wanted to change this very negative image and so he would have been conscious of how his actions were being perceived.

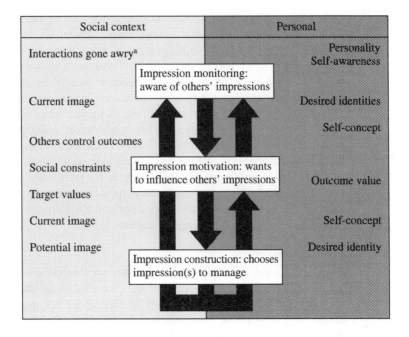

Figure 1.1 Three-component model of social psychological processes involved in impression management
Source: Based on Leary and Kowalski, 1990; Leary, 1993
Note: [a]Social context and personal variables are placed at point(s) in the process they are most likely to influence

The second process in Leary's model is impression motivation. It seems safe to assume that Steven Jobs recognized that a key to the success of his new company was improving his public image and ensuring his product was perceived positively. Thus, his impression motivation was high.

The selection of an image to construct is the final process in Leary's model. Jobs needed to be perceived as an effective business person and his product as useful and reliable. In contrast to the eccentric image he presented in Apple's early years, Jobs became very conscious of his physical appearance. It was written about him at that time, "Rarely is he seen in jeans and sandals and never in the office in such attire; instead he wears elegant European suits tailored to fit his slender frame and he looks like a successful executive"

(Butcher, 1989, pp. 216–217). The image of the Next computer also seems to have been carefully constructed. About $100,000 was spent on a logo long before the computer was ready for manufacture. The critical role of quality for product success in today's markets led Jobs to want to delay the release of the computer until it was running without failures. To be perceived as a successful businessperson and to have developed a powerful and high-quality computer probably would have been important for Jobs' personal sense of self and also how he wanted to be perceived. By choosing an image of an orthodox businessperson, he was conforming to the values and norms of the business community which may have made securing financing and building customer relations easier. If he could construct the image of high quality for Next, it would go a long way toward moving Next into a good position in the computer market.

IS IMPRESSION MANAGEMENT GOOD OR BAD?

The term "impression management" implies something disturbingly Machiavellian. However, we all know that how we present ourselves influences the course of our social interactions. Moreover,

> we know that our motives are not necessarily dark and manip-
> ulative . . . Although [impression management] surely can be used
> for unprincipled ends, more frequently it serves fairly benign
> aims.
>
> (Weatherly and Beach, 1994, p. 416)

As we shall see in Chapters 4 and 5, some of the most noteworthy examples of impression management are instances when it is used to get someone out of trouble at home, with friends, or at work. The field of impression management is much broader, however. Each of us, even those not in trouble of some sort, engage in impression management as a normal part of our daily lives. Historically, impression management has also been viewed as "bad" because it has been linked with *Machiavellianism*, the self-interested manipulation of another for one's own purposes. However, self-interest is only one of many motives for impression management. People's impression management can be used to help others as much as harm them. John may agree with the opinions expressed by a potential benefactor to his university so that the benefactor donates money for student scholarships.

From this overview, it should be clear that impression management is neither inherently good nor bad but rather is a fundamental part of our social and work lives. Whether impression management is good or bad, ethical or unethical, really depends on why it is used and what it does; a decision that requires a judgment of the motives or consequences of the impression management as used in a particular situation. Consider the case of Elizabeth, who tries to be considerate of her subordinates' personal and professional needs as part of actively managing the impression of being a good supervisor. If Elizabeth is being considerate so that her employees become a more effective and productive workgroup, few would call her impression management immoral or bad. If she uses the trust gained from being a considerate supervisor to try and convince several employees to sign a lousy early retirement agreement, that would be another story! In these two situations the motivation behind the impression management determines whether it is good or bad.

DOES IMPRESSION MANAGEMENT IMPLY WE ARE SOCIAL CHAMELEONS?

A man will boast to one person of an action – say some sharp transaction in trade – which he would be ashamed to own to another.

(Cooley, 1964, p. 217)

Are we merely social chameleons constantly changing our identities regardless of who we really are? Or do we typically impression manage to "accurately" convey the type of person we are? The answer to both of these questions is "sometimes, yes; sometimes no." Leary (1993) has pointed out that as more and more rides on the outcome of successful impression management, the tendency to present images that would have a desired effect on an audience increases, even if the images are not accurate. Alternatively, when certain images are central to our sense of who we are, we are more likely to try to manage an impression consistent with our self-image, regardless of the situational constraints. Let us use the example of Dan, a would-be electronics expert, to illustrate how these factors interact. As the prestige of those in attendance at an important professional meeting increases, so would Dan's desire to manage a

BOX 1.2

Consistency in impression management

Actions speak louder than words

Many of us have heard from our parents that "actions speak louder than words." Manufacturing companies today are increasingly recognizing the wisdom of this saying in managing an impression of quality. One of the factors leading to the decline in market share of the US car industry is said to have been the poor perceived quality in American cars relative to those manufactured by the Japanese. Some American car companies responded with increases in the quality of their products and advertising that described the changes. Yet their old negative image remained and that kept people from buying the cars.

One car company, the Chrysler Corporation, realized that it would take more than verbal claims of increased quality. Instead, they said they would back up their claims with action. An advertising campaign they had at the time said, "Buy one of our cars ... Take it home, and within thirty days, if you don't like it for any reason, bring it back and we'll refund your money" (Iacocca, 1984, p. 181). Certainly, backing the claim of quality with a promise of this type of action is a lot different from just making the claim.

At about this same time, Chrysler's financial troubles were widely publicized. While those in the company felt the problems would be turned around with the increased quality of their product, the sales had yet to arrive. However, the company's suppliers were becoming reluctant to ship parts for the improved products because the bills were not being paid. "At the same time we had to keep the suppliers shipping their stuff to us, even when we didn't have enough money to pay them. The first thing we needed to do was convince them that we weren't heading into bankruptcy. You can't fool suppliers. They know your business very well. We brought them in. We showed them our future products. We let them know we were here to stay. We asked them to stand by us" (Iacocca, 1984,

---

Box 1.2 continued

---

p. 186). This strategy was effective, presumably because even though the company's claims that they would soon turn the financial picture around were easy to make, actually becoming familiar with the product and its performance carried more weight. Impression management words are more effective when bolstered by impression management deeds.

In another example of how actions can make for effective impression management, Eleuthere Irenee Du Pont, a creator of the huge Du Pont corporation, built his family's house next to the powder yard as a way of convincing workers and the community that the danger from the production of gunpowder was not serious. Later he backed up his claims of being committed to his employees by caring financially for the survivors of a blast that leveled the powder mills (Du Pont de Nemours and Company, 1952, p. 22).

---

good impression also increase. If he suspected the prestigious audience members would value his knowledge of new electronics components he would be more likely to manage that impression, whereas if they seemed to view electronics experts as overly specialized nerds he would probably choose to keep his talents quiet. Alternatively, if Dan felt he had invested much time and effort in becoming an electronics expert, and this was an important part of his self-concept, he would be more likely to present that image regardless of the audience. If it was just something Dan had picked up and he cared little about, he would not. Thus, in certain situations, we are likely to act like chameleons and change the identities we present to fit our surroundings. In other situations, with traits we consider important, we are not.

It should be noted that consistency in impression management can be important because inconsistency can lead an audience to question the accuracy of all communications. We previously pointed out how some at Apple felt Steven Jobs was not a good manager. He would say one thing and do another which made them feel they "couldn't believe a thing the guy said." Thus, consistency in impression management is important to managers of organizations. One way managers can make impression management be seen as consistent and credible is to make "actions speak louder than words," as described in Box 1.2.

DOES EVERYONE USE IMPRESSION MANAGEMENT?

> Most interaction goals are mediated by the actor's attempts to manage the general impressions others form of him or her as a person.
>
> (Jones, 1990, p. 168)

> Concerns with face are salient in virtually all encounters.
>
> (Holtgraves, 1992, p. 141)

Although there are cultures in which its occurrence is less prevalent than in the United States or Western Europe (Hu, 1944), impression management, in our view, is a universal phenomenon. As we shall see in Chapter 6, while everyone uses impression management, there are individual differences in the form, frequency, and success of impression management attempts. Certain people are more likely to try impression management. Certain people are better at it than others. Some people are more aware of the impression management attempts of others.

According to a perspective called *evolutionary psychology*, impression management behaviors are universal because they evolved as a way of regulating human friendship behaviors. Friendship serves to support human survival through a *norm of reciprocity* – we help others and expect that they will help us. However, the give and take of reciprocity can be damaged if one of the parties cheats. Impression management serves as a signal that one is sincere about giving to others and also helps us detect when others may be insincere. As Pinker (1994, p. 3) writes, "In humans, the talkative species, long-term reciprocity creates an arms race of impression management. Everyone tries to show signs of integrity (exceeding that in actual behavior) while developing hypersensitive radar for such hypocrisy in others."

DO WE CONSCIOUSLY MANAGE CERTAIN IMPRESSIONS?

There is no compelling psychological reason why impression management must be either duplicitous or under conscious control. Impression management may be the product of highly overlearned habits or scripts, the original functions of which people have long forgotten.

(Tetlock and Manstead, 1985, pp. 61–62)

The entire process of self-presentation gradually becomes overlearned, automatic, and hence unconscious.

(Baumeister and Hutton, 1987, p. 72)

The issue of how conscious we are of our impression management attempts is one that is still the subject of much debate. From reading this text you may initially think we are implying that all impression management strategies are consciously selected and performed and that we are always aware and in control of our impression management behaviors. Certainly some impression management behaviors are conscious. We may plan and rehearse our impression management in preparation for important interactions like a job interview or first date. However, the reality is that much of our impression management is automatic; it occurs without awareness or with very little attention being devoted to it. Some of the most automatic behaviors are those we perform very frequently in the same situation, that are not of great difficulty and the ones we have performed successfully in the past. Because many of our behaviors fit in this category – like showing respect toward authority figures, not making rude gestures when our supervisor can see us, or keeping our shortcomings to ourselves or close friends – we may not be consciously aware of much of our impression management. This may explain why when asked, very few people acknowledge the amount of impression management they do on a daily basis. They are engaging in impression management, but are not aware of it.

We can consider impression management behaviors we do automatically as being our *impression management habits*. Many nonverbal behaviors such as grimacing when not being promoted or smiling when receiving a performance award fall in this category. As we shall see in Chapter 3, even though nonverbal behaviors often occur without our awareness, studies have shown that when we are consciously trying to create certain impressions, we use nonverbals effectively to accomplish our objectives (DePaulo, 1992).

We go off "automatic pilot" and pay closer attention to our impression management when we think the consequences of our behavior could be very good or bad, as would be the case when making a formal presentation at a business meeting, or when we suspect the image we are trying to present may be challenged, as might happen if we said something stupid during a job interview (Leary and Kowalski, 1990). In these situations we think more about impression management tactics, their performance, and how the audience might react to them. Apparently, this contemplation of impression management renders us more cautious in the images we choose to present, making us reluctant to present overly positive images. On the other hand, when we are managing impressions automatically, research has shown the impressions tend to be more positive (Paulhus, Graf, and VanSelst, 1989). We seem to have an unconscious bias to present ourselves positively.

DOES IMPRESSION MANAGEMENT REALLY WORK?

Given all the time, money, and effort people and organizations put into impression management, it seems clear they think it will work. Although the times we have failed in our impression management attempts probably stick out more in our minds – the muffed job interview, getting caught shopping on a "sick day" – most of the time we do it pretty well. Research has shown that people are quite good at using impression management to communicate their internal experiences (DePaulo, 1992).

As we shall see in Chapters 4 and 5, impression management not only works to make people view us more positively, it also is remarkably effective at damage control when we screw up. In a scenario study of US Senators, some explanations for illegal or unethical actions given by the accused were effective in altering the way they were perceived (Riordan, Marlin, and Kellogg, 1983). In fact, people were very forgiving of those who gave "the proper" explanations for their behavior.

DOES IMPRESSION MANAGEMENT AFFECT THE IMPRESSION MANAGER?

It is easy to think about impression management by focusing only on how it affects others. After all, a primary purpose of impression management is to influence the impressions others have of us. Yet, engaging in impression management also affects how we think about ourselves. To illustrate the effect of impression management on the impression manager, let us look at a study of people who reported "playing dumb" across a variety of situations (Gove, Hughes, and Geerkin, 1980). The researchers found that the people who played dumb the most often were also the ones with the poorest mental health. Similarly, Tennen and Affleck (1991) concluded that people who are quick to blame others for their failures (a common form of defensive impression management) are not very well adjusted. This means the employee who always says "it's not my fault" or "it's not my job" may ultimately suffer for blaming others.

Impression management can also have positive effects on the impression manager. Training in the self-fulfilling prophecy as described in Box 1.1 is a good example of some very positive effects of impression management. In fact, the impact of impression management probably falls on a continuum of adaptive to dysfunctional. It is also true that a total lack of impression management would be seen as maladaptive. A friend involved in career counseling recently retold in amazement the story of a student who refused to dress up for an interview or to think about those things he might mention to an interviewer to present himself in a more positive light. In fact, he felt it would be wrong of him to appear to be anything else than what he was every day, to give answers that had been premeditated in any way, or even to hold back something an employer might want to know. As you might suspect, this individual is still unemployed!

A CONCLUDING NOTE

We hope this introductory chapter has given you a sense of what the rest of this book holds in store. We will discuss many aspects of organizational impression management not included in this chapter. The questions we raised will be addressed in greater detail. You will come away with an understanding of what organizational impression management is, and is not; the various tactics and strategies of impression management, the reasons they are used, when they are most likely to occur; and the effects impression management has on audiences and impression managers. First we will deal with impression management strategies for looking good, followed by strategies to avoid looking bad. Differences among individuals in their tendencies to engage in impression management and how to measure those differences will follow. Applications of impression management to the area of human resource management will be outlined. We conclude with a presentation of new, emerging, and future areas of impression management research and practice. We hope you will come to share our enthusiasm for this exciting new area in organizational behavior and gain a clear understanding of how influencing the impressions of others is an integral part of virtually all organizational functions.

2 *Ingratiation*

WINNING FRIENDS AND INFLUENCING PEOPLE

He was a poor Missouri farm boy, shy and not very athletic. He suffered from feelings of inferiority and eventually got involved in public speaking so that people would notice him. The poor farm boy became a teacher of public speaking and, in 1936, published a book outlining his recipe for success. Neither the author, Dale Carnegie, nor the publisher, Simon & Schuster, expected the book to sell much; the original printing of *How to Win Friends and Influence People* was just 5,000 copies. Much to their surprise, the book became one of the great bestsellers in world history! At the time of Carnegie's death in 1955 the book had sold nearly five million copies, eventually being second only to the Bible in nonfiction sales. By 1987, *How to Win Friends and Influence People* had sold 15 million copies, had been translated into over 35 languages, and the motivational course inspired by Carnegie's writings had graduated over three million students in 69 countries. The Carnegie course became very popular in the corporate world with many management professionals and trainees completing the basic course as well as targeted courses in customer relations, sales, and the "executive image" (Abrams, 1991; Johnson, 1987). One measure of the popularity of Carnegie's message in the corporate world is that 80 percent of the Fortune 500 companies have paid for Carnegie training for at least some of their employees (Abrams, 1991).

While Dale Carnegie's success was phenomenal his message was simple: "smiling sincerely, paying honest compliments, and avoiding the use of the personal pronoun" (Johnson, 1987, p. 28), was the formula for winning friends and influencing people. Carnegie stressed the importance of praising others and noted that one of the most effective selling techniques is to make other people like you (Schlenker, 1980). Like the expansive view of impression management, Carnegie believed that one could both be sincere and expert in interpersonal influence; that while social influence could be used deceptively, it did not necessarily have to be deceptive.

Dale Carnegie's simple formula for success shares much with the focus of this chapter: *ingratiation* – tactics and strategies aimed at making others like you. However, Carnegie's common-sense analysis of ways of winning friends and influencing people, although appealing, has been largely unexamined (Abrams, 1991, p. E17). Like Erving Goffman's views of impression management described in Chapter 1, they are based on Carnegie's own insights and experiences rather than on systematic research. In contrast, the ingratiation tactics described in this chapter have been the subject of much scientifically oriented research by psychologists, sociologists, and organizational and management scientists. We summarize this research and systematically apply its findings to organizational settings.

Like Carnegie, impression management theory assumes that a basic human motive, both inside and outside of organizations, is to be seen by others in favorable manner and to avoid being viewed negatively (Rosenfeld, Giacalone, and Riordan, 1995). These attempts to be seen favorably or positively are called *acquisitive* impression management, while defensive tactics that seek to minimize deficiencies and avoid looking bad are called *protective* impression management (Arkin, 1981). Both acquisitive and protective impression management tactics can be *directly* applied by the parties involved or occur *indirectly* through some form of association (Cialdini, 1989). In this chapter we describe the most studied acquisitive impression tactic – ingratiation. Other acquisitive tactics, both direct and indirect, will be reviewed in Chapter 3. We will present the various protective impression management tactics in Chapters 4 and 5.

INGRATIATION: AN OVERVIEW

> Performance is important; you've got to perform. But ingratiation does something more. It gives you an edge.
>
> Psychologist Ronald Deluga (quoted in Odom, 1993, p. E-12)

Ingratiation is the most common and most studied of impression management techniques. Ingratiation was first described by Edward E. Jones (1964), one of the pioneers of impression management research. Linda Ginzel, formerly one of Professor Jones' students, provides a "behind the scenes" look at his profound influence on her career and impression management research.

• • • •

Behind the Scenes

Linda E. Ginzel
Graduate School of Business, The University of Chicago

As I write this I am mourning the tragic and unexpected death of my advisor and mentor Edward E. Jones. It is impossible to describe how I became interested in the topic of impression management and the nature of my research without knowledge of his profound impact. As a Ph.D. student at Princeton, Ned taught me how to think about interpersonal perception within the framework of experimental social psychology. He introduced me to both the study of attributional logic: How do people infer the causes of behavior? and its flip side: How do people elicit desirable attributions?

My first experiments, with Ned Jones and Bill Swann, explored people's intuitive understanding of attributional reasoning and investigated the conditions necessary for people to behave as attribution theories predict they should. The results demonstrate how difficult it is for people to identify accurately the impact of their own behavior in shaping the behavior of others. Since that time, I have been intrigued by this powerful notion: What we observe in others is often shaped by our actions, yet we tend to treat these reactions of others as independent of our own influence.

As I became more and more interested in understanding the

reciprocal nature of interpersonal perception and social interaction, I also shifted my focus from attitude attribution to judgments of task performance and ability. I took time off from my Ph.D. studies and worked as an internal management consultant for Mutual of New York. It was there that I discovered the relevance of social psychology in an organizational context and began to develop the idea of a dynamic evaluator–performer feedback sequence. I returned to graduate school and conducted an experiment which demonstrated that evaluators underestimate the impact of their own behavior, resulting in biased performance judgments (Ginzel, 1994). A second related experiment focused on the active role that performers (i.e., targets of evaluation) play in conveying a desired impression to the evaluator. Research in this area has interesting implications for the different strategies employed in managing impressions of competence versus likability in performance-relevant settings.

I took my first job at Stanford's Graduate School of Business and made the transition from social psychology to organizational behavior. It was during this time that I became interested in organizational impression management due in large part to my colleagues Bob Sutton and Rod Kramer. During my two years there, we had lively discussions about the role of the organizational audience in shaping the impression management process. Ultimately, we developed the idea that organizational impression management is a process of reciprocal influence and conceptualized impression management as a negotiated "settlement" involving organizational actors (top management) and the targets (members of the organizational audience) of their influence attempts. I also became interested in what I refer to as self-presentation by proxy, involving situations when a third-party makes competence claims on behalf of another.

For the future, I hope to better understand the attributional reasoning that underlies interpersonal relations and the strategic use of attributional logic for impression management. By studying the reciprocal nature of interpersonal perception and social interaction, I am returning to a theme that Ned Jones (with John Thibaut) introduced us to almost 40 years ago.

• • • •

Ingratiation refers to a set of related acquisitive impression management tactics that have as their collective aim making the person more liked and attractive to others (Jones, 1990). Thus, we might call ingratiation "attraction management" (Pandey and Singh, 1987). As originally conceptualized by Jones (1964), ingratiation was defined as "a class of strategic behaviors illicitly designed to influence a particular other person concerning the attractiveness of one's personal qualities" (p. 11). The ingratiator subscribes to the philosophy that, "you can catch more flies with honey than vinegar."

While Jones' original view was that ingratiation was inherently "illicit" ("ingratiating actions are illicit because they are directed toward objectives not contained in the implicit contract which underlies social interaction;" Jones, 1964, p. 11), organizational theorists have increasingly destigmatized these various forms of attraction management. They have argued that ingratiation is a common, often effective means of organizational social influence (Ralston, 1985; Ralston and Elsass, 1989). As Liden and Mitchell (1988, p. 574) note, "the use of ingratiatory behaviors may not always involve devious methods to manipulate others ... In fact, an individual may not be consciously aware that he or she is using ingratiatory behaviors."

Rather than being illicit, we believe that ingratiation can have positive benefits in organizations and therefore should be sanctioned under certain circumstances. Judiciously used, ingratiation can facilitate positive interpersonal relationships and increase harmony within and outside of the organizational setting. In Chapter 8, we suggest that ingratiation may be crucial to members of racial/ethnic minority groups, women, immigrants, and expatriates who often need to please majority group members in positions of greater social power. By generating liking and feelings of good will, ingratiation may counter natural cognitive tendencies to stigmatize, stereotype, and devalue people who are different (Allison and Herlocker, 1994). Through achieving his goal – increasing liking and attraction – the successful ingratiator becomes familiar, activates norms of reciprocity, and goes from a stereotyped "outsider" to a liked "insider." Although organizations can suffer if they only reward "yes-men" and disdain criticism (Odom, 1993), ingratiation, in proper doses, can be a binding and unifying force, melding diverse subgroups in the face of tendencies that seek to divide them. As Ralston (1985, p. 478) has written, "In fact, it may be argued that moderate levels of ingratiatory behavior are beneficial to the organization in that it may be a form of social glue that builds cohesive work groups in the absence of compatibility."

Of all impression management tactics, ingratiation may be the one most immediately translatable to organizational settings. Because the need for ingratiation and the likelihood of its occurrence increase with increasing power differentials (Schlenker, 1980), the hierarchical organization is the breeding ground of ingratiation and the employee–supervisor relationship – one built on power differences – its most prototypical example (Deluga and Perry, 1994). The subordinate employee, often a person low in power resources, may have few other options except for ingratiation to influence the more powerful supervisor. A successfully ingratiating subordinate who has been able to make the target supervisor like her, has achieved a great deal since the supervisor is now more likely to reward and less likely to punish her (Schlenker, 1980). Thus, the ingratiating subordinate has achieved a measure of social influence and control over the powerful superior. By manipulating supervisors to like them, successful ingratiators limit their supervisor's options to punish and control. Employee ingratiation is therefore *power enhancing* in that it restricts the "degrees of freedom" or control that the target has over the subordinate (Kumar and Beyerlein, 1991).

Thirty years ago, this organizational dynamic was brilliantly described by Jones, "he [the ingratiator] may try to amuse his boss with a joke during a conference thus taking time which might have been spent in fulfilling the stated conference purpose of detailing market conditions in the Dubuque [Iowa] area. Insofar as such 'extracurricular activities' succeeded, he becomes attractive to the target person's eyes; and an important consequence of this gain in attractiveness is an enhanced ability to control the target person" (1964, p. 11).

More recently, Wayne and Ferris (1990) have suggested a *cognitive information-processing model* whereby subordinate ingratiation attempts can lead to a cycle of events that positively bias the basic nature of the employee–supervisor relationship. "[T]he successful use of ingratiation by a subordinate may lead a supervisor to form a positive impression of that subordinate and to attribute desirable qualities to him or her. On the basis of these positive attributions and impressions, the supervisor may categorize the employee favorably; doing so may influence the supervisor's immediate responses to the employee, such as affect, and later decisions about the employee, including performance ratings and behaviors related to exchange quality" (1990, p. 488).

Given the dynamics of most contemporary organizations, it is safe to say that ingratiation is a very common feature. One study found that more than one-quarter of managers indicated that they encountered ingratiation on a frequent basis (Allen *et al.*, 1979). This occurrence of employee ingratiation may be expected to intensify when: (a) resources are scarce; (b) individuals are very dependent on each other; (c) job criteria and performance appraisal criteria are subjective; and (d) objective personnel policies are few or not well enforced (Liden and Mitchell, 1988). In sum, ingratiation can be considered a form of upward influence in organizations whereby individuals from the bottom try to influence those above them on the organizational ladder (Ralston, 1985).

Far from being a simple prescription, however, successful ingratiation is an interpersonal minefield that requires skill to prevent detection and avoidance of the attribution that one is a deliberate manipulator. Research on ingratiation suggests a number of methods, techniques and strategies associated with increased probabilities of success. The nature of ingratiation, its organizational implications, and specific forms are discussed below.

TYPES OF INGRATIATION

Opinion conformity

When Aristotle said, "birds of a feather flock together" he intuitively saw what social scientists have extensively documented: similarity breeds attraction. According to Donn Byrne's law of attraction (Byrne, 1971), the greater the proportion of similar attitudes that two people share the more they will like each other. Ingratiators often capitalize on the similarity–attraction relation by becoming "social chameleons:" experts in the art of opinion conformity. They express opinions or act in ways consistent with another person's attitudes, beliefs, and values so as to increase liking (Bohra and Pandey, 1984; Ralston, 1985). An organizational example was provided in his autobiography by Lee Iacocca, the noted former US auto industry executive. According to Iacocca (1984, p. 98), conformity to the proper executive image really mattered to Henry Ford, II, when he was the CEO of Ford Motor Company: "If a guy wore the right clothes and used the right buzz words, Henry was impressed. But without the right veneer, forget it."

There is also research supporting the effectiveness of opinion conformity. According to the results of a study of 152 supervisor/

subordinate pairs (described by Odom, 1993), opinion conformity is the most common and most effective form of ingratiation in organizations (flattery was least popular and least effective). The conclusion was that opinion conformity and other forms of "kissing up" to the boss work, even though the tactics themselves are sometimes transparent to observers and the bosses themselves. As Odom (1993, p. E-12) writes, "They [ingratiation tactics] work because it is human nature to appreciate compliments, to want reassurance that your attitudes are correct and to like the people who admire you. So even when the boss knows you are kissing up, it still pays off – literally – in positive job evaluations, promotions, and higher pay."

Like other forms of ingratiation, opinion conformity thrives on power differentials such as those between bosses and subordinates. In an early ingratiation study, Jones and his colleagues showed that opinion conformity occurred only when a supervisor had the power to evaluate a subordinate's performance (Jones *et al.*, 1965, p. 165). They had respondents rank the effectiveness of advertising slogans in increasing sales. Respondents later overheard a supervisor express either the values of group cooperation or of independence in accomplishing work tasks. The supervisor was either to have the power to evaluate the respondents' performance on the task or not. On an attitude survey completed after they found this out, respondents expressed opinion conformity only when the supervisor had the power to evaluate their performance.

In general, the greater the difference in power between two people in an organizational setting the greater the likelihood that the lower status individual will imitate the attitudes and behaviors of the higher status person. An applicant being interviewed for a job by an avowed vegetarian may offer that she eats very little red meat. A male employee transferred to a female supervisor may claim he deplores the prevalence of sexual harassment. A graduate student seeking a dissertation topic may cite evidence supporting her mentor's pet theory. In a study demonstrating organizational opinion conformity, female job applicants tailored their nonverbal and verbal behaviors to match the views of women held by their interviewer (von Baeyer, Sherk, and Zanna, 1981). When the male interviewer was known to hold views congruent with the traditional female stereotype, female applicants gave more traditional responses to questions about family and relationships, spent more time on their physical appearance and were less assertive in their verbal and nonverbal behaviors than when the interviewer held less traditional attitudes. We will have more to say on impression management in job interviews in Chapter 7.

As with many organizational impression management tactics, opinion conformity is often strategically applied to fit the ingratiator's goals. A study by Jellison and Gentry (1978) illustrates this point. In a simulated job interview situation, some role-playing applicants were informed that the interviewer hired people he liked while others learned that he hired individuals he did not like. On a later selection test, applicants adjusted their attitude statements to the "hiring philosophy" of the interviewer: they matched attitudes when the interviewer hired those he liked and expressed divergent views when they thought the interviewer hired those he did not like.

In addition to power differentials, availability of resources in an organization affects the occurrence of opinion conformity. The more limited resources are, the more ingratiation tactics such as opinion conformity are likely to occur (Liden and Mitchell, 1988). This contention was supported in a study by Pandey and Rastogi (1979). Individuals participated in a hypothetical job interview in a situation that was either competitive (20 job applicants available for 10 jobs) or noncompetitive (20 job applicants available for 40 jobs). More opinion conformity occurred in the competitive situation.

The expression "it's lonely at the top" suggests that leaders may become isolated from the realities of their subordinates' lives. Roy Baumeister (1989) has described a phenomenon called the *boss's illusion* that shows how opinion conformity can lead managers and supervisors to have distorted views of reality. According to Baumeister, the behaviors, attitudes, and values of leaders often become standards that are followed by others. One example is the popularity of red ties in the US because they are favored by President Bill Clinton. As Baumeister (1989, p. 65) notes, "If bosses present themselves as energetic, athletic persons, for example, the subordinates may start to drop remarks about their weekend jogging marathons or after-hours racquetball conquests. If bosses present themselves as casual mavericks – or as strict, staunch adherents to organizational policy and prestige – the subordinates may follow suit." This matching of attitudes and behaviors to those of the boss is, of course, textbook impression management in the form of opinion conformity. The boss, however, often thinks that a subordinate's actions reflect "real" views rather than being strategic impression management. "Bosses may think that subordinates are really similar to themselves, when in fact the subordinates' behavior is simply a reflection of their influence" (Baumeister, 1989, p. 65). The boss's illusion refers to this misreading of subordinates' real views by their superiors.

The boss's illusion may have negative consequences when a subordinate leaves for another job. Freed from the influence of the former boss they may no longer act or think like the boss does. The boss may be predictably dismayed by this "sudden" turnaround. "If they [subordinates] revert to other patterns when the boss' influence ends, and the boss learns this, the boss may perceive them as disloyal and hypocritical" (Baumeister, 1989, p. 65). The boss's illusion, Baumeister suggests, may be one reason why, as Daniel Levinson (1978) has noted, that once-close mentoring relationships (e.g., graduate students and dissertation advisors) often sour and end on a discordant note.

Successful opinion conformity
Two strategies have been associated with successful opinion conformity.

1   *Mixing disagreement with agreement.* Because all ingratiation tactics risk backfiring if too obvious, successful opinion conformity is best if disguised and complicated. One approach is to mix agreement and disagreement with the target's attitudes (Jones, 1990). Disagreement should be given unsurely on trivial issues while agreement is given confidently on important issues. Disagreeing with the boss over who is going to win the Wimbledon tennis tournament (a trivial issue) serves to enhance the credibility of later agreement with the boss's plans for a new marketing strategy (an important issue). Given previous disagreement, conformity appears to be sincere rather than strategic impression management. The effectiveness of mixing agreement and disagreement was shown by Jones, Jones, and Gergen (1963). They found that someone who occasionally agreed with a powerful target was liked better by the target than a person who agreed consistently.

2   *Yielding: Expressing initial disagreement and gradually changing to agreement.* The consistent "yes" man – someone who always agrees with the boss, runs the risk of being viewed as gutless or weak. One way to augment opinion conformity is to

initially disagree with the boss's views on an issue but gradually over time be "persuaded" as to the wisdom of his or her beliefs (Wortman and Linsenmeier, 1977). Yielding allows a person to simultaneously reap the benefits of opinion conformity – increased liking – while also managing the impression of autonomy – one is the kind of person who thinks for oneself.

Favor-doing

The second major category of ingratiation behaviors capitalizes on the simple truth that a good way to instill liking is by doing favors for others. The favor-doer hopes to capitalize on the *norm of reciprocity* which is a universal rule of social behavior suggesting that we should help or pay back those who help or do favors for us (Gouldner, 1960). Favor-doing – especially when the favor is unrequested – instills liking and an obligation to "try to repay in kind what another person has provided us" (Cialdini, 1993, p. 17). Many charitable organizations have found that donations increase when the original solicitation contains an unrequested gift such as customized address labels (Cialdini, 1993).

The ingratiator, however, typically seeks liking rather than an exchange of gifts. This leads to an intriguing possibility: from an ingratiator's standpoint the most effective type of favor-doing is one which *cannot* be readily reciprocated (Jones, 1964). The favor-doer seeks to "trigger a feeling of indebtedness" (Cialdini, 1993, p. 30) which can be exploited as a powerful means of social influence. So if you loan the boss ten dollars to buy lunch, he can easily repay the money later. However, if you install a new tape deck in the boss's car (something the boss cannot do himself), the favor may be "repaid" in increased liking and subsequent organizational rewards that increased liking may influence such as performance evaluations and promotions.

Other-enhancement: ingratiation through flattery and compliments

To Dale Carnegie, honestly praising and flattering others was a key to being successful. Research has shown that these forms of *other-enhancement* are an effective third category of ingratiation behaviors. We tend to like those who like us, praise us, give us positive evaluations, and bolster our self-esteem (Ralston and Elsass, 1989). The ingratiator exploits this simple and powerful social rule to increase the target's liking of him or her. An other-enhancer may manage the impression that she thinks the world of her boss. The boss's positive qualities such as efficiency, intelligence, and appearance are stressed, emphasized, and exaggerated, while negative traits like impatience, temper, and short-sightedness are minimized, distorted, or ignored. If properly disguised and strategically employed, other-enhancement can be a powerful means of getting ahead in an organization. Wright (1979, discussed in Ralston, 1985) claimed that successful executives at General Motors were those who most skillfully flattered their bosses.

Several studies have demonstrated the effectiveness of other-enhancement in organizations. In a classic work, Kipnis and Vanderveer (1971) placed research participants in a situation where they thought they were supervising workers manufacturing products on an assembly line. The participants were told they could send messages to and receive messages from the workers. In actuality, the nature of all the messages was controlled by the researchers to establish the experimental conditions. The messages were manipulated so that one of the hypothetical workers was clearly superior to the other two who both were average performers. One of the two average performers sent other-enhancing messages to the "boss." The messages indicated that the boss was a "nice guy" who could count on the subordinate for help and faster work if needed. Kipnis and Vanderveer found that the use of other-enhancement influenced ratings of the subordinate by the boss-respondents. The average other-enhancer received performance evaluations as high as that of the superior performer and better than the average noningratiating worker – even though their actual performances were the same as the noningratiating workers. Thus, other-enhancement had the rather profound effect of making the ratings of an average worker the same as someone whose actual performance was clearly better!

Other-enhancement was also found to be effective in a simulation study by Pandey and Kakkar (1982). They had role-playing work supervisors send "subordinates" a note explaining a job that the subordinate was to learn. The subordinates replied to the note in either an other-enhancing or nonenhancing manner. It was found that subordinates who sent supervisors the flattering replies were subsequently rated by the supervisors as more attractive, intelligent, and viewed as being more successful and promotable. They were also offered more help and recommended for higher wages. Thus, independent of performance, other-enhancement offers the potential for dramatically improving a person's organizational outcomes.

That successful ingratiation may be as important as actual performance in determining competence has also been suggested by the popular linguist Deborah Tannen as a reason for why men are often more successful than women in many work settings. In studying how men and women differ in their language patterns Tannen has claimed that men in work situations tend to engage in more ingratiating behaviors than women do, the impact being that men benefit more even though they aren't necessarily better workers. As Shapiro (1994, p. 59) summarizes Tannen's view, "she describes men in the workplace who boast and brag, take credit for others' accomplishments and shamelessly court the boss. It works: they get promoted. The women Tannen writes about are far more modest; they concentrate on doing a good job in the belief that it will be rewarded. They're wrong: it isn't." That ingratiation pays – literally – was also the conclusion of a recent study of supervisor–subordinate pairs (described by Odom, 1993). That study concluded that ingratiation gives an employee a 4 to 5 percent edge in their salaries over those who depend only on job performance.

Successful other-enhancement

While other-enhancement may seem plausible in theory, it is not always effective in practice. Because there are negative labels associated with obvious or excessive other-enhancement (see Table 2.1), the technique runs the risk of backfiring. Individuals may be hesitant to use other-enhancement for fear of being viewed negatively if this ingratiation attempt fails.

What makes for effective other-enhancement? Two approaches that increase the likelihood of success have been suggested (Jones, 1990; Schlenker, 1980; Wortman and Linsenmeier, 1977).

1   *Use of third-parties.* The risk of detection can be minimized if a third-party is used to deliver the flattering message (Liden and Mitchell, 1988). Linda Ginzel (see "Behind the Scenes," pp. 30–31) has aptly called this *self-presentation by proxy.* As Wortman and Linsenmeier (1977, p. 145) note, "If a manager is told by one of his colleagues that another colleague made favorable remarks about him, he is unlikely to conclude that the

Table 2.1 Risks of ingratiation: some negative terms associated with blatant other-enhancement

1	Sycophant	6	Back scratcher
2	Bootlicker	7	Kiss-up
3	Apple polisher	8	Brownnoser
4	Yes-man	9	Fawner
5	Toady	10	Flunky

Source: Based on O'Brien (1993, pp. 144, 146)

remarks were made to obtain his affection." Say Bob wants to tell his boss Karen that he really likes her and she is the best boss he has ever worked for. Rather than risk telling Karen this directly, Bob instead praises Karen to her secretary Val. The hope is that eventually Val will pass this on to Karen, and Bob will gain the benefits of other-enhancement without risking its dangers.

2   *Making compliments credible.* To be effective, other-enhancement must be credible. To maintain credibility, factors such as *timing, frequency,* and *discernment* should be considered. Timing means that the delivery of other-enhancement should not be linked to a desired goal. Asking for a promotion right after telling the boss how bright she is may make the strategic nature of the compliment obvious and thus, counterproductive. The frequency of other-enhancement is also a factor in its likely success. In general, other-enhancement is a tactic best used sparingly. If Liz gains a reputation as one who uses compliments all the time, this will likely undermine the effectiveness of her future attempts at flattery. In an organizational setting, if Edward is intent on ingratiating a specific target such as his supervisor, he is best advised to limit complimenting other people in the supervisor's presence. Lastly, effective other-enhancement should be discerning since indiscriminate other-enhancement is likely to fail. An effective approach is to mix flattery with criticism – the compliments should be in important areas and the negative comments in trivial areas or in acknowledged areas of weakness. For example, when Cathy points out to her boss Ralph, while returning from a business trip, that he is

driving too fast, the credibility of her also saying that Ralph's presentation at the company's annual sales meeting was fantastic is enhanced. It has also been found that other-enhancement is more likely to be effective when it stresses the target's personal effectiveness (Ralston and Elsass, 1989) or is for characteristics the target finds desirable but is unsure that he or she possesses them (Schlenker, 1980).

Self-enhancement

The fourth and final type of ingratiation is self-enhancement – directly using acquisitive impression management to make oneself be seen as more attractive (Schlenker, 1980). Through self-enhancement the ingratiator's best characteristics are made salient to target audiences. The goal of this form of ingratiation is to find out what the target thinks is attractive and claim it for oneself.

In organizational settings, self-enhancement is commonplace in job interviews (Rosenfeld, in press). The candidate who really wants a job in a sales department may stress how good he is at relating to people and how persuasive he is in conversations with others. This technique of playing up one's strengths may be effective. It has been found that job applicants who used impression management tactics that focused on themselves were rated higher than applicants whose impression management tactics focused on the interviewer (Kacmar, Delery, and Ferris, 1992).

While individuals will often engage in self-enhancement to please significant others, reality serves to constrain overly self-aggrandizing presentations (Schlenker, 1980). When information exists that could repudiate an overly positive claim, individuals will present themselves in a more accurate fashion, one that is closer to what they really believe (Schlenker, 1975). Cascio (1975), for example, found that exaggeration in résumés and application blanks was less likely to occur when the information could be verified by previous employers.

When reality constrains self-enhancement in one area, individuals may engage in *compensatory impression management*. Baumeister and Jones (1978) found that respondents who scored poorly on a personality test did not contradict this to an observer who knew of their poor performance. However, they engaged in compensatory impression management by exaggerating their personality descriptions for characteristics that the audience had no direct information

BOX 2.1

Exaggerated self-enhancement

Two real-world examples

An interesting example of the dangers of unchecked self-enhancement that came to light in the wake of the break up of the Soviet Union is the claim of longevity by residents of the former Soviet republic of Georgia. During the 1970s, Danon yogurt had a successful advertising campaign based on claims that residents of Georgia regularly lived past 100 years of age on a diet consisting largely of yogurt. A recent US Census Bureau study utilizing greater access to the former Soviet Union (and a greater ability to check the veracity of these contentions) found that the claims of longevity were due largely to the inaccurate reporting by the Georgian residents of their age! (Geier and Hawkins, 1993).

There also seems to have been some exaggerated self-enhancement regarding the performance of US-made Patriot missiles in shooting down Iraqi Scud missiles over Israel during the Persian Gulf War. *Newsweek Magazine* reported that the US military continues to claim that the Patriot missile had a 40 percent success rate over Israel ("Anti-Scud Duds", 1993). This despite an Israeli defense official informing US President George Bush in February 1991 that Patriots successfully intercepted only about 20 percent of incoming Scuds. Several days later, Bush claimed that the Patriot performed nearly perfectly. *Newsweek* reports that in 1993 Israeli defense officials acknowledged that the Patriots had knocked out one Scud at best and none at worst!

---

about. Therefore, one factor associated with successful self-enhancement is how much information the audience has about the claim and how easy it would be for them to check. The general rule as stated by Schlenker (1980, p. 188) is, "the more difficult it is for the audience to check the veracity of a self-presentation the more likely people are to self-aggrandize." In practice, the successful self-enhancer will acknowledge known weaknesses but make overly positive claims for things the audience knows little or nothing about. Box 2.1 presents several examples of overly positive claims that were later repudiated when more information came to light.

THE INGRATIATOR'S DILEMMA

The use of ingratiation is more skill than science; an interpersonal minefield fraught with constant danger and the risk of unpredictable explosions. If the boss comes to believe that Barbara's compliments and kind actions are simply attempts to win his favor, he may react negatively and come to dislike her more. The consequences of failed ingratiation are not neutral but rather they may place the ingratiator in a far worse impression management predicament – being disliked – than when he or she began (Arkin and Sheppard, 1990).

These dangers illustrate the concept of the *ingratiator's dilemma*. In general, the greater the person's need to engage in ingratiation, the more likely it is that the ingratiation attempts will be detected and fail (Jones, 1990). Rather than being used blindly, ingratiation often requires a person to engage in a complicated decision process. Jones and Pittman (1982) suggest that this decision to engage in ingratiation involves the consideration of motivational, cognitive, and ethical factors.

Motivational

The motivational component of ingratiation is called *incentive value*. It refers to how important it is for a person to be liked by the target. The greater the dependency of a person on a target, the greater the need for ingratiation. Incentive value goes up as the power difference between a person and a target increases. There will often be a greater incentive value for Ira to ingratiate himself with his boss than with his peers. Ira's incentive value will be particularly high if he needs the boss's support to get a promotion he really wants.

Cognitive

The cognitive aspect of the ingratiation decision is called *subjective probability*. It refers to how successful a person thinks an ingratiation attempt will be. Generally, the higher the subjective probability of success, the more likely it is that a person will attempt to ingratiate a target. Kara is more likely to compliment her vain management instructor on his lecture than she is her contentious business statistics professor. The vain management instructor is more apt to appreciate and agree with the flattering statement and reciprocate with increased liking of Kara. The contentious statistics professor is more likely to see the compliment as intentional ingratiation and discount its sincerity. Thus, there is a higher subjective probability associated with ingratiating the management instructor than the business statistics professor.

The ingratiator's dilemma can be thought of as the dynamic interplay between these motivational and cognitive components. As a person becomes more dependent on a target, his or her need or motivation to ingratiate the target increases. However, because dependency increases the *salience* of ingratiation attempts (they become more obvious and detectable) the cognitive part – the subjective probability of success – decreases as the motivational aspect increases. As Jones and Pittman (1982, p. 237) note, "the dilemma for the ingratiator is that the more important it is for him to gain a high-power target's attraction, the less likely it is that he will be successful."

Ethical

Assuming a person resolves the ingratiator's dilemma and concludes that it is worth the risk, one final aspect must also be considered. This is the ethical or moral justification for using ingratiation in a particular situation. This factor – known as *perceived legitimacy* – refers to the degree that ingratiation is considered appropriate in particular settings. For instance, a husband might avoid using ingratiation with his wife, or a worshipper his minister or rabbi, or a client her psychotherapist – not because they are incapable of the act, but because perceived legitimacy is low. Ingratiation in these settings violates norms stressing authenticity rather than strategic impression management.

Just as there are situations which constrain the use of ingratiation, there are other settings in which it is more appropriate. The perceived legitimacy or ethics of ingratiation depends on the situation or environment one encounters. We contend that organizational environments, for the most part, are settings that condone ingratiation. In the business world, salesmanship and trying to make others like you are legitimate ways of operating. Power differentials are inherent in the structure of most organizations and those low on the "food chain" often have few avenues of social influence other than ingratiation. As

Jones and Pittman (1982, p. 238) insightfully write, "Ingratiation is likely to be perceived as legitimate in settings where self-salesmanship is sanctioned by the individualistic norms of the business world."

RESOLVING THE INGRATIATOR'S DILEMMA: FACTORS ASSOCIATED WITH SUCCESSFUL INGRATIATION

Avoiding blatant ingratiation: adopting a complicating strategy

Although successful ingratiation can never be guaranteed, our analysis of the ingratiator's dilemma suggests that blatant ingratiation may be worse than doing nothing at all. Blatant ingratiation is often easily detected, leading targets to view the ingratiator as having ulterior motives (Jones and Pittman, 1982). A more successful approach is to adopt a *complicating strategy*. The ingratiator may act modest or even denigrate herself to "even things out." The key is to be modest and self-denigrating on things that are trivial or unimportant while being self-enhancing on core issues (Schlenker, 1980). The aim of this complicating strategy is to use modesty and self-denigration to increase the credibility of subsequent ingratiation attempts. While describing to his boss all the extra hours he has logged on the road selling insurance, Bill jokingly suggests that one reason he needs a raise is to pay for several speeding tickets he got: "I guess I'm a lousy driver but a great salesman" he says, in effect bolstering the validity of job-relevant ingratiation – selling insurance – by admitting a flaw on a job-irrelevant characteristic – driving ability.

Is a complicating strategy enough to make ingratiation work? Are bosses so blind that they can't see ingratiation attempts for what they really are? The answer to these questions is often, surprisingly, "yes." Because targets – bosses, supervisors, CEOs, etc. – have a need to be liked (we all do!!), they are often more likely to view ingratiation attempts as sincere than are others observing the same interaction. It has been found that targets are more hesitant to attribute ingratiation attempts to ulterior motives than are other observers (Jones and Pittman, 1982). Even though all his colleagues view Reg's conversations with his boss, Deborah, about the latest exhibits at the art museum as blatant "sucking up," Deborah buys into it and thinks Reg is a sensitive, nice guy – so unusual for a man in her department to like fine art!!

Disclosing obstacles to successful performance

A wise person once said "success has many fathers but failure is an orphan." From the ingratiator's perspective, the motivation to associate with success is powerful since everyone likes a winner and ingratiators want to be liked. But direct self-enhancement following success runs the risk of being perceived as haughty or boastful. Giacalone and Riordan (1990) found that by disclosing obstacles a person could gain credit for success without being perceived as overly pompous. They had respondents read a fictional account of a manager of a hospital research project who had discovered a cure for a fatal disease. The manager either disclosed obstacles to success – indicated at a press conference that the cure was found despite a fire in the lab and budget cuts – or was modest – said the discovery couldn't have been made without the support and help of colleagues. The results showed that the manager who disclosed obstacles to success was given more credit and recognition for the discovery than one who was modest.

Reducing salience of power differentials

Although differences in power increase the need for ingratiation, they also raise the likelihood of detection. Therefore, it is best to make ingratiation attempts when these power differentials are *not* salient. Complimenting the boss on what a fine family he has may work better at the annual company holiday party than the day before performance appraisals are conducted. Telling an interviewer during a job interview that she has nice taste in clothes may backfire, while the same statement during a chance encounter in a shopping mall may be viewed as sincere.

A CONCLUDING NOTE

This chapter has reviewed different ways that people use ingratiation tactics to get others to like, reward, and view them favorably. Although many ingratiation tactics may seem simple or obvious, our review has found that they can be effective means of social influence among coworkers, supervisors and subordinates, and even among strangers meeting for the first time. In addition to ingratiation, there are a number of other acquisitive impression management tactics that are used both in and out of organizational settings. We consider these in Chapter 3.

3 Beyond ingratiation
Other acquisitive impression management techniques

A TOAST TO TOASTMASTERS

The name Ralph C. Smedley is probably not familiar to all but the most serious of trivia experts. Smedley was neither an impression management researcher nor was he an organizational theorist. Yet his efforts seven decades ago had a profound impact on the practice of managing impressions in organizational settings. Seventy years ago, in a basement of a YMCA building in Santa Ana, California, Smedley founded Toastmasters International, an organization dedicated to helping people make effective public presentations. Today, Toastmasters has over 8,000 chapters and more than 170,000 members worldwide. It has also become very popular with businesses, many of which allow their employees to attend meetings on company time. Toastmasters still advocates the simple principles of public speaking proposed by Smedley: practice, plenty of feedback, and addressing a group just as one would address a single person (Hamashige, 1994).

Both employees who seek to improve their presentation skills at Toastmasters, and employers who support their involvement, realize that, in today's corporate world, effective presentations are important vehicles for managing impressions of the individual and the organization. A poor presentation may damage the employer's image and limit the employee's chances for promotion to management or other executive positions.

In Chapter 2 we focused on ingratiation – a series of techniques that all share a common impression management goal: making others like you. While ingratiation has been the most studied of acquisitive impression management tactics it is by no means the only one. The goal of members of Toastmasters, particularly those from the business world, is not just to be liked following a successful presentation, but, more crucially, to be viewed as competent and knowledgeable. This form of acquisitive impression management is known as *self-promotion*.

In Chapter 3 we look at ways other than ingratiation that individuals and organizations use to manage positive impressions. We describe these other acquisitive tactics, the impressions they seek to achieve, and their applications to organizational settings. We also consider how individuals utilize the principle of association while engaging in impression management and how nonverbal behaviors may influence the impressions people try to make.

SELF-PROMOTION

While at first glance, self-promotion may seem to be another form of ingratiation, it has a different goal. In contrast to the ingratiator who wants to be liked, the self-promoter wants to be seen as competent (Jones, 1990). According to Giacalone and Rosenfeld (1986, p. 321), "The self-promoter tries to make others think he or she is competent on either general ability dimensions (e.g., intelligence) or specific skills (e.g., ability to play a musical instrument)."

Self-promotion tactics may work hand-in-hand with ingratiation attempts or may conflict with them. For example, assume that Marie is being interviewed by Jerry for a job as an aerobics instructor at the local health club. Upon first meeting Jerry, she smiles and compliments him on his well-developed muscles (ingratiation). During the interview, Marie also "sings her own praises" – in glowing terms she describes her extensive previous experience teaching aerobics in other clubs (self-promotion). Marie's behavior illustrates that in organizations it is often in a person's best interests to be both liked and seen as competent. While individuals use self-promotion to make others think they are more competent, a related tactic described in Box 3.1, called *window-dressing*, is used at the organization level to achieve similar ends.

Though self-promotion and ingratiation may go hand-in-hand, they are not always equally achievable. One study of conversation patterns (Godfrey, Jones, and Lord, 1986) found that it was easier to be a successful ingratiator than a successful self-promoter. This may be because getting people to like you through ingratiation is

BOX 3.1

Window-dressing on Wall Street

Just as individuals engage in acquisitive impression management tactics such as ingratiation and self-promotion to make themselves liked and viewed as competent, so do organizations or institutions attempt to enhance their images as being competent, fiscally reliable, and caring. One such tactic is called *window-dressing*. Individuals and organizations that use window-dressing engage in a form of superficial or expedient manipulation to make themselves look better publicly. One recent example involved the New York Stock Market.

After a long and steady period of gains, the New York Stock Market experienced a dramatic decline during the first quarter of 1994 – with losses running at about 10 percent of their previous highs. Towards the end of the first quarter of 1994 (March 31), it was reported in the popular press that portfolio managers – individuals who manage large corporate investments (e.g., pension funds, insurance companies) in the stock market – were engaging in window-dressing. Usually, portfolio managers have to issue reports to investors every three months. However, as March 1994 approached, the general decline in the stock market left many portfolios with stocks that had done poorly. Window-dressing refers to the last-minute practice of purchasing stocks that have done well and selling stocks that have done poorly so that the overall portfolio presented to investors looks better than it would had these late adjustments not been made. While window-dressing may have helped the reputations of portfolio managers and the firms they represent, it had the impact of hurting the stock market even more: the increased sales of "losers" resulted in the market falling even more on the last days of March 1994.

(Craig and Rosato, 1994)

---

frequently a *reactive process*. The ingratiator can defer to the target, mumble agreement, and engage in positive nonverbals such as smiling. Self-promotion on the other hand tends to be a *proactive process*. If Maurice wants to convince the boss of his competence, he can't sit back and rest on his laurels – he has to actively say or do something.

There are times when self-promotion and ingratiation attempts are at cross-purposes. The ingratiator who acts modestly, or passively agrees with his boss's opinions, may not be viewed as very smart, independent, or competent (Jones, 1990). Successful or aggressive self-promotion attempts also run the risk of making others feel jealous or resentful. If one of our work colleagues is viewed as smart, competent, and intelligent, what does that say about us? While many people acknowledge the computer savvy and brilliance of Bill Gates, the founder and head of Microsoft, Gates is also widely disliked for the aggressive and highly competitive way he does business.

It has been suggested that successful self-promotion may also be intimidating (Jones and Pittman, 1982). While we may like competent people up to a point, at some level they become scary and fear-inducing. We may hesitate to publicly disagree with a Nobel prize winner in economics even when we have found an error in his calculations.

Research has shown that self-promotion is quite common, especially when the claims are for important audiences or occasions. In an early study, Gordon and Stapleton (1956) had high school students take a personality test either as part of a job application or for a guidance class. They found higher scores were obtained when the test was to be for the more important job application. Hendricks and Brickman (1974) found that college students overestimated their expected course grade if their teacher was to see it but were more accurate if a peer was to see it.

Self-promotion also is more frequent when the claims are not likely to be challenged or discredited. In an organizational study, Goldstein (1971) compared the job applications of candidates for a nurse's aide job with their records of previous employment. It was found that over half of the applicants exaggerated their length of service and pay at their previous jobs.

Given these findings, we would expect that the occurrence of self-promotion would increase when people have the opportunity to publicly impress a higher status target about their competence. This was demonstrated in a field experiment using full-time New York state legislative interns (Giacalone and Rosenfeld, 1986). The interns were sent a survey that they were told to complete while either anonymous or identified (i.e., names included) and were to return it either to a fellow intern (low status) or to the director of the internship program (high status). The survey asked the interns to rate themselves on items related to their competence, abilities, and traits. It was found that the interns exhibited the most self-promotion (i.e., had the highest self-ratings of competence) when their surveys had identifying information and would be returned to the director.

INTIMIDATION

While the ingratiator wants to be liked, and the self-promoter wants to be seen as competent, the goal of the intimidator is to be feared. The intimidator tries to gain social power and influence by creating an identity of being dangerous – one whose threats and warnings are to be obeyed, or negative consequences will occur (Arkin and Shepperd, 1990). As Jones and Pittman (1982, p. 238) note, "the intimidator advertises his available power to create discomfort or all kinds of psychic pain."

Intimidation is more likely to occur in nonvoluntary relationships such as the one between supervisors and subordinates. The supervisor's ability to influence or control a subordinate's salary, performance evaluations, and promotions often creates an atmosphere of intimidation – one where it is clear that noncompliance will have severe consequences. Rather than being inherently good or bad, intimidation like ingratiation is often a natural outgrowth of the social structure of organizations. Subordinates need to use ingratiation because they usually have little power; they have no better way of influencing others than by manipulating liking. Superiors (e.g., management), who by definition control power resources, have less reason to want to be liked. Indeed, to a person in power, being liked too much is a risky business – it can reduce compliance by lessening respect and fear. Social psychologists have found that people who like each other are not as likely to use threats. Thus, the library director who becomes overly "chummy" with her staff may lose their respect and fear, undermining the effectiveness of her power base. The intimidator who can't or doesn't back up threats may be viewed as weak and impotent.

In many ways, intimidation is the opposite of ingratiation (Jones and Pittman, 1982). While the ingratiator dangles a carrot, the intimidator wields a big stick. Successful intimidation often makes the intimidator less rather than more liked. While ingratiation may bring people together, intimidation drives them apart; if used indiscriminately or excessively it can reduce organizational cohesiveness.

Though intimidation is the opposite of ingratiation, successful intimidation often elicits ingratiation. The *intimidator's illusion* is that the intimidator may come to think that his or her behavior is liked and accepted when in fact it is loathed and detested. The liking and acceptance presented in response to intimidation is in reality strategic impression management – an attempt to counter or neutralize the intimidator's influence attempts. While Jane "gladly" agrees to work late to finish a presentation for her boss, Mr Grumps, she secretly despises him for constantly dumping work on her at the last minute. He takes her smiling agreement as both a sign of his successful management style and as a further reason to view Jane favorably. Mr Grumps later recommends that Jane receive a large bonus. Her smiling acceptance has influenced Mr Grumps's behavior more favorably in her direction than if she had frowned and complained – actions that would have been more reflective of her "true self."

In organizations, intimidation is typically a form of *downward influence* – flowing downhill from higher power to lower power individuals. There are cases, however, where those lower in status can intimidate those above them. Jones and Pittman (1982) refer to this use of intimidation by those low in status as *counterpower*. It has been suggested that lower-class, inner-city, African–American males in the US may adopt an intimidating "cool pose" – actions that advertise hypermasculinity, toughness, and a willingness to use violence – as a way of gaining social power in the face of limited educational and employment opportunities (Freiberg, 1991).

In organizational settings, an incompetent handicapped worker who vows to sue if not promoted, or an elderly employee who lets it be known that he will file an age discrimination claim if disciplined for unauthorized absences, use intimidation even though they themselves are weak. A case of counterpower intimidation we witnessed involved a woman who had openly flirted with and willingly participated with her male colleagues in "dirty joke" sessions. Later, when her work performance was criticized, she claimed to have been the victim of sexual harassment during those joke sessions. Her intimidating tactics successfully kept her supervisor from taking disciplinary action. Given the high personal costs associated with filing sexual harassment complaints, we suspect such blatantly false sexual harassment claims are uncommon. However, they do in some ways quickly shift the power to the "victim" and therefore can be a potent source of counterpower.

EXEMPLIFICATION

Exemplification involves managing the impressions of integrity, self-sacrifice, and moral worthiness (Jones and Pittman, 1982). The exemplifier is the boss who shows up early and stays late, the coworker who takes work home everyday, and the colleague who never takes a vacation. Exemplifiers volunteer for difficult assignments. They willingly suffer to help others. They go beyond the call of duty.

From an impression management perspective, exemplification often involves *strategic self-sacrifice*. There is method to the exemplifier's martyrdom. The exemplifier attempts to influence and control through inducing guilt or attributions of virtue that may lead to imitation by others. The exemplifier often wants others to know how hard she is working. Exemplifiers will let you know that they haven't had a day off in months, that they worked all weekend on the Annual Report, or that a killer migraine didn't keep them away from their desks.

Because exemplifiers need to "advertise" their behavior, they run the risk of being viewed by others as sanctimonious. Also, if their behavior doesn't live up to their lofty claims, they may be seen as hypocrites. In the Fall of 1994, there were a number of media stories reporting that the well-known American football player, Barry Sanders, was the unmarried father of a $5\frac{1}{2}$-month-old son. What made the item newsworthy was that Sanders was once a spokesperson against premarital sex and had said in interviews that he was celibate. After being questioned about this apparent contradiction between his public statements and private actions, Sanders indicated that he no longer speaks about the premarital sex issue! Box 3.2 gives some additional examples of private behavior that didn't match public exemplification.

BOX 3.2

Practicing what they preach, *not*!!

Exemplification in public and private

In 1993, US President Bill Clinton made speeches advocating personal responsibility and the virtues of family-type values. At the same time, widespread media accounts appeared alleging that he had extra-marital affairs and accused him of sexually harassing a former state employee while governor of Arkansas. Similarly, the Reverend Jimmy Swaggert, a popular US television evangelist, had the sincerity of his religious preaching questioned after he was caught soliciting a prostitute. Because the "flesh is weak," the exemplifier's most difficult chore may be living up to the identity that he has so carefully crafted (Gilbert and Jones, 1986).

An organizational example of public exemplification that didn't match private behavior occurred in Dallas, Texas, in 1981. Oak Communications surveyed members of the community to determine what sorts of cable television services the residents wanted. The survey results indicated that adult programming that involved sex and nudity came off very low. However, when cable subscribers could privately sign up for the adult channel, 60 percent did!

This sort of public exemplification may be a cross-cultural phenomenon. In 1993, the British Broadcasting Corporation decided to air a documentary about Chairman Mao Tse-Tung, the former leader of Communist China (Tuohy, 1993). The documentary was aired over the objections of the Chinese government to the documentary's unflattering portrait of Chairman Mao as a leader who held markedly different views of sex and women in private than in public. "In public, Mao espoused the cause of women's rights ... In private he collected, used, and discarded concubines by the hundreds. The image promoted by the Communist authorities of Mao as an ascetic, almost puritan figure, could not have been further from the truth" (Tuohy, 1993, p. A4).

SUPPLICATION

Supplication is the acquisitive impression management strategy of last resort. The supplicator exploits his own weakness to influence others. We might say that supplicators are adroit at managing the impression of incompetence, or "looking bad" (Becker and Martin, 1995). By advertising their incompetence, supplicators attempt to activate a powerful social rule known as the *norm of social responsibility* that says we should help those who are in need. When Betty lets Sam know that she can't sleep at night because she is intimidated by the firm's new computer system, Sam offers to teach her how to use it. When Bob, a new employee at the Kraft Day Care Center, tries unsuccessfully to change baby Drew's diaper, his supervisor Karen jumps in and does it for him. Negotiation expert Stephen M. Pollan claims this "I-need-your-help" approach is an effective bargaining tactic in business negotiations for things such as increased severance pay after being fired. It works, he recently noted, because "Asking for help is like apple pie – nobody can say no" (Overstreet, 1994, p. 2B). Thus, successful supplication is the opposite of self-promotion; we get help from others if they believe we can't help ourselves.

There are limits, however, to how much people will help supplicators. If overused, the supplicator may gain a reputation as a malingerer, one who would rather feed at the public trough than do things for himself. Supplication works best when it is associated with *compensatory exchanges* (Jones, 1990). For example, José may be a statistical and computer whiz but may lack presentation skills, while another member of his workgroup, Willy, may be "Mr Slick" in public but lack quantitative abilities. Through compensatory exchanges, José helps Willy with the quantitative part of the quarterly report, while Willy expertly presents the results to their boss.

INDIRECT IMPRESSION MANAGEMENT

At the height of his wealth and success, the financier Baron de Rothschild was petitioned for a loan by an acquaintance. Reputedly, the great man replied, "I won't give you a loan myself; but I will walk arm-in-arm with you across the floor of the Stock Exchange, and you soon shall have willing lenders to spare."

(Cialdini, 1989, p. 45)

It is clear that acquisitive impression management has its risks; the best laid plans of mice and managers may backfire. Therefore, it often is prudent for the impression manager to use indirect means. We owe much of our knowledge of indirect impression management to the work of Robert B. Cialdini.

Cialdini and colleagues have found that individuals will utilize associations with positive others for impression management purposes, even when the associations are due to chance or are trivial. Indirect impression management is based on the simple premise that we can influence how others view us by managing information about things and people we are associated with (Cialdini, 1989). The indirect impression manager lives by the slogan, "you are judged by the company you keep."

Indirect impression management utilizes the *association principle* which states that individuals will attempt to maximize their links to desirable things and minimize associations with disfavored images. People associate themselves with desirable things through behaviors or statements known as *claims* (Schlenker, 1980). By being attached to something positive, the person hopes that others will view him positively as well – even if the connection is casual. Indirect impression management also capitalizes on the principle of *evaluative generalization* (Schlenker, 1980) which says that people linked to positive entities will themselves often be rated positively. Politicians and advertisers are well aware of the power of positive associations and often hire celebrities to endorse their products. When US President Clinton delivered his plans for health-care reform to the US Congress in October 1993 one freshman Congressman from San Diego, California, was reported in the press to have shown up early, avoided socializing with others, carefully observed the seating arrangements and chose a chair directly behind the one set aside for the President, one that would be within "camera range" of the President.

Advertising is full of examples of indirect impression management. For many years, pop star Michael Jackson appeared in advertisements for Pepsi, a relationship that was quickly terminated after Jackson was accused of allegedly sexually molesting a young boy. The *New York Times* reported that the noted marine explorer Jacques Cousteau was suing a California dairy for 1.2 million dollars because the dairy had portrayed its mascot cow on a billboard wearing flippers and a wet suit as "Jacques Cowsteau" ("For

California cow, one caricature too many," 1993). Lawyers for Cousteau indicated that the marine explorer felt that people seeing the billboard would think that Cousteau was endorsing the dairy's milk when in fact he was not.

This notion of association with a positive other implying endorsement underlies much of indirect impression management. After being hired as a junior partner in a law firm, Lloyd's colleagues noticed this sort of indirect impression management. Lloyd always bought the best suits, ate in the best restaurants, drank the finest wine, drove an expensive sports car, lived in a posh neighborhood, and dated women from well-to-do families. Lloyd would likely subscribe to a cardinal principle of indirect impression management, "What we do is often less important than whom we do it with" (Cialdini, Finch, and De Nicolas, 1990).

In one of Cialdini's more famous studies of indirect impression management, he and his colleagues found that on the Monday following college football games, students wore more school-related items (e.g., sweatshirts, buttons) when the school had won the previous Saturday than when they had lost (Cialdini *et al.*, 1976). They were also more likely to use the pronoun "we" in describing the school's victory than defeat. This form of impression management by association is called *basking in reflected glory* (BIRG).

While the students in this BIRGing study had some connection to the victorious school, indirect impression management occurs even when associations are accidental. This was demonstrated for a phenomenon called *boosting* (Finch and Cialdini, 1989). Boosting refers to the tendency for individuals who are somehow associated with a negative other to rate that person's character more positively. For example, although both former US President Jimmy Carter's brother Billy and President Clinton's half-brother Roger were widely portrayed as uncouth publicity-seekers by the press, their presidential siblings publicly boosted them. In the Finch and Cialdini (1989) study, respondents were given an unflattering description of Rasputin, the Mad Monk of Russia. Half of the respondents learned that they had the same birthday as Rasputin, while the others were not given any birthday information. It was found that those who shared a birthday with Rasputin rated him less negatively. From an impression management perspective, viewing Rasputin as less negative lessens the impact of being associated with a stigmatized other.

Although the boosting phenomenon has not been studied in

organizations, one area where it might apply is to diversity issues (see Chapter 8). For example, do members of minority groups, or women engage in boosting for underperforming members of their groups? While white males are not typically held responsible for the work performance of other white males, this may not be true for minority group members and women – newcomers to more powerful positions in many corporations. One prediction would be that a minority executive may engage in boosting more for the unexcused absences of a minority subordinate than a white executive would for a white subordinate.

According to Cialdini (1989), a factor that increases indirect impression management in organizations is *setbacks*, especially those that reflect on a person's self-esteem. For example, assume Kyle is an up-and-coming salesman in a public relations firm. However, Kyle's abrasiveness recently alienated one of his firm's clients and he lost a major account. While informing his boss that he has just lost this important advertising client, Kyle makes sure to stress how prestigious the firms that he still has accounts with are, and how much better they are than the client that he lost. Kyle is engaging in a form of indirect impression management called *burnishing*, which involves stressing the favorable features of something we are positively linked to (Cialdini, 1989). That burnishing increases following failure was demonstrated by Cialdini and Richardson (1980). They found that students who thought they had failed a creativity test were more likely to describe the academic, cultural, and social environment of their school in glowing terms than those who thought they had done well on the test.

ACCLAIMING

The desire to engage in impression management is especially strong following success. One application of the association principle is that people will try to stress, highlight, exaggerate, or distort their relationship to successful outcomes to bolster their public images (Schlenker, 1980). According to Schlenker (1980, p. 163), acclaiming tactics, "are designed to explain a desirable event in a way that maximizes the desirable implications for the actor."

There are two forms of acclaiming: *entitlements* and *enhancements*. Entitlements are attempts to maximize responsibility for positive events. They are especially likely to occur when responsibility for the positive outcome is either ambiguous or unclear (Schlenker, 1980). For example, when the present authors were all graduate students working in the same social psychology laboratory we observed the following scenario: A graduate student would propose an idea for a research study at a meeting attended by other graduate students and our mentor/advisor. A year or two later, after the project was done and was about to be published, the graduate student who had come up with the idea (and done all the work) was surprised to find that he had three other people claiming that they merited coauthorship. "I helped you come up with the idea," said one. "You based your project on my past work," said another. "I helped you with the stats," claimed a third. Success has many fathers (and mothers) and our journal articles often had many extra authors due to this entitlement phenomenon. Of course, all three authors of this book claim that they have done the lion's-share of the work, an entitlement that may change in intensity depending on how success-ful it turns out to be!

Enhancements try to maximize how desirable a positive occur-rence is. When Valerie claims that the award-winning advertising campaign was "her own" idea rather than giving credit to her campaign team, her claim is an entitlement. When Bob remarks that his son Farrell didn't just graduate from "any business school" but got his degree from the best one in the country, Bob is offering an enhancement.

Research on acclaiming has typically focused on entitlements. A cross-cultural study (Rosenfeld, Giacalone, and Bond, 1983) found that entitlements, if challenged, can backfire. In that study, US and Hong Kong Chinese students read scenarios describing a medical research team that had discovered a cure for a serious disease. Some of the students read that the assistant project director called a news conference and claimed that he had the idea that led to the break-through. This entitlement claim was either confirmed or challenged by subsequent statements made by the project director. Respondents then evaluated the assistant director. Interestingly, while the ratings of the assistant director were somewhat more positive when he made an entitlement than when no entitlement was given, the differences between entitlement and no entitlement conditions for both American and Hong Kong Chinese students were not statistically significant even when the entitlement was confirmed. However, when the entitlement claim was disconfirmed, the ratings of the assistant director were significantly less positive for both Americans and Hong Kong Chinese. Apparently, using entitlements can backfire when they are not substantiated by accompanying evidence.

Bob Giacalone (1985) applied this backfiring notion to organizational settings. He warned that employees who engage in *random entitlements* run the risk of "slipping" when they thought they had put their best foot forward. How can entitlements be made more effective and less risky? Giacalone advises using the principle of *third-party impression management* (also known as *self-presentation by proxy*) we noted to be effective for ingratiation attempts. In a study using a version of the medical discovery scenario described above, Giacalone (1985) found that the assistant director was seen as more intelligent, successful, competent, and moral when he was the beneficiary of this third-party entitlement: A hospital spokesperson announced at a news conference that the assistant director should be credited with the discovery. Third-party entitlements were more successful than no entitlements or entitlements that the assistant director made on his own behalf.

NONVERBAL IMPRESSION MANAGEMENT

The employment manager of a large New York department store told me she would rather hire a sales clerk who hadn't finished grade school, if he or she has a pleasant smile, than to hire a doctor of philosophy with a somber face.

(Dale Carnegie, 1936, p. 67)

Dale Carnegie recognized the importance of smiling as a potent way of making people like us. Today we realize that many different types of *nonverbal behaviors* can be used in the service of impression management. Facial expressions, touching, body orientation, posture and interpersonal distance can strongly influence the impressions we form of others and they of us (DePaulo, 1992). Marie is encouraged when her boss Pat nods and smiles during her presentation of a proposed new marketing strategy. Stephanie thinks her boss Jules looked bored and skeptical when she argues for a long-overdue raise and promotion. Her boss's "nonverbals" make a clear impression; Stephanie doubts her plea will be successful. Table 3.1 provides six reasons why nonverbal behavior plays an important role in impression management.

Table 3.1 Six reasons why nonverbal behavior is important for impression management

---

1 **Irrepressible**
   Explanation: It's hard to not make an impression nonverbally. Even if people don't move, their posture may send signals.
   Example: Jim, a manager, tightens up when a female employee who has charged him with sexual harassment enters the office.

2 **Linked to emotion**
   Explanation: Certain nonverbal behaviors such as facial expressions are automatically linked to emotions such as fear. These emotional reactions may more directly convey an impression than corresponding verbal statements which are more under voluntary control.
   Example: When Katie discovers that her coworker Kurt has been promoted instead of her, she verbally congratulates Kurt. Her facial expressions, however, convey how disappointed and mad she really is.

3 **Less accessible**
   Explanation: People know less about their own nonverbal behaviors than others do. Other people see our expressions but we don't. This less accessible feature of nonverbal behavior may constrain the use of intentional nonverbal impression management since people can't control what they are unaware of.
   Example: Paul passes his coworker Jack at the company cafeteria several times a week. Paul is often preoccupied and rarely makes eye contact or acknowledges Jack's presence. Jack interprets these nonverbals as conveying dislike for him, while in actuality Paul doesn't realize the negative vibes he is giving off.

4 **Off-the-record**
   Explanation: Nonverbal behavior is elusive. It is more difficult for people to describe what nonverbals occurred or to repeat them compared with verbal behaviors. Therefore, people may be more likely to risk expressing something nonverbally that they would be hesitant to express verbally. If there are negative consequences they can deny that it happened or that they meant it.
   Example: Ted is attracted to Nancy, one of the secretaries in the typing pool. When she walks by, he leers and stares at her. When Nancy later complains to Ted's boss, he denies that he has done anything wrong.

5 **Communicates unique meanings**
   Explanation: There are some meanings that can't be easily expressed in words.
   Example: Josh finds the negotiations with the union over a new contract to be very frustrating. When Sally asks for his impression of how things are going he looks upward and throws both his hands up as if to say, "God only knows!"

Table 3.1 continued

---

6 **Occurs quickly**

Explanation: Many nonverbal behaviors are quick reactions to events such as learning that you have won the lottery or someone has died. The quickness of nonverbal behavior increases its perceived sincerity since lack of time does not provide much opportunity for faking. Thus, nonverbal behaviors may convey more sincere impressions than words. *Example*: After learning that she has cancer, Martha, an unpopular vice-president of a small manufacturing firm, calls a meeting to announce her retirement. Steve is in the back watching the audience's reactions. Although some people seemed shocked, Steve is surprised to see a number of expressions of relief and even some happy reactions. Later, of course, everyone verbally expresses how shocked and sorry they are at the news!

Source: Based on DePaulo (1992)

In addition to nonverbals such as facial expressions and body orientation, other types of nonverbal expression such as dress (Rafaeli and Pratt, 1993), office design (Ornstein, 1989), and seating arrangements (Riess and Rosenfeld, 1980) can be used in the service of organizational impression management. For example, Rafaeli and Pratt (1993) contend that the way individuals in an organization dress can convey powerful messages about the nature of the organization and the type of people who work there. Outsiders may use the way members of an organization dress as a cue to evoke *cognitive associations* that influence the impression formed of the organization. When Don is sent to a business meeting in southern California, he is surprised at how casually the employees are dressed. Don would never dream of wearing jeans and sandals to work, let alone to an important business meeting. "These people must not be very serious about their work," he concludes. At the same time, Paul, Don's California counterpart, is struck by how dressed up Don is. "Another of those uptight Washington, DC-types," Paul concludes. "I'm glad I don't have to work with that stuffed shirt every day."

A CONCLUDING NOTE

This chapter has reviewed ways other than ingratiation that people and organizations attempt to manage positive impressions. When used skillfully, sparingly, and properly, these acquisitive impression management tactics often work – whether for an employee attempting to get a promotion or for an organization trying to increase its profit margin. In addition to using impression management to make positive impressions, people use a full range of protective impression management tactics when faced with identity-threatening situations called predicaments. Protective impression management is the focus of Chapters 4 and 5.

4 *Protective impression management I Using excuses and justifications to repair spoiled identities*

A stigmatized organizational identity can affect how members view themselves and their work, as well as how others view and interact with them ... Members of potentially stigmatized organizations often employ a range of interactional strategies to minimize the possible costs associated with their identity.

(Cain, 1994, p. 43)

Offer quick and clear explanations, and, by all means, avoid any appearance of a cover-up.

(Hedges, Walsh, and Headden, 1994, p. 43)

DAMAGE CONTROL AT FOOD LION

Food Lion was the fastest-growing supermarket chain in the United States. That was until they were the target of an exposé on the television news-magazine show *Prime Time Live* in November, 1992. Using hidden cameras, the show documented how Food Lion doctored old meat and sold it as being fresh. They reported that the supermarket chain used barbecue sauce to help sell old chickens and even dipped bad meat into bleach to make it seem fresh! Supermarket workers were shown to have removed and doctored "sell by" tags that indicate the last day meat can be sold (Miller, Smith, and Mabry, 1992).

Surely, caught so red-handed, you would expect that Food Lion would be finished – their goose literally being cooked! Would anyone ever purchase meat from Food Lion again? The answer surprisingly was "yes"! Food Lion quickly mobilized an all-out *damage control* campaign to restore their image. According to Miller *et al.* (1992), this campaign involved the following steps:

1   *A denial statement.* Tom E. Smith, the President and CEO of Food Lion, quickly issued a statement denying the charges. He said, "these lies have got to stop."
2   *Attacking the attackers.* The day after issuing the denial, Smith claimed, in a conference call to stock analysts, that *Prime Time*'s sources lacked any credibility because they were union sympathizers.
3   *Admission of some blame.* Food Lion aired a television commercial that said although "a problem can exist," their company had good procedures and policies.
4   *The best defense is a good offense.* Food Lion went on the offensive by putting their response to the charges on videotape and sending 60,000 copies to company employees. The employees were encouraged to watch the tape with family and friends. It was suggested that employees invite friends over for a party and serve them Food Lion food!

Faced with potentially fatal accusations, Food Lion's tactics were a very aggressive form of *protective impression management* – steps aimed at repairing spoiled identities. And like many of the protective impression management tactics we describe in this chapter and the next, they were remarkably effective. Though Food Lion's sales went down immediately after the *Prime Time* exposé, they showed consistent increases after the damage control campaign began. As we shall see in this chapter and in Chapter 5, defensive impression management tactics, if applied correctly (e.g., Food Lion's damage control campaign was quick and aggressive), can help snatch a semblance of victory from the jaws of apparent defeat.

PREDICAMENTS

No organization or individual is perfect. Mistakes, screw-ups, blunders, and boners characterize social and organizational life. Ed spills his coffee on the boss's new suit. Elizabeth shows up late for an important meeting. Charlie erases accounting data from the company's main computer.

In impression management terms, Ed, Elizabeth, and Charlie all

Table 4.1 Categories of predicament-generating behaviors

---

1 *Doing something that shouldn't be done*
Example: Though Charlie was unfamiliar with the company's new accounting system, he still tried to run some analyses on it to answer a question his boss had. The result was he erased some key data from the system.

2 *Not doing something that should be done*
Example: Because Elizabeth was late for a meeting, she had no time to prepare hard copies of her presentation for potential clients.

3 *Doing things badly*
Example: Being late also resulted in Elizabeth not having time to research her sales pitch adequately. It "bombed": the clients found her sales pitch confusing and difficult to follow. And, they still are annoyed that she showed up late!

4 *Being caught "red-handed"*
Example: Charlie is so upset at losing the accounting data that he sneaks into the office on the weekend and tries to change the company's main accounting program to cover up his mistake. Unaware of the recently installed security system, his unauthorized attempt is detected soon after he logs on to the system.

Source: Snyder, Higgins, and Stucky (1983)

face a *predicament*. According to Schlenker (1980, p. 125), a predicament is "any event that casts aspersions on the lineage, character, conduct, skills, or motives of an actor." Snyder, Higgins, and Stucky (1983) have identified four general categories of predicament-generating behaviors. These are presented in Table 4.1.

Predicaments are *identity risk factors*; a person's reputation, image, and self-esteem may be tarnished. The offender finds himself in a *sticky situation* (Snyder, Higgins, and Stucky, 1983). Unless dealt with, the offender may be viewed negatively by others, face sanctions, punishments, and be denied future benefits and rewards.

In real-world settings there are often financial consequences to being blamed for predicaments, including loss of profit, pay, and denial of bonuses (Crant and Bateman, 1993). Some companies who are represented by professional athletes have even gone as far as to purchase "image insurance" to protect themselves. The policies, which can cost up to 2 percent of the total revenue involved, protect the firm if something negative happens to the athlete's reputation. If the athlete commits a crime, an indecent act, or does something degrading or offensive to the community, the company is paid off (Hiestand, 1991). Most individuals and organizations, however, cannot afford image insurance. Instead, they make use of a series of protective impression management behaviors described below.

REMEDIAL TACTICS

They earn their living by sticking Happy Faces over unpleasant realities [description of a *communications professional*, a new term for a public relations *spin doctor*].

(Bleifuss, 1994, p. F-13)

Politicians call the protective form of impression management *damage control* or *rezoning*. Impression management theorists often refer to these image-repair efforts as *remedial tactics*. They are attempts "to deal with the predicament, offering the audience, real or imagined, an explanation of it or an apology for it that can place the actor and the event in a different perspective. By so doing, the actor attempts to minimize the negative repercussions of the predicament" (Schlenker, 1980, p. 135).

Remedial tactics that follow predicaments try to ward off a potentially negative impression in one of four ways: reducing the negative impression, negating it, neutralizing it, or redefining it as positive (Giacalone and Rosenfeld, 1984). Faced with the predicaments mentioned above, Ed, Elizabeth, and Charlie quickly engage in *facework*. Ed apologizes profusely and offers to pay the dry-cleaning bill. Elizabeth complains about the monster traffic jam that caused her lateness. Charlie blames his error on a flaw in a newly installed software package.

There has been much recent attention to the types of remedial impression management engaged in following predicaments. In the remainder of this chapter we describe *excuses* and *justifications* – protective impression management tactics known jointly as *accounts*. In Chapter 5 we will consider the other protective forms of impression management as well as their organizational implications.

ACCOUNTS

Predicaments give birth to remedial tactics that aim to reduce the negative impact of the failure event on the person's identity. These actions, typically verbal repair statements occurring after the predicament has occurred, are most commonly known as *accounts* (Scott and Lyman, 1968). Table 4.2 describes a number of other terms that have been used to describe these forms of verbal damage control.

Accounts have been defined as "statements made to explain untoward behavior and bridge the gap between actions and expectation" (Scott and Lyman, 1968, p. 46). The offender uses accounts to try to obtain the best possible deal under the circumstances. In the absence of an account, significant audiences will likely reprimand, think less of, or in some way punish the transgressor. Accounts are attempts to avoid this worst case interpretation of the offending behavior and manage the best impression possible under the circumstances (Schlenker, 1980). "An effective account is one that the receivers find credible, and through which the account-giver is forgiven or is exonerated of blame, avoids negative evaluation, avoids penalties, and avoids conflict" (Braaten, Cody, and DeTienne, 1993, p. 220).

As these characteristics of an effective account indicate, the function of an account is not necessarily to make individuals look good as much as it is to avoid having them look bad. Consider the case of Steve, a pharmacist who is caught pilfering medicine from the drug store that employs him. If he says nothing he likely will lose his job, be demoted or, at best, be continuously monitored. However, Steve offers an account: "My wife is suffering from cancer and needs the medicine to help relieve her pain." If the account is accepted, the consequences to Steve (compared with saying nothing) will not be as bad.

As we saw with our opening Food Lion story, organizations as well as individuals offer accounts. According to Bies and Sitkin (1992), organizational accounts often follow on the heels of *failure events* – actions such as budget cuts and layoffs. Unexplained, these failure events can cause an organization great harm – trust and cooperation will be lowered and organizational performance and productivity decreased. Failure events can be made less organizationally harmful if acceptable explanations for bad outcomes are offered. No one likes a pay cut, but, as one study to be described later found,

Table 4.2 Verbal damage control

A number of different terms have been used to describe the types of verbal statements individuals give when faced with predicaments.

Term: *Motive Talk*
Source: Mills (1940)

Definition: Motives to Mills were not internal processes but were words that addressed the anticipated impact of questionable conduct . People use a "vocabulary of motives" to justify their actions.

Term: *Neutralization*
Source: Sykes and Matza (1957)

Definition: According to Sykes and Matza, verbal statements can be used to "neutralize" unacceptable behavior and make it appear as not too deviant from accepted norms and societal practices.

Term: *Accounts*
Source: Scott and Lyman (1968)

Definition: Accounts are verbal devices that explain unanticipated or untoward actions. They consist of excuses and justifications.

Term: *Quasi-Theories*
Source: Hewitt and Hall (1973)

Definition: These are explanations offered on an *ad hoc* basis in problematic situations to give these situations order and hope. For example, a corporate consultant unable to find work attributes his lack of success to "market forces" resulting from a bad economy.

Term: *Aligning Actions*
Source: Stokes and Hewitt (1976)

Definition: When social interactions or verbal conversations prove problematic people use verbal strategies to "align" or make the problematic actions seem consistent with or motivated by cultural expectations and societal standards. The person faced with a predicament tries to show that she is still part of the social order even though she may have acted in such a way as to violate it.

---

a good account for a pay cut resulted in less employee theft than a comparable situation where no account or a perfunctory account was offered (Greenberg, 1990).

While individuals typically use accounts to extricate themselves from predicaments, managers in organizational settings may need to use accounts as a necessary means of maintaining their authority. Although managers have much power over their subordinates, their success depends to an extent on the degree of support and cooperation their employees give them. Since managers often cannot endorse all their subordinates' requests for raises, promotions, or outstanding performance appraisals, the use of accounts to maintain order becomes a daily part of the successful manager's repertoire. Through accounts, a manager tries to make his or her tough decisions seem fair, justified, and necessary (Bies and Sitkin, 1992). If accepted, subordinates will continue to perform and produce. If accounts aren't offered or lack in credibility, then negative outcomes such as lowered morale, turnover, theft, and sabotage may increase. Thus, the use of accounts – often thought to be a sign of weakness – can actually enhance the power and authority of managers in a manner parallel to the way that ingratiation serves as a means of heightened social influence for the powerless (see Chapter 2).

It is important to realize that it is not simply the offering of an account but whether it is accepted that determines its effectiveness. Rather than viewing accounts as stand-alone forms of protective impression management, it is useful to think of them as *account episodes*. Schonbach and Kleibaumhuter (1990) describe four phases that comprise a typical account episode: (1) *Failure Event*: A predicament occurs where an individual may be held responsible by an observer. (2) *Reproach Phase*: The observer reacts either with a look or statement that communicates some disapproval to the individual. (3) *Account Phase*: The individual offers an account aimed at reducing the potential negative impression. (4) *Evaluation Phase*: The observer evaluates and accepts or rejects the account. If accepted, the negative impression is lessened and the parties can continue positive future interactions. If rejected, a negative impression is formed and unpleasant consequences may follow. For example, say that Ted, a white male fileclerk, is overheard telling anti-black jokes by Shirley, his black supervisor. As the company's personnel policy bans racist or sexist remarks, Ted's overheard racial jokes qualify as a failure event – he faces a serious predicament. Shirley's facial scowl and angry departure signal reproach, and heighten the need for Ted to engage in damage control. He quickly seeks out Shirley and says he was only repeating something he heard at a local pub and didn't mean to offend anyone. Although still

BOX 4.1

Accounts as sources of organizational information

Because accounts may be biased by employees' impression management concerns at the time of the incident, they are often dismissed as not being good sources of information. However, accounts can be rich sources of information about incidents such as those involving unethical behaviors or industrial accidents. In those situations it is often difficult to obtain accurate information because people rarely feel free to openly discuss their own or others' actions and motivations (Szwajkowski, 1992).

By looking at individuals' accounts surrounding unethical acts, we can learn, for example, what conditions people think would excuse or justify certain actions. People may pick the accounts they use because they assume they would be accepted, i.e., they appeal to accepted norms for behavior in that situation. Even if the accounts are not the real reason for a behavior, they convey what the individual thinks would be an acceptable reason for the behavior. "I'm not cleaning up the garbage because it's not my job," is more likely to be heard in an organization that has a powerful union presence because it would be a more acceptable reason for failing to act than it would be in a small family business.

Sometimes employee accounts identify things the organization is doing that employees feel excuse or justify unethical behavior. Accounts may signal the likelihood of future ethical lapses even though the reasons given were not the real reasons for the particular act in question. An enlightened organization would want to stop doing those things believed to be justifying or excusing unethical behavior. For example, it has been found that frustrated employees were more likely to commit acts of sabotage than individuals not frustrated (Spector, 1975; cited in Giacalone and Knouse, 1990). If, in listening to employees' accounts of recent problems, they are describing situations in which they feel they were trying to do the right thing but were frustrated by other employees, supervisors, policies, or

Box 4.1 continued

procedures, trying to change those frustrating factors would be one way to reduce the possibility of future sabotage. Suppose Linda knows she has an excellent product but Steve the quality control supervisor keeps it tied up with endless testing. When asked why her product hasn't been marketed yet, Linda goes into a "blaming frenzy" pointing to Steve and others in the firm as the reason for the delays. Dealing with Linda's accounts for the delays as a potentially rich source of information rather than just as an excuse or an attempt to blow off steam may ultimately prevent the realization of Linda's fantasy of putting a lethal virus in the company's mainframe computer.

Accounts can also serve as information sources about the potential causes of accidents. Employees involved in an accident are often more in touch than management or outside investigators with factors that did or could have led to the accident. Even though the factors might be used as excuses by a negligent person trying to get off the hook, those same factors may be potential sources of future accidents and therefore are worth checking out. Suppose a chemical spill was due to Stan's carelessness, but Stan claimed it was due to the faulty equipment that often breaks down. If Stan's accounts were listened to as a source of information, they could stimulate an investigation that reveals equipment badly in need of repair. Even though the equipment was not the actual cause of the spill in question, the account may serve to get the repairs made and thereby prevent future accidents.

Finally, listening to accounts can reveal individuals' understanding of company policies. In the United States there are laws and regulations that can hold organizations liable for violations even if the individuals involved did not intend or were unaware of the consequences they produced. For example, supervisors are responsible for preventing sexual harassment even if they did not know, but should have known, it was happening. Similarly, the Environmental Protection Agency can file charges against someone who illegally disposed of waste, even if the individual did so without knowing that what

Box 4.1 continued

> was being done was wrong. From the organization's perspective, if problems of sexual harassment or improper waste disposal arise, and employees or managers are attempting to excuse their behaviors by saying they weren't aware anything wrong was going on, it points to the need for additional training: They need to know that lack of intent or ignorance will not protect them or their organization from legal responsibility.

miffed, Ted's account strikes Shirley as sincere. She also admires Ted for coming to her directly rather than avoiding the issue. Since Ted has never been heard to make remarks like this before, Shirley accepts his account and takes no further action. Just as Shirley drew inferences about Ted based on his accounts, organizations can use accounts as rich sources for information that is often difficult to obtain in other ways. Box 4.1 describes the information potential of organizational accounts.

While we have discussed accounts in general, impression management theorists have described two specific types of accounts: excuses and justifications. They are reviewed in detail below.

EXCUSES AND JUSTIFICATIONS

A public relations professional recently noted, "It is easier and less costly to change the way people think about reality than it is to change reality" (Bleifuss, 1994, p. F-13). Excuses and justifications are verbal impression management tactics commonly used following predicaments. The offender acts as his own public relations agent trying to change the way people think about bad events rather than changing the events themselves.

Excuses and justifications differ in the assignment of responsibility. An *excuse* admits an action was wrong but the person denies that she is responsible. A *justification* accepts responsibility for the action, but the person denies that the act was bad (McGraw, 1991).

Excuses are attempts to reduce responsibility as much as possible for failure events. Schlenker (1980) views the excuse-maker as someone who tries to get the best deal obtainable under the circumstances. Excuse-makers seek an impression management plea-bargain. The transgressor, in Schlenker's view, can't totally eliminate responsibility for the predicament but can reduce it as much as possible, cushioning the blow to where the damage is minimized. Consider the following excuses. When Harvey drops an expensive office computer, he says it was the bad lighting that made him trip. When Gwen is questioned by the company comptroller as to why she purchased expensive office furniture, she says her boss demanded she order the best stuff. When Lloyd is asked why he hired Ivan, an incompetent intern, he says that based on Ivan's good grades and prior experience he didn't know Ivan would turn out so bad.

Justifications, in contrast, try to redefine the questionable action so that it doesn't appear to be as bad. When Stan, an employee in an organizational consulting firm, is asked by his boss why he has been overcharging an oil company client, Stan justifies his misdeed by claiming that the oil company underpaid him in the past and it has a reputation for trying to cheat consultants out of their full fees. In essence, Stan is claiming that stealing from a thief is really not wrong and he should not be viewed negatively for it.

A TYPOLOGY OF EXCUSES AND JUSTIFICATIONS

Scott and Lyman (1968) have proposed a typology of excuses and justifications that are useful both to organizational researchers and practitioners. We review the major categories.

Types of excuses

1   *Appeal to accidents.* An attempt is made to reduce responsibility by claiming that the predicament was an accident. Appealing to an accident is an effective excuse if the accident is rare and doesn't occur again often. If Darla spills coffee on her coworker Danni once, it can be excused as an accident. If it happens a lot, Darla may not be easily forgiven by Danni.

2   *Appeal to defeasibility.* This excuse maintains that the person wasn't fully informed about what occurred and so can't be held fully responsible. A supervisor confronted with excessive long-distance calling by his subordinates may contend that no one told him what was going on. If he knew, he surely would have acted.

3   *Appeal to biological drives.* To avoid responsibility, the excuse-

makers claim an uncontrollable biological factor compelled them to act. In an interview study, Scully and Marolla (1984) found that convicted rapists made frequent use of excuses which claimed that uncontrollable outside forces made them "do it." In a more typical organizational scenario, after making a pass at Jan at the company holiday party, Norman says that he was so turned on by her that he couldn't control himself.

4   *Scapegoating.* This type of excuse involves blaming others for causing the predicament. When caught cheating on a promotion exam, Lauren says she had to cheat because the exam was poorly constructed by her incompetent professor and therefore unfair.

Types of justifications

1   *Denial of injury.* The individual acknowledges doing the act, but justifies it because there was no harm or damage caused. Barry admits he used the company car for a personal trip to Las Vegas, but claims it's no big deal since no one else needed the car and he didn't damage it.

2   *Denial of the victim.* The behavior is justified on the grounds that the victim deserved it. Some supporters of Paul Hill, a man who shot and killed an abortion doctor in Pensacola, Florida, claimed that his action was justified because the doctor was, in their view, killing innocent babies and had to be stopped.

3   *Condemnation of the condemners.* The claim is made that others do the same thing or worse and get away with it. Judith is accused of using company-earned frequent-flyer airplane tickets for personal use. She admits violating organization policy, but claims her actions are justified since many supervisors in the organization are doing the same thing and getting away with it.

4   *Appeal to loyalties.* The negative action is justified because it helped another to whom the person feels loyal. G. Gordon Liddy justified his role in the Watergate burglary, and subsequently maintained silence about his crimes, out of loyalty to former US President Richard Nixon.

EXCUSES AND JUSTIFICATIONS: RESEARCH EVIDENCE

The offering of accounts may very well be a universal human tendency – when faced with a predicament people tend to explain it. One study found that only 7 percent of individuals who were asked to recall things they wish they hadn't said indicated that they did nothing, and most of those who did nothing were hoping that their "regrettable message" would not be noticed (Knapp, Stafford, and Daly, 1986). It seems not to matter how irrational the action or even how ludicrous the account is. Some people seem to operate according to the principle that an absurd account is better than none at all. Bernstein's (1993) analysis of excuses offered by psychology students found that in one class, 14 of the 250 students claimed that their grandparent died before the final!

Researchers have noted that there are dangers in the overuse of excuses. The short-term gain provided by an excuse may result in long-term harm to the excuse-maker's identity. While a single excuse can provide short-term relief from a specific predicament, excuses may result in long-term identity damage. Excuses "are effective in exonerating the account-giver of blame for a specific act. However, the claim that one is not responsible for actions can adversely affect the excuse-maker's public image by creating (or maintaining) an image that he or she is not committed to or involved in the organization, and that he or she is not competent to plan and execute actions in such a way as to perform work successfully" (Braaten, Cody, and DeTienne, 1993, p. 222).

Despite these dangers, research has shown that excuses and justifications are very common. For example, Wood and Mitchell (1981) found that nurses who offered excuses for incorrect nursing procedures (e.g., indicating that not checking a patient's vital signs was due to factors beyond their control) were perceived by nursing managers as being less likely to fail in the future.

With workplace violence on the rise in many organizations, it is of interest to note that even individuals accused of the most heinous violent crimes use accounts to excuse and justify their actions. When Ray and Simons (1987) interviewed 25 convicted murderers they found that 18 offered excuses for their actions and six gave justifications. While few of the murderers thought their crime was OK, they offered excuses, such as being drunk and on drugs or stressful life events (e.g., unemployment, divorce), or justifications like claiming they killed in self-defense. Henderson and Hewstone (1984) also found accounts to be common among convicted felons incarcerated in a maximum security prison, but in contrast to the previous study they found justifications were more common than excuses. While the prisoners tended to accept responsibility for their crimes such as murder and assault, they offered justifications for their occurrence. Thus, individuals will offer excuses and justifications for what may seem to an observer to be senseless, violent acts.

While it may be hard to relate to the accounts of convicted murderers, we all have missed a class or a day of work and have needed to explain our absence to a teacher, boss, or coworker. When Kalab (1987) looked at the accounts offered by students for their absences, he found that excuses were more common than justifications. Illnesses were the most commonly offered excuses. While students also used accounts such as family responsibilities, other classwork, oversleep, and accidents, Kalab notes that claiming illness is a particularly good excuse in that it can be used repeatedly and is not immediately met with skepticism. This would also seem to be true of organizational excuses and justifications for absence. While car trouble or a faulty alarm clock may work occasionally, such excuses quickly become old and ineffective if used repeatedly. Being sick, however, is viewed in many organizations as a legitimate excuse for missing work and, unless there is some reason for doubt (e.g., being sick on Mondays and Fridays exclusively), it will usually be effective. We know of one employee who changed a planned vacation day to sick leave after hearing that some of his coworkers had recently gotten the flu!

Another common breeding ground for accounts occurs following poor performance on tests. Albas and Albas (1988) found that students who did poorly on an exam – they were called "bombers" – tended to conceal their performance or avoid encounters with "aces" – those who did well. However, when they encountered other bombers they typically engaged in a mutual account session that the authors called a "pity party." Once again, excuses were more common than justifications. Especially when the grade distribution was low, the bombers engaged in excuses in the form of scapegoating to reduce their responsibility for doing poorly. They blamed the teacher for being a sadist, slave driver, or incompetent. Of course, as instructors ourselves, we doubt that any of our students would ever offer such "lame" excuses!

The work of Catherine Riordan and her colleagues (e.g., Riordan, Marlin, and Kellogg, 1983) suggests that excuses may be less risky than justifications. In one study she and her colleagues looked at how accounts influenced psychologists' perceptions of unethical research practices. The psychologist respondents to this study read scenarios in which a psychologist was charged with faking data or plagiarizing part of a research publication. They found that the unethical action was viewed less negatively following an excuse than a justification. Also, the act was seen as more likely to occur in the future following a justification. Why might justifications be riskier than excuses? Riordan and associates suggest that when acts are clearly bad, justifications may fail because they try to claim that the action was OK. The audience may disagree and view the person negatively as a result. Excuses, in contrast, commit organizational actors to better behavior in the future regardless of whether the audience accepts the contention of lessened responsibility or not. Indeed, future behavior was predicted to be more negative following a justification than an excuse (Riordan, Marlin, and Kellogg, 1983).

If an act is clearly bad, it may be harder to justify it than to excuse the perpetrator's responsibility for committing it, since determining a person's responsibility is often less clear than knowing whether an act is bad or good. Because it is often harder for audiences to determine the responsibility of the actor than to characterize the act, excuses tend to be believed, even when they are false. Bernard Weiner and his colleagues had college students recall instances where they offered excuses for predicaments such as showing up late to a party (Weiner *et al.*, 1987). They found that respondents perceived 88 percent of their excuses to be believed and only 12 percent to be disbelieved by their target audiences. Interestingly, of the 28 excuses that were disbelieved, 13 were actually true and 15 were false! The practical lesson may be that following clearly negative actions, an excuse is more likely to work than a justification.

EXCUSES AND JUSTIFICATIONS IN ORGANIZATIONS

When identity-threatening or stigmatizing events befall an organization, leaders typically provide explanations for those events that are intended to minimize damage to the organization's image and their own reputations.

(Ginzel, Kramer, and Sutton, 1993, p. 228)

While excuses and justifications are common features of everyday social interaction, they are also frequently used in organizational settings. Since many organizational decisions are made in private, employees often can evaluate how fair a decision is only through the type of account used to explain it. If managers do not explain decisions or if their accounts are inadequate, subordinates may draw "worst-case" scenarios and conclude that decisions are unfair even when they are not. In organizations, more than in daily social interactions, accounts serve a necessary and positive function. According to Robert Bies and colleagues (e.g., Bies and Sitkin, 1992), accounts, particularly in the form of excuse-making, serve as a *legitimatization strategy* in organizations. That is, managers need to offer accounts to legitimize their actions to subordinates in order to maintain authority. Since a manager can't possibly agree to all requests for raises, promotions, transfers, etc., she must explain her decisions (i.e., offer accounts) or risk losing the support and cooperation of those who work for her. Managers who successfully offer accounts for organizational predicaments, minimize the destructive aspects of these failure events (Bies and Sitkin, 1992).

That excuse-making is a "normal" way of doing business can be seen through the results of a 1990 study by Robert Bies conducted with middle managers in ten companies (discussed in Bies and Sitkin, 1992). The managers were asked to recall instances where bad news (e.g., financial losses, budget cuts) was given to subordinates or bosses. Bies found that the managers gave an excuse every time they were the bearers of bad news – regardless of whether they were delivering it to their bosses or subordinates. In addition to telling those directly affected by the bad news, the managers offered excuses about the bad news to key powerful others in the organization to build a *coalition of supporters*. They also engaged in excuse-making as a public-relations activity to those who had witnessed or had heard about the bad events. Thus, managers were "hyper" excuse-makers, using this form of protective impression management to legitimize their status and authority within the organization. Bies and associates found that managers typically offered multiple excuses following failure events in organizations rather than depending on a single excuse.

One reason that excuses may be so common in organizations is that they are often remarkably effective in reducing the potential damage of failure events. Bies and Sitkin (1992) cite evidence indicating that excuses make: (a) employees more accepting of being underpaid, (b) budget cuts seem more justified, (c) individuals more accepting of rejection for a job, and (d) poor performance evaluations appear fairer. Giacalone (1988) found that accounts improved the perceived leadership ratings of a male library director who had misappropriated funds.

CHARACTERISTICS OF EFFECTIVE EXCUSES

Not all excuses are equally effective. Factors that have been associated with successful excuse-making in organizations are perceived adequacy, normativeness, and perceived sincerity. Successful excuses also can reduce anger in the aggrieved party.

Perceived adequacy

To be effective, an organizational excuse must be seen as adequate. The perceived adequacy of an excuse refers to whether it is viewed as logical and reasonable under the circumstances. Adequate excuses fit the facts and are sufficiently detailed so as to be convincing (Greenberg, Bies, and Eskew, 1991). Excuses which lack in perceived adequacy may be seen as arbitrary and be counterproductive.

Greenberg (1990) looked at the effect of perceived adequacy of explanations on employee theft in manufacturing plants following a temporary 15 percent pay cut. In one plant, the pay cut was announced with no explanation, in a second plant a minimal explanation was offered, while, in a third plant, a detailed "thorough and sensitive" explanation of the reasons for the pay cut was given to employees. The results showed that a detailed explanation for the pay cut resulted in less theft than a minimal explanation. One reason individuals given adequate explanations for the pay cut stole less is that they perceived the pay cut as less unfair than individuals who received a minimal or no explanation for it.

Normativeness

The study just described points to an important aspect of accounts: Their effectiveness often depends on people's expectations for how actions *should* be explained. This is what we mean by an account's *normativeness*. As the study above demonstrates, when an organization takes an action that has significant harmful effects on employees, a detailed account is expected. Anything less results in adverse reactions.

Certain accounts seem to be seen as appropriate for certain actions and not for others. If Martha is late for work, saying her son had a cold is usually an acceptable account. If Martha is late for an important job interview, trying to excuse her tardiness with her son's illness would not be as effective. People's impressions of the appropriateness of certain accounts stem from a common understanding of the situation and norms for behavior in those situations. In the case of a job interview, it would be expected that some back-up child care arrangements would have been made. Given this, the sick-child excuse isn't as effective in that situation.

It turns out that giving accounts that are normative may be more important than whether the account is truthful. In a study of perceptions of Senators accounting for their illegal and unethical actions, it was the accounts "that other people might offer for that behavior" that led to relieving responsibility for negative acts and in recharacterizing the actions in a less negative way (Riordan, Martin, and Kellogg, 1983). This perceived normativeness was more important than whether the account was seen as being the "real" reason for the predicament-causing behavior. At least in this situation, accounts believed to be the ones most people would offer produced more positive perceptions than those that were seen as closer to the truth. An implication of these findings is that we may get out of being perceived badly following predicaments by merely showing we know the acceptable way to explain our actions. Knowing the acceptable explanation may be more important than truthfully explaining those actions.

Perceived sincerity

To be effective, organizational accounts also have to be believed. Subordinates have to perceive that management's explanation is truthful and that managers really mean what they say (Greenberg, Bies, and Eskew, 1991). The importance of perceived sincerity was demonstrated in a study by Bies, Shapiro, and Cummings (1988) that looked at reactions by subordinates to management's refusals of their budget requests. They found that the perceived sincerity of the manager in communicating the excuse was associated with less subordinate anger, less perceived injustice, fewer complaints, and less disapproval of the boss. Interestingly, the excuse alone – a claim of extenuating circumstances – was not independently associated with any of these positive outcomes. Thus, the way a manager offers an account may be as important or more important than the content of the explanation. In this vein, Giacalone and Rosenfeld (1984) recommend that managers should properly "stage" their accounts so that the excuses and justifications they offer appear to be well planned. They found that accounts offered by a library director for an erroneous decision were more accepted if associated with decisions that were portrayed as well thought out and proper.

That sincere excuses were associated with less subordinate anger in the Bies, Shapiro, and Cummings (1988) study supports an important affective or emotional consequence of excuses noted by Bernard Weiner and his colleagues (e.g., Weiner *et al.*, 1987). According to Weiner, excuses, in addition to managing impressions, can also serve as effective means of emotion or anger management. In a field study with college students, they found excuses that were believed were associated with less anger even when they were not true, while excuses that were not believed were associated with increased anger even when they were true. Mort's boss will likely not be as angry if he believes Mort's excuse that he was late for an important sales meeting because he had to take his pregnant wife to a doctor. This will be true whether Mort actually was late for the meeting because of this reason or if his excuse was made up.

A CONCLUDING NOTE

When faced with predicaments, individuals and organizations react with a variety of protective impression management behaviors aimed at reducing the damage to their fragile identities. This chapter has focused on excuses and justifications – after-the-fact damage control tactics known as accounts. Though there is long-term danger in their overuse, excuses and justifications appear to be effective means of reducing the negative fallout from image-threatening events.

In addition to accounts, individuals and organizations use other types of protective impression management known as disclaimers, self-handicapping, and apologies. Also, to enhance the credibility of protective impression management, indirect means such as minimizing the association with negative others or enlisting third-parties to assist in damage control may be used. We consider these forms of protective impression management in Chapter 5.

5 Protective impression management II Disclaimers, self-handicapping, apologies, and indirect tactics

WALKING A TIGHTROPE

> In the first 24 hours after the crash, USAir – like all airlines after a crash – had to walk a tightrope between damage control for the company's image and expressing complete compassion for the victims.
>
> (Schmit and Jones, 1994, p. B-1)

On September 8, 1994, USAir Flight 427 was on approach to its landing in Pittsburgh, Pennsylvania. Suddenly the airplane lost control and crashed, killing all 132 people aboard. For USAir it was the fifth deadly crash of one of its airplanes in the past five years. There was immediate media focus on the safety of USAir's planes and speculation about the future viability of the company.

In response to this terrible disaster, USAir quickly and effectively implemented a well-planned and rehearsed crisis plan; one that simultaneously tried to protect the company's image while tending to the needs of the victims' families. Phone banks were set up to deal with the flood of calls, spokespersons appeared on television news shows to deflect criticisms, and two employees were assigned to each victim's family. While not denying the magnitude of the tragedy, USAir representatives insisted that the company's airplanes were safe. At a press conference the next day, USAir's CEO claimed that had he thought the airplanes unsafe he would have grounded the entire USAir fleet. Thus, even in the midst of a great tragedy USAir engaged in protective impression management, an effort designed to help the company survive. And, indeed, USAir's damage control was effective. Although there were no immediate indications of what caused Flight 427 to fall out of the sky, within a few days, media focus and the public's interest had lessened, and USAir's operations were back to normal. The company had walked an impression management tightrope and survived (Schmit and Jones, 1994).

In the last chapter, we reviewed a study that found that managers made excuses to powerful people within the organization in advance of the delivery of bad news to build a "coalition of supporters." Similarly, USAir acted quickly to try to control the damage to their corporate image *before* it spread. As these examples illustrate, individuals and organizations often don't wait till the flames of predicaments spread and consume them, but may ward off potential damage by acting quickly following crises or by engaging in "preemptive strikes" in the face of anticipated problems. In Chapter 5 we review two of these anticipatory impression management tactics: disclaimers and self-handicapping. We also consider the protective tactic of last resort: an apology, and conclude with a review of indirect defensive impression management.

DISCLAIMERS

A *disclaimer* is a form of anticipatory excuse-making that occurs before a predicament. Sociologists Hewitt and Stokes (1975, p. 3) have defined a disclaimer as, "a verbal device employed to ward off and defeat in advance doubts and negative typifications which may result from intended conduct." As the disclaimer described in Box 5.1 shows, perceived sincerity is as important to disclaimers as it is to excuses.

Jung (1987) found that disclaimers increased in advance of probable failure: they were more likely to occur when individuals expected to do poorly on a test. Disclaimers involve impression management by prognostication, anticipation, and premonition. A disclaimer is a form of predicament insurance purchased right before the disaster. If the predicament does not occur, then people can claim they were being modest or cautious (Jung, 1987). Disclaimers nip predicaments in the bud, they put out image-threatening fires before they engulf us, they alter the meaning of future actions so as not to damage our fragile identities. "Don't get me wrong, some of my best friends are Mexican, but Juan is a lazy thief and should be fired,"

BOX 5.1

Lame disclaimers

Although disclaimers are very common, they are not always believed. Consider the following example. At one time, according to Lee Iacocca, high-level employees from Ford Motor Company were sent to solicit donations from executives at other larger companies connected with the auto industry. The executives were asked to donate money to one of Henry Ford's pet projects, a huge office/shopping complex that was to revitalize downtown Detroit. Ford was often a very big customer of these companies. The executives sent to solicit funds would say, "Now, I'm not here in my capacity as head of purchasing" – even though they were doing millions of dollars of business with these companies each year. "I'm coming to you as the personal representative of Henry Ford ... and my visit has nothing to do with Ford Motor Company." Apparently some of the executives being solicited didn't buy this lame disclaimer and burst out laughing. One thought the symbol for the office complex should be a twisted arm because so much of the money came as a result of undue pressure by these Ford executives! (Iacocca, 1984, p. 107).

Miles tells his boss Dee. The hope is that Dee won't consider Miles a bigot, even though his comment could lead to that impression. "I think you should decide for yourself, but I'd transfer to another department if I worked for your nutty boss," Jules tells Jack. In this way, Jules can offer the advice but avoid the blame if Jack transfers and things don't work out.

As these comments illustrate, disclaimers are very common forms of anticipatory impression management. Hewitt and Stokes (1975) describe five major categories of disclaimers that help us to appreciate their breadth and functions.

Types of disclaimers

1   *Hedging*. A hedge is a verbal statement which signals "minimal commitment" to a future behavior. A hedge indicates that the

future behavior is not very important to a person's identity. "I'm not very good in math," says Joyce, "but I'll take a job in the accounting department if it will get me a promotion." Hedging also occurs when leaders voice tentative support for a position counter to their own to avoid losing the support and commitment of their subordinates who may react negatively to an overly aggressive one-sided advocacy. "Yes, I can see why some people would want to start a union here, they have done some good in the past," says Dorothy, a CEO of a mid-size corporation. "However, given our current economic situation a union would clearly hurt the bottom-line."

2   *Credentialing.* In some instances, a person knows that something they are about to do or say will be viewed negatively. To avoid a negative impression, the person claims a special "credential" that allows him to say or do something bad without being viewed negatively. "I'm a Jew," Morris says, "so when I say that the Jews control the movie business in Hollywood, you know its true." Morris is using "Jewish credentials" to avoid being labeled a bigot by others.

3   *Sin licenses.* The person who uses a sin license is trying to be the justifiable exception that proves the rule. By paying homage to the rule, the taint of being viewed as a rule breaker is avoided. "I know it's against the company nepotism policy to hire relatives," says Donn, a corporate vice-president, "but my daughter Kathleen is such a super word processor and we are really short of secretarial help."

4   *Cognitive disclaimers.* It's generally good impression management to be viewed as rational and sane even when we do things that might be seen as bizarre. A cognitive disclaimer tries to accomplish this avoidance of labels such as "crazy" or "irrational." "You may think I'm nuts," Maria tells her boss Andrea, "but I found my productivity has improved since I began taking megadoses of bee pollen and antioxidant vitamins last month."

5   *Appeals to the suspension of judgment or affect.* This form of disclaimer attempts to delay judgment and the negative emotional reaction often accompanying predicaments until the questionable action is put into context. Tom tells his boss Linda, "Before you get mad about the lost advertising account, listen to why it won't hurt us in the long run."

SELF-HANDICAPPING: SETTING UP OBSTACLES TO SUCCESSFUL PERFORMANCE

> I was struck by the strategic benefits that one could derive from "tying one hand behind their back" prior to entering a contest they knew they would lose ... I recalled a variety of occasions when, as a summer bartender at an affluent country club, I heard members excuse crude or inept actions by claiming, "I didn't realize how much I had had to drink."
>
> (Steven Berglas, quoted in Rosenfeld and Garrison, 1991, p. 176)

There has been much attention given to a particular form of protective impression management called self-handicapping. According to Tice and Baumeister (1990, p. 443) self-handicapping involves "placing obstacles in the way of one's task performance so as to furnish oneself with an external attribution when future outcomes are uncertain." Simply put, the self-handicapper places impediments or barriers in the face of success. In this way, self-handicappers provide themselves with a double impression management payoff: if they succeed, the value of their success is heightened; if they fail, the negative impact is weakened. Assume that Mary and her boss Connie decide to play tennis. Connie has heard that Mary is a good tennis player and is somewhat unsure of her own tennis ability. As they begin to play, Connie mentions that she pulled a muscle in her leg last week and is having trouble running at full speed. Connie's statement is a classic self-handicap. If she beats Mary it will be in spite of the sore leg; if she loses she can blame it on the injury and not on her lack of ability.

Since self-handicapping is especially likely to occur in situations where success and failure are important and people feel that their competence or self-worth is on the line, it is not surprising that competitive athletes engage in self-handicapping. Rhodewalt, Saltzman, and Wittmer (1984) found that golfers and swimmers who scored highly on a measure of self-handicapping practiced less before big tournaments than before lesser ones. When the event was unimportant, high and low self-handicappers practiced about the same. In this way, if they won the important event, they could claim victory even though they didn't practice very hard; if they lost, they had the excuse of lack of practice ready in the wings. It has been found that withholding effort for events on which a person is to be evaluated is a common form of self-handicapping (Tice and Baumeister, 1990).

As the quote by Steven Berglas indicates, the self-handicapping construct can help us understand the strategic benefits of alcohol and drug use. Say that Martin is sent by his company to an off-site, two-week training course. Martin enjoys the course but is somewhat worried about how he will do on the final exam. While the other students stay in and study hard, Martin goes out, hits the town, and gets drunk. He takes the exam with a hangover and barely passes. While Martin's behavior may seem on its surface to be self-destructive, it also is an effective form of self-handicapping. Martin can blame his mediocre test performance on excessive drinking and not on the more threatening lack of ability. He can tell himself and others that had he not gone out and partied he would have done better. Also, the drinking has helped "bolster" his barely passing test performance. Since he was able to pass the exam even with a hangover, the implication is that had he been sober and studied more, he certainly would have done better. Of course, the possibility that Martin would have done as poorly had he been sober is not considered – we, the audience, just won't know – which is precisely what the self-handicapper seeks to accomplish!

The strategic benefits of "shooting yourself in the foot" are not limited to drug and alcohol abuse, but may apply to other *acquired* or *claimed* impediments (Arkin and Baumgardner, 1985) such as illnesses, bad mood, obesity (Baumeister, Kahn, and Tice, 1990), and traumatic life events (DeGree and Snyder, 1985). For example, students who scored high on a hypochondriasis measure reported more physical illness symptoms when faced with an evaluative task than those scoring low on the hypochondriasis measure (Smith, Snyder, and Perkins, 1983). Hypochondriacs, it seems, strategically used illness symptoms as a form of self-handicapping.

It has also been suggested that *procrastination* – putting off things that are needed to reach goals – is a form of self-handicapping (Ferrari, 1991, 1992; Lay, Knish, and Zanatta, 1992). Consider the case of Marlene who writes software manuals for a large consulting company. Marlene procrastinates – she throws herself feverishly into other tasks. She is the head of the employee recreation committee, spending hours, days, nights, and weekends planning for the company picnic or the annual holiday party. Marlene is a devoted member of the company diversity committee, she writes a plan suggesting how the firm can attract more women and minority employees. Marlene spends hours testing new software products, and is always available to help junior colleagues in need of a mentor. In short, she is the perfect employee except for the fact that she isn't doing her main job of writing software manuals very well! From a self-handicapping perspective, Marlene's procrastination makes total sense. Worried that her writing will be evaluated negatively by her bosses, colleagues, and readers, she uses time as her impression management ally. Eventually, Marlene's procrastination causes her to miss a deadline. "But, I've been so busy, I haven't been able to work on those manuals," she tells all who are interested and some who aren't. Eventually, she gets the manual done, but it takes several all-night work sessions and a couple of weekends. But her dawdling has not been for naught. Her delaying has cushioned the blow and provided a defense ("I didn't have enough time to do a better job!") against criticism of her writing ability. And, Marlene's bosses are so happy to finally have a product that they aren't very critical. Also, the fact that she could get it done in a last-second panic gets her brownie points for producing under pressure. Marlene tells her coworkers that she did the best she could under the circumstances and given more time in the future she'd surely do better!

Research on self-handicapping began with a laboratory study conducted by Steven Berglas and Edward E. Jones (1978). They had college students take a test that supposedly measured their intelligence. The students were told they would be given one of two drugs before they took an equivalent form of the same test to see if the drugs affected their test performance. Some of the students had solvable problems as part of the first test, while others were given problems that were unsolvable. Despite these differences in types of problems, all students were told they had done well on the first test. The students were then given a choice between one of two drugs: "Actavil," a drug that was claimed to improve intellectual performance, and "Pandocrin," a drug that supposedly hampered intellectual performance. In support of the self-handicapping notion, male students who had unsolvable problems on the first test, tended to choose Pandocrin – the drug that hurt performance, while those who had solvable problems chose Actavil – the performance-enhancing drug. Being told they succeeded on a test containing unsolvable problems led students to be unsure about their ability and uncertain whether they would do as well on the second test. Rather than find out, they chose to protect their intellectual identity from failure by choosing a drug that supposedly hurt performance. The drug provided a form of impression insurance. If they failed the second test it could be blamed on the drug. If they aced it again, their interpersonal stock would further rise because they had overcome the intellectually harmful drug.

Self-handicapping needs to be used sparingly to maintain its effectiveness. The athlete who constantly cites injuries may be viewed as a malingerer; the employee who drinks before big meetings may be seen as untrustworthy; the procrastinator who always misses deadlines may lose future choice assignments. In this vein, Smith and Strube (1991) found that self-handicappers were perceived more negatively by others than non-handicappers were. Thus, the short-term gains offered by self-handicapping need to be balanced by the long-term bad impressions a self-handicapping "life-style" may create. Diana's claim of a bad headache before a big corporate presentation may be an effective tactic once; however, her career may suffer if she repeatedly claims to have headaches in similar future situations.

Given how important success and failure are to the corporate bottom line, we would expect self-handicapping to be a common form of organizational impression management. Surprisingly little research, however, has looked at self-handicapping in organizational settings. One exception is a study conducted by Crant and Bateman (1993). They note that because receiving credit for success and avoiding blame for failure are often tied to tangible outcomes such as promotions and bonuses, the motivation to manage impressions of success and failure is usually very high in organizations. Manipulation of impressions of success and failure through self-handicapping was demonstrated in a field study conducted at a large accounting firm in New York City. The respondents (accountants and supervisors) read scenarios that described an audit of a client's firm by a staff accountant named Richard Emmitt who was portrayed as using self-handicaps. For example, one self-handicap involved telling the boss that the audit would be difficult because the client had a new computer system that had bugs that needed to be worked out. In the scenarios, Emmitt was portrayed as having conducted a successful audit – it took him fewer hours than had been budgeted; or an unsuccessful audit – he needed more hours than had been budgeted. Interestingly, it was found that Emmitt's self-handicapping was effective following failure but not after success. He was blamed less for failure but he also received less credit for success. The principle that self-handicapping enhances success in addition to cushioning failure was not supported in this organizational application.

APOLOGIES

There are some situations where a person cannot use excuses, justifications, disclaimers, or self-handicapping to extricate himself from a predicament. The thief who is caught red-handed; the manager who forgets to attend the CEO's birthday party; the professor whose wife finds him in bed with a voluptuous graduate assistant. In these cases, the protective impression management tactic of last resort – an *apology* – is the offender's only hope (Lazare, 1995). An apology is an admission of responsibility, blame, and regret that tries to obtain a pardon from the target audience (Schlenker, 1980). By profusely apologizing for being late to a job interview, Wendy hopes her prospective employer will not consider her tardiness as indicative of her "real" nature as a worker. Wendy is attempting to capitalize on a feature of an apology called *splitting*. A successful apology will split the individual into the "bad me" – the one who was late for the job interview – and the "good me" – the one who realizes her transgression and won't do it again in the future. A courtroom example of splitting was provided in March 1994 by Danny Rolling, a serial killer convicted of the mutilation murders of five college students in Gainsville, Florida. In an effort to avoid the death penalty Rolling said, "I regret with all my heart what my hand has done." In essence Rolling's "good" heart was expressing remorse over what his "bad" hand had done.

While we may think of apologies as single acts such as saying "I'm sorry" after bumping into a coworker at the copy machine, or "pardon me" after burping at the company picnic, a more complex apology sequence is often used for serious predicaments. Schlenker and Darby (1981, p. 272) have described a five-component apology sequence. We illustrate the steps with the case of Tim, an employee who gets drunk at the company New Year's party, damages some expensive furniture, and tells loud, dirty jokes that many of the other people find offensive.

1   *Statement of apologetic intent.* After getting drunk at the party,

Tim tells his boss's secretary that he's really sorry and would like to apologize to the boss for his behavior.

2   *Expression of remorse.* During a meeting with the boss, Tim indicates how ashamed of his behavior he is and how sorry he feels. Tim tells the boss that he has had trouble sleeping at night since so making a fool of himself.

3   *Offer of restitution and redress.* Tim offers to pay in full the cost to the company of replacing the damaged furniture.

4   *Statement of self-castigation.* Tim says he feels worthless and understands if the boss needs to discipline him. "No one feels worse about this than I do," says Tim.

5   *Request for forgiveness.* Lastly, Tim begs the boss not to fire him and to forgive him this one lapse. He promises never to let anything like this happen again.

Apologies have only begun to be studied in organizational settings. One area where apologies are often stressed as a way of doing business is during service encounters such as between flight attendants and airline passengers, and waiters or waitresses and restaurant customers. Goodwin and Ross (1992) had students read scenarios of several service encounters (e.g., dental office, airline, auto mechanic) that had an unexpected delay. In one of the scenarios a mechanic tells a customer that a car repair promised by 5.00 p.m. that day won't be ready till 4.00 p.m. the next day. The service provider either offered or did not offer an apology and indicated that the customer would get a 10 percent discount or said there was nothing that could be done about it. The results showed that an apology alone was not enough to increase ratings of fairness or satisfaction. However, when a 10 percent discount was offered, an apology resulted in greater ratings of fairness and satisfaction than no apology. It may be that in real world settings saying you are sorry is not enough unless accompanied by some tangible restitution. Apparently, apologetic words work best if accompanied by apologetic deeds.

While many managers may hesitate to show remorse or admit that they have done wrong, the judicious use of apologies may actually be a characteristic of an effective leader (Lazare, 1995). Ave (1994) described the winning entries in a "best–worst boss" essay contest. While one of the characteristics of the best boss was an ability to admit mistakes, worst bosses tended to blame their mistakes on

BOX 5.2

Reducing the negative effects of destructive feedback

Most managers are taught that it is important to tell employees how they are doing through some form of regular feedback. *Constructive feedback*, according to Robert Baron (1990), can enhance worker motivation and performance. But while telling employees that they are doing well while offering some pointers for improvement is not very hard, many managers find it difficult to provide *negative feedback*. In fact, many managers avoid giving negative feedback because it may harm their future relations with employees or cause employees to be upset.

But avoidance doesn't make the problem go away. Instead the manager's annoyance may build and build until it explodes in a burst of *destructive criticism*, which "is often biting, sarcastic, and harsh" (Baron, 1990, p. 235). As you might imagine, the manager's outburst results in anger and tension in employees. Employees' performance may suffer and they may refuse to change.

What can be done? In two studies, Baron (1990) looked at different ways of reducing the negative organizational impact of destructive criticism. In the first study undergraduate research participants were asked to prepare an advertising campaign for a new shampoo product. An accomplice of the experimenter then looked at their work and gave preplanned criticism to the participants that was either constructive or destructive. When providing destructive criticism the accomplice was threatening and inconsiderate and said things like "I don't think you could be original if you tried" (p. 237).

After the destructive criticism, the research participants were exposed to four different conditions:

1   Incompatible responses: participants rated humorous cartoons rather than focusing on the campaign or the criticism.
2   External attribution: participants were given an account – they were told that most people do poorly on the task.

Box 5.2 continued

3   Apology: participants were told by the experimenter that the accomplice regretted his harsh comments and was sorry.
4   Catharsis: participants were given a chance to "get even" by rating the accomplice.

Baron (1990) found that the apology and external attribution (account) conditions were most effective in reducing the negative impact of destructive criticism. Respondents in these conditions were less angry at the accomplice, were happier, and were more likely to view their evaluations as fair than were those in the other groups.

Baron's second study used actual managers and non-managers in organizational settings such as banks and tele-communications companies. The respondents completed a survey that asked them to imagine that they had received destructive criticism from a colleague and they had to rate how effective the four countering actions used in Study 1 were in reducing their negative reaction to the criticism. Baron found results similar to those obtained in Study 1: both managers and nonmanagers rated the apology and account as the most effective of the four interventions. Thus, protective impression management tactics (apology, account) proved more effective than traditional behavioral techniques (incompatible response, catharsis) in reducing the negative effects of destructive criticism.

Source: Baron (1990)

subordinates. Box 5.2 describes how apologies can also help managers lessen the impact of destructive feedback.

INDIRECT PROTECTIVE IMPRESSION MANAGEMENT TACTICS

The nature of bad news infects the teller.
                    William Shakespeare, *Antony and Cleopatra*

In Chapter 3 we saw how individuals use the principle of association to claim positive impressions for themselves. This form of indirect impression management can also be used as a protective tactic. People will try to minimize their links to negative events or people. They will distance themselves from failure, and downgrade unsuccessful others with whom they might be associated. After Jody's subordinate Mitch is caught stealing from the company safe, Jody says she never wanted Mitch to work for her in the first place, had never trusted him, and was trying to get him fired. In this way, Jody is trying to minimize the natural tendency of other people to link Mitch's sleazy behavior to her. "Don't associate me with that creep," her words indicate, "I think he's a slimebag too!" Cialdini (1989) has called this tendency to "advertise" one's negative links to an unfavorable other, *blaring*. In a laboratory demonstration of blaring, Cooper and Jones (1969) found that individuals expressed attitudes that were dissimilar to another person when that person had been obnoxious to the experimenter. By proclaiming differences from an obnoxious other, the blarer is trying to have people view him more favorably.

While blaring works by minimizing the connections to a stigmatized other, Cialdini and his associates also noted some indirect tactics to minimize or devalue the person with whom we are connected. They called the tendency to exaggerate the bad qualities of someone with whom there is a negative association, *blasting* (Cialdini and Richardson, 1980; Cialdini, 1989). "You can promote Bob over me," Carol tells her boss, "but I want you to be aware that most of the people in this department have said they would quit before they would work for an incompetent like him!"

As we saw in Chapter 3, impression management techniques such as entitlements often work better if offered by third parties (Giacalone, 1985). Public relations firms have used third-parties to argue against laws or regulations that they have been hired to defeat. This form of blasting is called *white hats* (Bleifuss, 1994). White hats involves enlisting the help of groups with no apparent association to an issue to argue against it. The lack of association makes the blast more credible. Bleifuss (1994) provides the following example. A public relations firm was hired by several auto manufacturing companies to help defeat a proposed requirement for stricter anti-pollution devices on automobiles. The firm got the assistance from elderly and handicapped representatives by convincing their members that the anti-pollution regulations would result in smaller cars being built that would be hard for them to get into, and from parents who were convinced that more fuel-efficient station wagons would be too small to accommodate their families. With the opposition of the elderly, handicapped, and many parents, the proposed legislation was defeated. In essence, the public relations firm had used third-party blasting. They blasted the legislation to the handicapped, elderly, and parents, who in turn blasted it to their elected representatives.

In addition to blasting negatively associated others, individuals may try to distance themselves from failure, a tactic called *cutting off reflected failure* (CORF) (Snyder, Lassegard, and Ford, 1986). In one study, students were given success, failure, or no feedback on a problem-solving task they worked on together. It was found that those who failed tended to engage in the most CORFing – they were less likely to take part in their group's presentation and less likely to wear group identifiers (Snyder, Lassegard, and Ford, 1986).

Bob Giacalone (Giacalone, 1987; Giacalone and Knouse, 1988) has applied these notions of protective indirect impression management to perceptions of women managers in organizations. Giacalone reasoned that because female managers are often viewed as less successful than men or otherwise negatively stereotyped in organizations, male managers would be more likely to blast a female manager, especially if she fails. In one of several related studies, Giacalone (1987) had undergraduate business students read short descriptions of a corporate vice-president who was blamed for a decision that led to a huge financial loss for a fictitious company. The manager was portrayed as being either male or female. Giacalone found that while female students' ratings of the manager did not differ as a function of the manager's gender, males' ratings did. Males rated themselves less similar to a failing female manager than to a failing male manager. In a second study, Giacalone and Knouse (1988) found that this tendency of males to disassociate from a failing female manager occurred primarily in male respondents who had negative attitudes toward women. In this study the males whose connections to females were already the weakest, seemed to be first to blast the failing female manager. It suggests that when things get tough in organizations, prejudicial attitudes may have even more negative effects on organizational functioning.

A CONCLUDING NOTE

In this chapter we have described disclaimers, self-handicapping, and apologies, three types of protective impression management that individuals and organizations use in addition to accounts. As with acquisitive impression management, the danger exists that overly aggressive or obvious tactics may be ineffective or backfire. Thus, indirect means are also used in the service of damage control and image repair.

While the full repertoire of both acquisitive and protective impression management behaviors are available to all, not everyone engages in impression management in the same way or with equal proficiency. There are a number of different impression management behavior patterns or personality traits based on the type and frequency of impression management used and the skill or lack of skill in engaging in it. How these differences in impression management style are measured, and what their implications are for organizations is the focus of Chapter 6.

6 *Measuring impression management*

In a personnel selection situation, for example, a correlation between self-reported motivation and a measure of impression management has a number of plausible interpretations. A stylistic interpretation would suggest that chronic impression managers are faking high motivation. Alternatively, the nature of the position (e.g., public relations) may be such that chronic impression managers would continue to be motivated and are, therefore, ideal candidates.

(Paulhus, 1991, pp. 23–24)

DIFFERENT STROKES FROM DIFFERENT FOLKS

In the previous chapters we learned of the many ways that individuals and organizations engage in impression management – both to look good and to avoid looking bad. But while everyone manages impressions, they don't all do it in the same way. Researchers refer to these individual variations in impression management tendencies and behaviors as differences in *style* (Arkin, 1981). Styles are characteristic ways people manage impressions. Styles are one way to capture the idea of *individual differences* in impression management. We might say that different folks use different strokes to manage their impressions. Consider the following four examples:

Ted is a consultant who speaks his mind, and is confrontational in his approach. When a company hires him to help solve organizational problems he tells them what he thinks, despite how they might feel about it. He disregards how the people in the organization tend to act toward each other. This was particularly true of his interaction with the Caty Carpet Company. Caty had a culture with one rather implicit rule which Ted knew about: Never directly challenge Caty employees. One day when Ted was at a meeting, one Caty executive made a statement with which Ted disagreed. Ted looked at him, stood up and pointing at him said, "Prove it." The Caty executives had never seen such confrontation in their organization before. Their contract with Ted was soon terminated. As one Caty executive noted, "Ted apparently thinks that he can act and say anything he wants. He is wrong. He can act that way in other companies, but not at Caty."

Dawn is an executive who is constantly trying to put her best foot forward. She is quick to tell about her expertise in statistical process controls and human resource databases, although she privately tells her husband that "It is all an act. I know very little about those areas, but they are hot topics now, so I learned the buzzwords and make up the rest." Her assistant Leigh has the same level of inexperience as Dawn, and also claims the same degree of expertise. Yet Leigh is different: she really believes that she is an expert in these areas. As a colleague Vince notes, "I think that if you hooked Leigh up to a lie-detector, you would see that she isn't lying. She believes that she has the expertise. Unfortunately, she cannot do the work."

In what was to become a highly publicized dismissal, Gerry's company, Minks, Inc. was about to lay off Gerry and an entire group of mid-level managers for what they called "corporate incompatibility." When Glenn, Gerry's friend in public relations, came by to ask him what he intended to do, Gerry said he was planning how he could market himself to prospective employers after all the bad publicity. "There aren't many choices," Gerry finally concluded, "It's all a sales job. These days you've got to make it seem like you've got every skill a company would ever want or you don't have a chance."

Sidney is an engineer at a major manufacturing company. He is known as an employee who is moving up the organizational ladder rather quickly. What is his secret? Sidney is an ingratiator. He is quick to do favors for the executives, and knows how to agree with his boss on appropriate topics. He is well liked and that gives him an edge over colleagues who are not well liked. When promotions are on the line, his "friends" (the executives he has helped) are quick to remember and reward him.

Ted, Dawn, Gerry, and Sidney are all engaging in organizational impression management, but in very different ways. As we shall see in this chapter, Ted is a low self-monitor, someone whose deeds correspond closely to his beliefs. Dawn is high in the trait of impression management: she knowingly deceives others to make herself look good. Gerry's style is one of high attributive impression management – he tends to use impression management to ascribe positive characteristics to himself. Finally, Sidney is a hyper-ingratiator. He tries to move up by "kissing up."

In this chapter, we present four measures of impression management that correspond to the styles of Ted, Dawn, Gerry, and Sidney. These measures illustrate the ways that impression management might be assessed, how assessment provides us with an understanding of the varied nature of impression management, and how such assessment could be utilized by organizations.

MEASURES OF IMPRESSION MANAGEMENT

The measures we have chosen differ in their focus. The *Self-Monitoring Scale* (Snyder, 1974) is the most popular measure of impression management behavior, focusing on the extent to which individuals differ in their attentiveness and responsiveness to social cues. The focus is on both the choice to engage in impression management and how successful the person is at it. The *Balanced Inventory of Desirable Responding* (BIDR) (Paulhus, 1991) is a measure that conceptualizes impression management as a process driven by two rather different tendencies. On one hand is the tendency to deliberately convey a distorted image of oneself to others (what some have cynically viewed as describing all impression management). The BIDR also measures the extent to which individuals give overly positive statements about themselves that they actually believe. The *Self-Presentation Scale* (Roth, Snyder, and Pace, 1986) is a measure of whether individuals tend to use impression management which focuses on the positive characteristics that they hold, or on the denial of negative characteristics. Lastly, the *Measure of Ingratiatory Behaviors in Organizations Settings Scale* (MIBOS) (Kumar and Beyerlein, 1991) focuses on the extent to which individuals use the various tactics of ingratiation (see Chapter 2) in supervisor–subordinate relationships.

Self-Monitoring Scale

> From the early stages of deciding where to work and in what capacity through the ending of one's association with an organization, self-monitoring may influence the types and qualities of interactions between individuals in an organization.
>
> (Snyder and Copeland, 1989, pp. 17–18)

Some people, both inside and outside of organizations, appear to be *social chameleons*: individuals who change their attitudes, perspectives, and behaviors so as to fit into the social situations at hand. Others, as the story of Ted shows, do not adapt to the constraints of the social environment.

The Self-Monitoring Scale most directly assesses the degree to which people act like social chameleons. It measures the extent to which individuals in social situations actively monitor and control their public behaviors and appearances. For example, in an organizational setting, when a manager asks the opinions of employees about a new performance appraisal system, high self-monitoring employees may carefully control what they say and adjust their response to fit what the manager wants to hear. Others who are low self-monitors may offer their opinions and beliefs in a manner that is close to what they actually feel irrespective of what they think the manager's position is. The complete Self-Monitoring Scale is presented in Table 6.1.

Gabrenya and Arkin (1980) have described the high self-monitor as having five key tendencies. First, high self-monitors will have a strong concern for the social appropriateness of behavior. Second, they will show a greater attentiveness to the behavior of others as cues for their own impression management. Third, high self-monitors will possess a greater skill at modifying and controlling their own impression management. Fourth, they will use impression management skill in more circumstances. Finally, the high self-monitor will exhibit different behaviors in different situations.

On the other hand, low self-monitors tend to behave in a way which coincides with how they feel. Their behaviors are determined more by their actual attitudes, beliefs, and feelings, rather than the particular situation at hand. Low self-monitors are far less attentive to the social appropriateness of their self-presentations, perhaps because they lack the necessary skills to be effective impression managers. As such, they tend to be cross-situationally more

Table 6.1 The Self-Monitoring Scale

1 I find it is hard to imitate the behavior of other people.
2 My behavior is usually an expression of my true inner feelings, attitudes, and beliefs.
3 At parties and social gatherings, I do not attempt to do or say things that others will like.
4 I can only argue for ideas which I already believe.
5 I can make impromptu speeches even on topics about which I have almost no information.
6 I guess I put on a show to impress or entertain people.
7 When I am uncertain how to act in a social situation, I look to the behavior of others for cues.
8 I would probably make a good actor.
9 I rarely need the advice of my friends to choose movies, books or music.
10 I sometimes appear to others to be experiencing deeper emotions than I actually am.
11 I laugh more when I watch a comedy with others than when alone.
12 In a group of people I am rarely the center of attention.
13 In different situations and with different people, I often act like very different persons.
14 I am not particularly good at making other people like me.
15 Even if I am not enjoying myself, I often pretend to be having a good time.
16 I'm not always the person I appear to be.
17 I would not change my opinions (or the way I do things) in order to please someone else or win their favor.
18 I have considered being an entertainer.
19 In order to get along and be liked I tend to be what people expect me to be rather than anything else.
20 I have never been good at games like charades or improvisational acting.
21 I have trouble changing my behavior to suit different people and different situations.
22 At a party I let others keep the jokes and stories going.
23 I feel a bit awkward in company and do not show up quite so well as I should.
24 I can look anyone in the eye and tell a lie with a straight face (if for a right end).
25 I may deceive people by being friendly when I really dislike them.

Source: Snyder (1974).

consistent in their attitudes, beliefs, feelings, and behaviors across situations (Snyder, 1987). For example, Ted, the consultant described in the opening to this chapter, is a low self-monitor. He stated his beliefs as he felt them, regardless of the sentiments against open confrontation in the organization culture.

Mark Snyder, who authored the Self-Monitoring Scale, provides a personal, "Behind the Scenes" look at self-monitoring.

● ● ● ●

Behind the Scenes

Mark Snyder

Twenty-some years ago, as a graduate student in psychology, I discovered this quotation from the works of W.H. Auden: "The image of myself which I try to create in my own mind in order that I may love myself is very different from the image which I try to create in the minds of others in order that they may love me." Why, I asked myself then, and continue to ask myself today, do some people have so much in common with the state of affairs described by Auden? Why do some people seem to be living lives of public illusion, forever striving to create images, always trying to control the impressions they convey? My attempts to answer these questions have grown out of a long-standing fascination with the differences between reality and illusion – the contrast between the way things appear to be and the reality that often lurks beneath the surface. As a psychologist, I wanted to understand this world of appearances, to discover how and why people deliberately choose their words and deeds to create images appropriate to particular circumstances, to appear to be the right person in the right place at the right time.

This creating of images in the minds of others, this acting to control the impressions conveyed to others, is no doubt practiced to some extent by just about everyone. But for some people, it is almost a way of life. These people are particularly sensitive to the ways they present themselves in social situations. Indeed, they carefully observe their own performances and skillfully adjust these performances to convey just the right image of themselves. I call these people *high self-monitors* because of the great extent to which they are engaged in monitoring or controlling the images of self they project in social interaction. In contrast, other people, known as *low self-monitors*, think of themselves as consistent beings who value congruence between "who they are" and "what they do." They are not so concerned with constantly assessing the social climate around them. Instead, they can be expected to speak their minds, vent their feelings, and bare their souls, even if doing so means sailing against the prevailing winds of their social environments.

To identify people high and low in self-monitoring, I have developed the Self-Monitoring Scale, an inventory of true–false statements. Over the years, studies of self-monitoring have taught us that self-monitoring meaningfully influences people's views of themselves and the world around them, their behavior in social situations, and the dynamics of their relationships with other people. Among the life domains where the self-monitoring orientations are evident are the activities of people in organizations, particularly those in which people find employment and in which they pursue their careers. Researchers have examined how people choose occupations compatible with their self-monitoring orientations, how self-monitoring reveals itself in personnel selection interviews, and how high and low self-monitors fare when it comes to matters of job performance and job promotion. With the insights gleaned from such research comes the potential for more informed decision-making and planning, both on the part of individuals and organizations.

• • • •

Self-monitoring has been linked with a variety of organizationally related processes including job choice (Snyder and Gangstead, 1982), personnel selections tasks (Smith and Davidson, 1983; Snyder, Berscheid, and Matwychuk, 1988), job performance (Caldwell and O'Reilly, 1982; Giacalone and Falvo, 1985), and leader emergence (Garland and Beard, 1979). For example, Latham (1985) found that high and low self-monitors differed in how they looked for jobs. While high self-monitors tended to use social connections (e.g., friends) to find jobs, low self-monitors used more formal means such as employment agencies. These results have implications for organizational recruitment. In order to attract the full range of potential employees, Snyder and Copeland (1989) suggest that organizations should use both formal means such as job advertisements and agencies that would tend to attract low self-monitors, and informal means such as friends and acquaintances of current and former employees to attract high self-monitors.

It should be noted that job selection is not only affected by the self-monitoring orientation of the applicant but also is influenced by the self-monitoring level of the job interviewer. Snyder, Berscheid, and Matwychuk (1988) had college students act as evaluators in a job selection task. They found that evaluators tended to make hiring decisions that matched their own self-monitoring styles. The decisions of high self-monitoring evaluators favored appearance over the applicant's personality, while low self-monitoring evaluators tended to make their decisions based on the applicant's personality and temperament rather than their appearance.

Self-monitoring has also been applied to the area of leadership. Dobbins *et al.* (1990) investigated the role that self-monitoring plays in leader emergence. Groups consisting of a female high self-monitor, female low self-monitor, male high self-monitor, and male low self-monitor were asked to work on a salary allocation task. Respondents then completed questionnaires that asked them to choose a leader from the group. They found that high self-monitors were more likely to emerge as leaders than were low self-monitors. However, other studies have found the relationship between self-monitoring and leadership to be inconsistent (Anderson and Tolson, 1989).

Although self-monitoring impacts a number of organizational processes, neither high nor low self-monitors are at a distinct organizational advantage overall. It really depends on the nature of the work and the demands of the job. As Snyder and Copeland (1989, p. 13) write, "one may be led to believe that when it comes to performance on the job high self-monitors have better chances for success than low self-monitors. However, this is not necessarily the case. Low self-monitors may be more effective in job performance than high self-monitors in those occupations that call for their characteristic interpersonal style. For example, an occupation that requires an employee to be relatively self-motivated and capable of performing duties without a great deal of supervision or interpersonal contact may find better employees in low self-monitors than in high self-monitors."

The balanced inventory of desirable responding

The *Balanced Inventory of Desirable Responding* (BIDR) consists of 40 items designed to measure two very different aspects of the impression management spectrum: impression management (IM) and self-deceptive enhancement (SDE) (Paulhus, 1991). On this scale IM is the tendency to deliberately over-report desirable

Table 6.2 Balanced Inventory of Desirable Responding (BIDR)

1   My first impressions of people usually turn out to be right.
2   It would be hard for me to break any of my bad habits.
3   I don't care to know what other people really think of me.
4   I have not always been honest with myself.
5   I always know why I like things.
6   When my emotions are aroused, it biases my thinking.
7   Once I've made up my mind, other people can seldom change my opinion.
8   I am not a safe driver when I exceed the speed limit.
9   I am fully in control of my own fate.
10 It's hard for me to shut off a disturbing thought.
11 I never regret my decisions.
12 I sometimes lose out on things because I can't make up my mind soon enough.
13 The reason I vote is because my vote can make a difference.
14 My parents were not always fair when they punished me.
15 I am a completely rational person.
16 I rarely appreciate criticism.
17 I am very confident of my judgments.
18 I have sometimes doubted my ability as a lover.
19 It's all right with me if some people happen to dislike me.
20 I don't always know the reasons why I do the things I do.
21 I sometimes tell lies if I have to.
22 I never cover up my mistakes.
23 There have been occasions when I have taken advantage of someone.
24 I never swear.
25 I sometimes try to get even rather than forgive and forget.
26 I always obey laws, even if I'm unlikely to get caught.
27 I have said something bad about a friend behind his or her back.
28 When I hear people talking privately, I avoid listening.
29 I have received too much change from a salesperson without telling him or her.
30 I always declare everything at customs.
31 When I was young I sometimes stole things.
32 I have never dropped litter on the street.
33 I sometimes drive faster than the speed limit.
34 I never read sexy books and magazines.
35 I have done things that I don't tell other people about.
36 I never take things that don't belong to me.
37 I have taken sick-leave from work or school even though I wasn't really sick.
38 I have never damaged a library book or store merchandise without reporting it.
39 I have some pretty awful habits.
40 I don't gossip about other people's business.

Source: Paulhus (1991).

behaviors and under-report behaviors that are undesirable. SDE is the tendency to give overly positive reports. SDE differs from IM in that respondents actually believe their positive SDE self-reports. The BIDR is presented in Table 6.2.

The distinctions between IM and SDE can be seen in the following example. Let us look at Steve, an employee with a mediocre work record who is seeking employment. Steve responds to a question by an interviewer in which he is asked to "describe the credentials you possess that make you most qualified to do this job." Steve proceeds to provide a lengthy answer about his education at Oxford, his ten years of experience with his previous organization, the accomplishments he has achieved in his time with the company, and the enormous respect he receives for doing a similar job with his present company. In fact, while Steve did go to Oxford, his grades were average. His experience and accomplishments are hardly noteworthy, and his coworkers and supervisors find him acceptable at best. Thus, an objective observer would listen to Steve's response and conclude that it was not entirely accurate. The question is why? One interpretation, that of IM, is that Steve is an outright liar, intentionally faking his responses for the sake of creating a positive impression and getting the job. Another interpretation, that of SDE, is that Steve may actually believe what he said, perhaps because he has little self-insight, is not in touch with reality, or is very self-centered. It could also be that both processes are at work in Steve's case, perhaps a little bit of other-deception is mixed in with some self-deception. The BIDR is therefore designed to measure the extent to which each of these dimensions – deception of others, deception of oneself – is driving the socially desirable responses Steve is giving.

Responses to the BIDR are categorized along these two dimensions. The first 20 items of the BIDR measure SDE, the remaining 20 items measure IM. Going back to our opening scenario, it seems that Dawn, the executive using buzzwords to feign expertise, would score highly on IM, while her assistant, Leigh, who falsely believes she is an expert, would likely have a high SDE score. A person who scores high in SDE is likely to endorse items on the BIDR such as "My first impressions of people usually turn out to be right," and "I don't care to know what other people really think of me." Conversely, a person who scores high in IM is likely to endorse items such as "I have never dropped litter on the street," and "I don't gossip about other people's business."

In a "Behind the Scenes" look, Delroy Paulhus gives us a more personal view of his work on the BIDR.

• • • •

Behind the Scenes

Delroy Paulhus

A researcher interested in impression management and self-deception faces a special hurdle in composing a background profile. That hurdle involves overcoming the skepticism of the reader who assumes that I, like many researchers, conduct research on my own most prominent tendencies. Whatever the reason, I have long been fascinated by individuals who seem consistently to self-promote and wondered whether such individuals actually believe their self-promotion. This interest in impression management was aroused in graduate school at Columbia University – a program notable for its combined training in personality and social psychology. Because of this dual training, I was exposed to the impression management literature from both the situational and individual differences perspectives. Indeed, my dissertation examined both sources of variance in the phenomenon of cognitive dissonance. Strongly influenced by my graduate advisor, Harold Sackeim, I focused on separating the unconscious component from the conscious component of impression management. Several of my early publications argued that traditional measures of socially desirable responding actually confounded the two components. This distinction evolved over the years along with my new test instrument, the *Balanced Inventory of Desirable Responding* (BIDR). Ultimately, I settled on the labels, Self-Deception (sometimes also called Self-Deceptive Enhancement) and Impression Management, for the response styles measured by the BIDR.

I believe that this distinction is central to a number of issues in organizational behavior. These include personnel selection, workers' compensation, malingering, as well as control of desirable responding in research contexts. In personnel selection for example, few interviewers accept at face value the self-descriptions of job applicants. Often, however, interviewers fail to differentiate the applicant who knowingly dissembles from the one who exaggerates his/her qualifications because of over-confidence and optimism. The BIDR has proved to be an ideal tool for making such discriminations. In simulated job interviews, for example, my colleagues and I showed that the Impression Management scale, but not the Self-Deception scale, was sensitive to attempted faking. In actual personnel selection studies, the BIDR scales have been used to evaluate the ideal test conditions for minimizing desirable responding in US Navy recruits. More and more organizations are now incorporating the BIDR as a standard feature of their personnel selection batteries. Another common application of the BIDR scales is in evaluating self-report instruments used in organizational research: some instruments correlate significantly with self-deception and some with impression management (Moorman and Podsakoff, 1992). None the less, statistical control methods should not be applied hastily. Often response styles such as impression management and self-deception are an essential component of the organizational concept being measured (Zerbe and Paulhus, 1987). In short, content and style are sometimes one and the same.

Finally, in looking back at this summary, I must admit that my own tendency to manage impressions played some part in the presentation. I'll leave it to the reader to judge whether self-deception also played a role – after all, I'd be the last to know!

• • • •

One recent organizational application of the BIDR has been in the area of computer surveys. A number of studies have used the scale to look at the implications of utilizing computers to administer organizational surveys (Booth-Kewley, Edwards, and Rosenfeld, 1992; Lautenschlager and Flaherty, 1990). These studies have addressed an issue that has both important theoretical and practical implications: to what degree are responses on computer surveys similar or different from those obtained on standard paper surveys? Over the past decade, some published studies (see Rosenfeld, Booth-Kewley, and Edwards, 1993 for a review) have reported that computer survey responses are more candid, less biased, and less influenced by impression management motives than responses given on paper surveys. These studies have, however, been difficult to replicate. Comparisons between paper-and-pencil and computer surveys have frequently yielded virtually identical responses.

The findings of studies that claimed computers either reduced the tendency to engage in impression management and those reporting no computer–paper differences were both challenged by Lautenschlager and Flaherty's (1990) findings. They compared responses of undergraduates on the BIDR completed in either computer or paper-and-pencil conditions. They found that students in the computer condition gave more socially desirable responses on the BIDR than their counterparts in the paper-and-pencil condition. Also, respondents who were identified had significantly higher scores on both scales than students in the anonymous condition. These results led the authors to conclude that individuals may be *more* likely to distort their responses on the computer and that "the administration of ... attitude questionnaires in organizational research may be adversely affected when converted from paper-and-pencil format. Increases due to impression management on such diagnostic measures may produce inaccurate and potentially misleading results" (Lautenschlager and Flaherty, 1990, p. 314).

Given the potential implications of this finding, Booth-Kewley, Edwards, and Rosenfeld (1992) attempted to replicate the study in a non-college environment. Male Navy recruits completed surveys in either a computer or paper-and-pencil condition, and their responses were either identified or anonymous. The results supported the finding discussed above that identified respondents had higher IM and SDE scores than anonymous respondents. Contrary to those findings, however, whether responses were made on the computer or on paper had no effect on either IM or SDE scores. Booth-Kewley, Edwards, and Rosenfeld (1992) concluded that computer vs. paper administration does not appear to alter scores on organizational scales in any consistent way. They argued that, where financial and logistical considerations allow, organizations are justified in using computer-based surveys instead of paper-and-pencil administration.

Recently, Rosenfeld, Booth-Kewley, Edwards, and Thomas (in press) again attempted to directly address these inconsistencies found in computer versus paper-and-pencil survey administration. Their study used paper and two computer conditions, linked and unlinked. The linked-computer condition was included to simulate the Big Brother Syndrome – an increasing fear that individuals have that their computer responses are being monitored or will be checked. Rosenfeld and his colleagues predicted that responses in the linked-computer (Big Brother) condition would be more socially desirable than those in the unlinked-computer and paper conditions. It was expected that this effect would be enhanced when respondents were identified rather than anonymous. In the Rosenfeld et al. (in press) study, male Navy recruits completed the BIDR. Scores on the IM subscale of the BIDR were higher in the identified than in the anonymous conditions. More importantly, in identified conditions, IM scores were significantly higher in the Big Brother condition than in the other two conditions. It was concluded that perceiving that one's responses are linked to a larger data base may activate the Big Brother Syndrome which may lead to greater impression management on computer surveys.

Self-Presentation Scale

Gerry's reply to Glenn in one of the scenarios opening this chapter, points to a different facet of impression management. While the BIDR distinguishes between impression management driven by conscious deception of others or self-deception, there is yet another way of conceptualizing differences in how individuals manage impressions. C.R. Snyder and his associates (Roth, Harris, and Snyder, 1988; Roth, Snyder, and Pace, 1986) have created an instrument which measures the tendency toward *attributive* versus *repudiative* tactics of impression management. The contrast between attributive versus repudiative tactics of impression management represents a basic distinction in the general *style* in which impressions are managed rather than in the underlying motivation to manage impressions. The essence of this style is that individuals will tend toward favorable impression management by either attempting to ascribe positive traits to themselves via the use of attributive tactics or deny the existence of negative characteristics through the use of repudiative tactics.

The *Self-Presentation Scale* (SPS) is a 60-item measure of the tendency to use either attributive or repudiative tactics. For each of the items, respondents indicate whether the statements made are true or false regarding themselves. The attributive measure has 30 items containing unrealistically positive statements. Because all of the statements are highly unlikely to be true, those responding "true" to these statements are seen as engaging in attributive self-presentations. The repudiative measure also has 30 items which describe undesirable characteristics that are likely to be true of almost anyone. Those responding "false" to these measures would also be engaging in self-presentation, but of a repudiative type. The complete SPS can be found in Table 6.3.

Table 6.3 The Self-Presentation Scale

1   My childhood was always happy.
2   I would lie to get out of trouble.
3   I contribute all I can to charity.
4   All of my successes can be explained by my abilities.
5   I sometimes think about attacking others physically.
6   Everyone thinks I am a calm person.
7   At times I feel like swearing.
8   I voice opinions on issues that I know little about.
9   I obey all laws.
10 I worry about things over which I have little control.
11 Before voting, I thoroughly investigate the issues and candidates.
12 My solutions to problems are original and effective.
13 I evaluate the physical attractiveness of people the same sex as myself.
14 I am loyal to my friends at all times.
15 Money is an important motivator for me.
16 I have thought of suicide as one way I could get back at those who have hurt me.
17 My shyness prevents me from meeting new people.
18 I argue only when I know I'm right.
19 I am always on time for appointments.
20 Pornography arouses me.
21 I am completely happy with the way my life is going.
22 My behavior is influenced by the expectations of others.
23 When angry, I sometimes feel like smashing things.
24 If I find something that is not mine, I make every effort to return it to the real owner.
25 I sometimes avoid people I do not wish to speak to.
26 When I was a child my parents were mean to me on occasion.
27 I always enjoy accepting new responsibilities.
28 When wronged, I sometimes want revenge.
29 I always practice what I preach.
30 I understand all of the problems of the disadvantaged.
31 My family life is totally happy and peaceful.
32 I have cheated on schoolwork in the past.
33 The success of others sometimes makes me jealous.
34 My friends and acquaintances are all exceptional people.
35 In my private thoughts, I laugh at the incompetencies of others.
36 I will always go out of my way to help others.
37 My parents always did what was best for me.
38 I have doubted my sexual adequacy.
39 I always help people who feel lonely.
40 My peers should follow in my footsteps.
41 I try to figure out what others think of me.
42 I am always courteous, even to disagreeable people.
43 I am willing to admit all of my mistakes.

Table 6.3 continued

44   I am completely honest.
45   I am sometimes rude to other people.
46   I am responsible for some of my failures.
47   I live by the highest moral standards.
48   Some of my thoughts are too bad to talk about.
49   I have deliberately hurt other people's feelings.
50   I am always kind to animals.
51   I feel sad sometimes.
52   I have felt hatred toward others.
53   I feel sexually attracted to many people.
54   Everyone thinks I am important and knowledgeable.
55   I worry about my own death.
56   Everyone likes me.
57   I am always trying to improve myself.
58   I feel resentful when I don't get my way.
59   I sometimes quarrel with family members.
60   I completely control my own destiny.

Source: Roth, Snyder, and Pace (1986).

Although the Self-Presentation Scale has been around since the late 1980s, to our knowledge no organizational studies have been developed using it. Still, the potential for diagnostic information from the SPS is clear. The ability to categorize individual styles of impression management could aid understanding of communication. For example, knowing whether an employee will tend to use repudiative or attributive self-presentation can help a manager anticipate and better understand the employee's behaviors and responses to success and failure feedback. Similarly, employment interviewers might be able to ask better questions (and follow-ups) if they were alerted, in advance, that the interviewee tended to self-present in either an attributive or repudiative manner. Also, the types of responses regarding employee turnover or other organizational phenomena given during an exit interview may vary depending on whether the interviewee tends to be an ascriber of positive traits or a denier of negative ones.

The Measure of Ingratiatory Behaviors in Organizational Settings (MIBOS)

Understanding the ability of employees like Sidney (the engineer described in our opening case-study) to ingratiate themselves to

Table 6.4 Measure of Ingratiatory Behavior in Organizational Settings (MIBOS)

1   Impress upon your supervisor that only he/she can help you in a given situation mainly to make him/her feel good about himself/herself.
2   Show him/her that you share his/her enthusiasm about his/her new idea even when you may not actually like it.
3   Try to let him/her know that you have a reputation for being liked.
4   Try to make sure that he/she is aware of your successes.
5   Highlight the achievements made under his/her leadership in a meeting not being attended by him/her.
6   Give frequent smiles to express enthusiasm/interest about something he/she is interested in even if you do not like it.
7   Express work attitudes that are similar to your supervisor's as a way of letting him/her know that the two of you are alike.
8   Tell him/her that you can learn a lot from his/her experience.
9   Exaggerate his/her admirable qualities to convey the impression that you think highly of him/her.
10 Disagree on trivial or unimportant issues but agree on those issues in which he/she expects support from you.
11 Try to imitate such work behaviors of your supervisor as working late or occasionally working on weekends.
12 Look for opportunities to let the supervisor know your virtues/strengths.
13 Ask your supervisor for advice in areas in which he/she thinks he/she is smart to let him/her feel that you admire your supervisor.
14 Try to do things for your supervisor that show your selfless generosity.
15 Look out for opportunities to admire your supervisor.
16 Let your supervisor know the attitudes you share with him/her.
17 Compliment your supervisor on his/her achievement, however trivial it may actually be to you personally.
18 Laugh heartily at your supervisor's jokes even when they are not really funny.
19 Go out of your way to run an errand for your supervisor.
20 Offer to help your supervisor by using your personal contacts.
21 Try to present your own qualities persuasively when attempting to convince your supervisor about your abilities.
22 Volunteer to be of help to your supervisor in matters like locating a good apartment, finding a good insurance agent, etc.
23 Spend time listening to your supervisor's personal problems even if you have no interest in them.
24 Volunteer to help your supervisor in his/her work even if it means extra work for you.

Source: Kumar and Bayerlein (1991).

others is the focus of the *Measure of Ingratiatory Behaviors in Organizational Settings* (MIBOS). The MIBOS (Kumar and Beyerlein, 1991) aims at a rather different aspect of impression management measurement than did the previous three scales. The MIBOS is a measure of "the frequency with which ingratiatory tactics are used by subordinates in superior–subordinate relationships" (Kumar and Beyerlein, 1991, p. 620). The measure can be broken down into four factors representing the ingratiation tactics of other-enhancement, opinion conformity, self-presentation (what we called self-enhancement), and favor rendering discussed in Chapter 2. The MIBOS, therefore, differs from the previously discussed measures in two distinct ways. First, the MIBOS is focused on particular impression management tactics rather than on the more global concepts of impression management response style or orientation. Second, the MIBOS is the only one of the measures that specifically focuses on organizationally related impression management. The complete MIBOS scale can be found in Table 6.4.

Watt (1993) did a study using the MIBOS in a bank setting. He asked subordinates to fill out the scale, and their supervisors to evaluate them on a performance evaluation instrument. Results showed that employees who engaged in more ingratiating behaviors (according to the MIBOS) were judged significantly higher in motivation, competence, cooperation, promotion potential, and overall performance by their supervisors. Thus, the MIBOS appears to show some utility in predicting whether ingratiation impacts overall performance appraisal, as well as specific aspects of that appraisal.

UTILIZING IMPRESSION MANAGEMENT MEASURES

How might impression management measures be used by organizational practitioners and researchers? In trying to illustrate the utility of impression management measures, the differing perspectives of these two groups is important to consider. On the one hand, business practitioners might be very interested in using impression management measures as part of their overall set of assessments. Practitioners would be interested in these measures generally from the perspective of how to change organizational processes. However, researchers would be interested in using these measures to study the impact of impression management on organizational functioning. Their interest would not be from a hands-on applied perspective, but from the standpoint of scientific inquiry. Thus, we will address the issues of practitioner and scholarly utility separately.

How organizational practitioners might use impression management measures

While the measures we have discussed are both interesting and potentially useful, relatively little has been done with them in actual organizations. In our view, there is much untapped potential for using measures such as these in organizations, both as measures of actual performance, and as moderators/mediators of self-report measures in organizations. The distinction between these two types of measures is an important one. *Hard measures* gauge actual performance, including such things as measures of performance appraisal, productivity, and training effectiveness, as well as measures of events such as absenteeism, tardiness, and medical claims filed. *Self-reports* involve perceptual or attitudinal concepts measured by surveys or interviews. Included in this would be measures of morale, job satisfaction, ethical climate, and organizational commitment. While impression management has been used extensively with self-report measures, very little has been done in response to hard measures explaining performance or other organizationally relevant outcome measures.

Individual differences in impression management and hard measures

There are a number of ways the scales reviewed above might be used to understand how impression management impacts hard measures in organizations. Table 6.5 provides some specific examples.

Impression management measures could be used to predict those positions in which different abilities and motivations can promote job success (Riordan, 1989). For example, in *boundary-spanner* positions – those that require an employee to work in a position requiring multiple roles (e.g., acting as a liaison between a union and management) – self-monitoring ability may have an impact, since such positions require closer scrutiny of situational variables. Indeed, high self-monitors were found to be more effective in boundary-spanning tasks than low self-monitors were (Caldwell and O'Reilly, 1982). Snyder and Copeland (1989, p. 17) suggest that an employer can use knowledge of differences in self-monitoring to gain different types of information from an exiting employee that can assist with

Table 6.5 Potential applications of impression management scales to hard performance measures in organizations

---

Self-Monitoring (SM)

Interviewing: High SM interviewers could be used to help detect candidate impression management as well as create an "appropriate" organizational image on the candidate.

Recruitment: Low SM recruiters could be used in realistic job previews so as to promote the most realistic/accurate view of the organization.

Behavioral Inventory of Desirable Responding

High Visibility Positions: In high visibility positions, individuals who have been assessed to have the requisite abilities can be screened for IM. Those low in this can be remedially trained. Alternatively, those high in SDE can be trained to be more aware of self-deception.

Self-Presentation Scale

Employee Feedback Interviews: Management awareness of the candidates' tendency to use repudiative or attributive self-presentational strategies can help to redirect the feedback toward realistic concerns and improve the efficiency of feedback.

Measure of Ingratiatory Behaviors in Organizational Settings (MIBOS)

Defensive Management: Knowledge of the degree of ingratiation in the organization can help in the training of managers to overcome dysfunctional and/or excessive impression management.

---

future selection decisions. "From a low self-monitoring employee, an employer may be able to determine what personality or behavioral characteristics of that employee did not mesh well with the particular job's requirements and use this information for future personnel decisions. From a high self-monitor, on the other hand, an exit interview might provide the employer with information about how an employee in a given occupation views the occupation's necessary vocational prerequisites."

Second, impression management measures could be used within work units and organizations to better understand the culture and/or facilitate organizational development and change. Imagine an organization in which certain departments are thought to be deficient on a particular criterion (e.g., productivity) and believed to have employees who are more interested in image than substance. Administering the MIBOS could tell us about the ingratiation tactics employees use to manage images for themselves and their departments and, by comparing them to scale norms, whether they were being used excessively. After having tested an entire department, we could develop a "profile" for the department – high in self-presentation, low in opinion conformity, etc. Thus, if in a particular department we knew that the strategy of opinion conformity was not used, but that self-presentation was a tactic which was used frequently, we would be able to help managers better identify self-presentation as a strategy, while opinion conformity would be comparatively less of a focus. This profile could then help increase management awareness so that the organization could more effectively interact with or overcome these tactics. If it could lead to rewarding actual output rather than superficial image, we would expect productivity to increase in the long run.

Also, impression management measures could help identify those employees who are interpersonally deficient in their impression management and in need of training. For example, if we found that an employee had a profile which showed he was probably engaging in very little acquisitive impression management (e.g., a low self-monitor, low on the BIDR, a low attributor of positive qualities on the SPS), we might want to take a look at helping this individual learn to put his best foot forward to represent the company positively (see Martinko, 1991). Training such individuals would not be intended to help them exploit others, but to present themselves, their work and the organization more realistically and effectively.

Individual differences and self-reports

Measures of impression management may also help explain the responses that individuals give to attitudinal, perceptual, and personality measures.

First, impression management measures may help us understand *whose* responses to self-reports will be biased. For example, if we knew that employees high in IM and employees low in IM were being given a measure of "employee morale," we would predict that the employees high in IM would be more motivated and more likely to distort the responses given to the employee morale measure than would the employees who scored low in IM. Thus, some statistical adjustments could be made to the responses of individuals who score high in IM if it was determined that they gave inflated responses to particular questions or overall measures.

Second, impression management measures may help us to better interpret the responses given in employee self-reports. If we found that employees tended toward an attributive rather than a repudiative style on the SPS, we might interpret agreement with positively worded self-report questions more conservatively, since such agreement would more likely be expected among those with an attributive style.

Third, impression management measures may help us to understand why some individuals will give biased responses on self-report measures even when they are anonymous. The BIDR, for example, can help us to determine whether biased responding exists because of a deliberate attempt to control one's image, or as a result of self-deception. One of the authors of this text is using the BIDR to understand why a group of "at risk" youths with few job-related skills report that they expect to get "very good jobs" when they receive their Graduate Equivalency Degrees. Are they trying to impress the interviewer? Are they deceiving themselves? The distinction may be important, since some in the impression management area have traditionally assumed that a reduction in impression management bias can be achieved by increasing the anonymity of responses (Giacalone and Rosenfeld, 1986). Unfortunately, employees who are high in the SDE component of the BIDR will not necessarily give less biased responses when anonymous (Rosenfeld, Booth-Kewley, Edwards, and Thomas, in press).

How organizational researchers might use impression management measures

In addition to being used as simple assessment/diagnostic tools for individual workers, impression management measures can also help researchers determine the role that impression management plays in the way employees in organizations work and interact.

Except in some specific areas of organizational research (e.g., job interviews, performance evaluations, exit interviews), the role of impression management has often been overlooked. These measures can help researchers understand more about organizations by providing insight into the extent to which impression management processes play a role in various organizational areas. In a very general way, the measures themselves raise some very interesting questions about how employee differences in impression management may result in different reactions to organizational processes and events. For example, would individuals who score highly on the MIBOS have quicker or smoother career paths? Are high self-monitors more likely to adapt to new environments after transfers to new jobs? Do those who score highly on SDE do better in times of organizational crisis since the scale is negatively associated with measures of neuroticism and depression?

Why would researchers wish to use impression management measures? Researchers focusing on impression management realize that there are basically two strategies to investigate its organizational impact. As the appendix on pp. 186–193 indicates, one strategy is to manipulate variables such as identifiability (anonymity or identification of one's responses) or the source of an evaluation (one's own manager or another manager). The manipulation of variables in organizational settings, however, can be disruptive or ethically questionable. For example, if we asked some employees to put their names on surveys, while asking others to remain anonymous, we might arouse suspicion, fear, or mistrust. Employees might ask how it was decided who would be identified and who would be anonymous. Similarly, if we attempted to show that interpersonal behaviors would change, based on whether one's own or another manager was the evaluator of those behaviors, we would be inconveniencing outside parties and perhaps causing still more suspicion about the "true" purposes behind the intervention.

A less intrusive strategy is to use the impression management measures we have described. Measures of impression management allow an organizational researcher to administer questionnaires and see how groups of individuals who are high or low in these traits perform in various tasks and settings. Utilizing this approach can provide us with a great deal of information about when impression management impacts organizational phenomena, when it does not, and when it actually hinders performance. Today employees are used to being tested. Therefore, using impression management measures as part of a larger organizational assessment can be done without overly disrupting organizational functioning or arousing undue suspicion or ill-will.

Using impression management measures in organizations: advantages and disadvantages

Although impression management measures have been underutilized or ignored by many organizational practitioners and researchers, we believe it is important to look carefully at the advantages and

Table 6.6 Advantages of impression management measures

- Provide quantitative information on which individuals can be compared.
- Are unbiased indicators of impression management, especially when such behavior is perceived by managers as nefarious or dysfunctional.
- Provide an empirical basis for evaluating impression management in individuals or groups, rather than the more political characterizations motivated by self-interest.
- Provide empirical data to justify managerial decisions.
- Provide respondents with significant insight into their own behaviors.

Source: The issues addressed herein are based on categories from Furnham, A. (1992). *Personality at work: The role of individual differences in the workplace.* London: Routledge, pp. 38–39

disadvantages of using these measures in organizational settings. Summarized in Table 6.6 are a number of advantages of measuring differences in impression management in organizations.

One important advantage is that using impression management measures may help managers make decisions that are supported by empirical data. For example, knowledge that an individual is a high self-monitor might lend support to a manager's decision to give him a boundary-spanning job, or one that involves lots of interaction with the public. Conversely, for an employee in a boundary-spanning position who is a low self-monitor, such knowledge may justify further training in interpersonal sensitivity and communication or transfer to a job that requires an ability to successfully work alone.

Another advantage is that measuring impression management can provide testers and respondents with some insight into their own behaviors. Using this as part of an overall seminar in communication, for example, may help to direct both the tester and respondent toward greater self-understanding and career development. We've found that one of the best ways to explain impression management measures to our students or clients is to have them complete the scales, score them, and then tell us whether their impression management "personality profile" really fits. Interestingly, most of the time it does!

While these advantages are appealing, disadvantages can also be encountered in using these measures. These are summarized in Table 6.7.

Table 6.7 Disadvantages of impression management measures

- Some respondents may be incapable of providing insight into themselves.
- Measures may be fakable.
- As knowledge of impression management testing becomes common, potential respondents can "practice" their responses in advance.
- The measures may have limited organizational validity. They may provide interesting but not significant insights into key organizational processes.
- Sample norms generated with non-working populations may provide misleading comparisons.
- Use of the measures may result in legal challenges.

Source: The issues addressed herein are based on categories from Furnham, A. (1992). *Personality at work: The role of individual differences in the workplace.* London: Routledge, pp. 39–40.

Inherent to almost any testing process involving self-ratings is an assumption that respondents are capable of providing insight into themselves. In fact, some individuals may lack an understanding of themselves sufficient to provide such insights. The SDE component on the BIDR is, in itself, a measure of this phenomenon.

Conversely, some individuals may have the insight to provide accurate responding, but may be *unwilling* to do so and fake their responses. For example, while an individual who has self-monitoring tendencies may recognize these in himself, he may be unwilling to respond truthfully when completing the scale, fearing that his responses would adversely impact the perception that his boss has of him.

In the future, with the potential for increased use of such measures by organizations, another problem may emerge. Individuals may go beyond unwillingness to tell the truth, and move more toward a manipulation of their responses so as to conform to organizational "criteria" of how they should respond on impression management measures.

A more serious concern is that the measures herein, as well as others related to impression management, have not been subjected to the rigorous validity studies required for many organizational purposes. When such tests are used to make critical personnel decisions, it is essential that we be able to show that tests measure in a consistent and unbiased way, factors important to job performance

Table 6.8 Measures of importance to impression management*

Measure	Sources	Characterization of measure	How characteristics could be related to impression management	Process impacting impression management
Bases of Power	See Hinkin and Schriesheim, 1989	Measures designed to ascertain bases of power	• Various bases of power, by their presence or absence, may *facilitate* particular forms of impression management • Impression management and various bases of power form a reciprocal relationship; impression management facilitates the base of power (e.g., expert), which, once gained, brings with it impression management potential	Power bases
Fear of Appearing Incompetent Scale	Good and Good (1973)	Measures the extent to which individuals are concerned with the maintenance of face	• Level of concern may impact the extent to which an individual will try to control activities and behaviors so as to maximize perceived level of competence	Self-esteem
Interaction Anxiousness Scale	Leary, 1983; Leary and Kowalski, 1993	Measures the extent to which individuals exhibit the tendency to be nervous in social encounters	• Greater concern with how people perceive them may motivate impression management attempts • Lower confidence in the effectiveness of their impression management • Greater motivation to make impressions (Schlenker and Leary, 1982)	Social anxiety (Leary and Kowalski, 1993) (Maddux, Norton and Leary, 1988)
Machiavellianism	Christie and Geis, 1970; Fehr, Samsom, and Paulhus, 1992	Measures the extent to which individuals behave in manipulative ways, have a cynical view of human nature, and disregard the parameters of conventional morality	• Machiavellians may tend to use impression management strategies with a distorted focus on self (Ickes, Reidhead, and Patterson, 1986) • Machiavellians will tend toward unethical impression management usage	Unethical decision-making strategies

Measure	Source	Description	Relevance to impression management	Construct
• Marlowe-Crowne Social Desirability Scale	Crowne and Marlowe, 1960	Originally designated as a measure of need for social approval; current thinking (Crowne, 1979; Millham and Jacobson, 1978) is that it is a measure of avoiding disapproval	• The desire to avoid disapproval may foster impression management behavior, both to avoid disapproval and/or garner approval.	Social desirability
Self-Handicapping Scale	Jones and Rhodewalt, 1982; Strube, 1986	Measures the tendency for an individual to engage in behaviors designed to protect self-esteem via the creation of appropriate barriers to performance	• Self-handicapping individuals will use various forms of impression management to emphasize impediments that inhibit performance	Self-esteem
Willingness to Communicate Scale	McCroskey, 1992	Measures the respondent's predisposition to approach or avoid communication	• A willingness to communicate positive information may facilitate self-presentation, while an unwillingness may deter observers from perceiving the communicator positively. Similarly, a willingness to communicate negative information may allow for some impression management flexibility, while an unwillingness virtually ensures a negative conclusion	Communication

Note: *These measures should by no means be construed as representing an exhaustive list of measures which could impact impression management in organizations. The measures listed herein are intended as a small sample of the many possible measures which could impact impression management. Many constructs (e.g., fear of negative evaluation) which have some overlap with similar constructs (interaction anxiousness) were not included in this list.

and other important organizational outcomes such as job satisfaction and turnover. Even the MIBOS measure, which has been used with a working sample and shown to be related to supervisors' perceptions of performance, has not been tested for variations within and between industries, professions, positions, or related to less subjective and independent measures of performance.

Additionally, the current environment of legalistic responses to various business practices, both from individuals (as lawsuits) and from government (in the form of legal restraints) may create headaches for organizations testing for impression management. The reaction to these measures will depend on whether these tests discriminate against particular groups, and/or can adequately predict job-related performance. At present, tests for differential or pre-dictive validity have not been made. Using these scales in certain applications without prior validation on organizational populations is legally risky and considered unethical by many.

Measuring concepts related to impression management

Those interested in measuring impression management behaviors might also want to measure related traits which may impact a person's willingness, desire, or motivation to use impression man-agement behaviors. Table 6.8 summarizes some of these related measures.

These measures provide additional insights into what motivates and fosters impression management usage. For example, Machiavel-lians may be more inclined to use impression management tactics for manipulative reasons, while those who are interactionally anxious might be poorer at managing the right impression.

Whether these measures are useful components of organizational impression management will require much more research and development. In fact, these measures, like the earlier discussed impression management scales, suffer from many of the same deficits that preclude organizational implementation. However, there are ways to address these potential problems.

Some suggestions for successful implementation

In order to successfully utilize impression management measures, a number of steps need to be taken.

1   *Validate measures on large organizational samples and develop adult-worker norms.* A major issue that managers must address prior to implementing impression management measures is the question of appropriate validation and development of adult-worker norms. With the exception of self-monitoring, the other measures we have discussed represent relatively new attempts at measurement. As such, much more development work is needed. Because many of the measures have used MBA students in their research samples, questions about the validity of the test for employed adult populations are a serious concern. It is essential that the validity of the measures be established for organizational populations. As these populations are sampled, norms can be developed which both increase the justification for the measures and protect against the potential legal liability of questionable norms and validity.

2   *Assess and determine differences within and between organizations/industries.* An important question remains regarding differences within and among organizations, as well as within and among industries: Will individuals in particular organizations and/or industries differ in the need, type, degree, and distribution of impression management traits in order to be successful? For example, does a company which focuses on cleaning services have any great need to employ individuals with certain impression management abilities? Would a retail store clerk require the same type or intensity of impression management as an advertising executive? The answer to these questions intuitively would appear to be no. Research needs to be conducted to make this determination.

3   *Assess impact.* The question for the practicing manager always remains the same: Is it worth it? In order to justify the expense and resources of measuring impression management-related phenomena, managers need to show that there is utility in the measures themselves. The practicing manager cannot afford the luxury of using measures of impression management to focus on issues that are obscure and of no practical value (e.g. anti-toothbrushing essays used in social psychology studies). It will be important to show *how* these measures are useful to managers. For example, do these measures affect the bottom line in any way? Do they predict which salespeople are more likely to be effective? Studies are needed which show a direct relationship

between the measures themselves and the desired performance.

4   *Market impression management as a positive organizational force.* As Rosenfeld and Giacalone (1991) have noted, the impression management perspective has gone from being viewed as extreme to being seen as a mainstream process in organizational settings. Still, there are detractors who associate impression management with nefarious and malevolent manipulation attempts. In order for organizations to fully use impression management measures, it will be important to market these measures as ethically and practically acceptable and positively contributing to the organization's bottom-line. Indeed, the field of organizational impression management needs to practice what it preaches: it could benefit from a good dose of positive impression management to disassociate from extreme and dysfunctional stereotypes and associate itself with positive organizational outcomes. While this may appear to be a simple suggestion, the negative ethical insinuations cast upon impression management still make association with it controversial in some circles.

A CONCLUDING NOTE

The measurement of impression management differences, and their organizational applications, is an area yet in its infancy. Much remains to be done both from a theoretical and an applied standpoint before measurement of individual differences in impression management can take its proper place within the study of organizational impression management. Still, we cannot help but see the enormous, untapped potential that lies before tomorrow's managers and organizational researchers. Hopefully this chapter has provided a starting point.

7 Impression management and human resource management

It is not enough to have great qualities; we should also have the management of them.

La Rochefoucauld

MANAGING DESIRABLE QUALITIES

La Rochefoucauld's statement has two basic premises – an assumption that great qualities are desirable, and that their management is essential. It raises a number of intriguing questions. For example, what are "great" qualities? Is La Rochefoucauld talking of physical qualities (like a well-conditioned body) or of attributes such as motivation and intelligence? Is the concept of greatness a subjective one, subject to the perceptions of those who have witnessed it? Who defines such greatness? Are the qualities self-defined, defined by a management hierarchy, by consensus, or by some long-held social traditions? And if an individual who has these qualities does not produce great achievements, who is to blame? The manager? The employee?

These are some of the questions that human resource managers, implicitly and explicitly, ask themselves daily. These questions pervade the basic functions of the human resource department – recruitment, selection, training, and appraisal – and are a source of confusion and frustration to the human resource manager. Why? We would argue that these questions involve *judgment calls*. These judgment calls are based on the perceptions that human resource managers have of their employees – perceptions often based not on

129

first-hand knowledge of the employee's objectively measured performance and ability, but on the impression that the human resource manager has of that employee; an impression that the employee has contributed to by means of his skillful or not so skillful impression management.

For human resource managers, impression management is a powerful force that is important to understand. Employees are not passive observers of their organizational destinies, they are players in the drama that pervades organizational life. As such, employees' attempts to create images of themselves and their performance must be a part of the overall process that assists or thwarts the human resource manager. For example, human resource managers must consider that it is probably incorrect to see performance evaluations as true indicators of actual performance. Rather, performance evaluations represent a more complicated matrix of actual performance, moderated by the impression management of the ratee (who has a stake in being seen positively), the impression management of the rater (whose stake may be a positive impression based on a perception of fairness, equity, etc.), as well as many other factors (Villanova and Bernardin, 1989; 1991). Thus, human resource managers need to understand how and why impression management affects their decision-making.

WHY HUMAN RESOURCE MANAGERS NEED TO UNDERSTAND IMPRESSION MANAGEMENT

Aside from any personal and intellectual interest that they may have in impression management, human resource managers should be interested in impression management for more practical reasons. These practical reasons are based on the pivotal role that impression management plays in much of the organization, specifically in terms of its impact, its potential to contribute positively and negatively to organizational functioning, fairness, functionality, cues, and stakeholders.

Impact

Human resource functions impact directly and forcefully on employee lives and careers. Human resource managers make decisions on a daily basis which impact salaries, benefits, promotions, layoffs, and other factors that have long-term repercussions in employees' lives. What is defined as "excellent performance" or "good customer relations" is a matter of *social reality* – a reality defined by consensus among people rather than an *objective reality* (Halle, 1965). For example, all employees present at the meeting in the boss's office would agree that the boss's desk is in his office; it can be physically verified. While the *function* of the boss's desk may be disputed, its existence is not. In contrast, the existence of excellent performance is interpretive in nature; it must be interpreted and gauged against some standard. For example, Michelle may distort information, provide a "best case" view of her mediocre performance, or supply evidence to help define her performance to benefit her career. Michelle's motivation to do so depends in part on the impact that managing the right impression may have on her. As such, impression management tactics are vital to Michelle's ability to define how she is perceived at work.

The new competence

It has been argued that impression management ability is a *new competence* (Wexler, 1986). In previous centuries, workers produced a tangible product which could be evaluated in and of itself. But, as Wexler (1986, pp. 253–254) notes, "While fewer and fewer people today are engaged in the production of foodstuffs and even fewer in manufacturing, more and more . . . are engaged in generating nothing that is tangible at all, indeed, in generating services, resulting in an entirely new game – one in which man no longer sutures his notion of competence in his struggle with things, but now and in the near future in his ability to impress upon people his or her worth." Human resource managers are entrusted with validating skills, abilities, and potentials that are not tangible, clearly defined and subject to the employee's ability to create the impression of having those skills and that they are useful, scarce, and excellent. For example, one of the authors viewed two talks by scholars from two universities in the United States. The first, from a non-Ivy League school, provided a thought-provoking presentation based on some rather creative scholarship. The second, a scholar from a prestigious Ivy League school gave a lackluster performance, was often boring, and meandered in and out of various topics. Still, he repeatedly referred to his Ivy-League lineage, his Ivy League colleagues, and the "great minds" of the discipline, who he subtly reminded us were also at Ivy League schools. Can you guess what transpired after the talk? As you may have guessed, the scholar from the non-Ivy League school received good reviews from the audience. But the scholar from the Ivy League school was even more impressive to some, even though they admitted that they understood little of what he said. Why? Members of the audience were impressed with his "credentials" – teaching at an Ivy League school. "If he is at a place like that," remarked one person, "he must be onto something good." The use of indirect impression management (being associated with Ivy League schools) "overwhelmed" the talk, leading to a positive evaluation of the talk and the scholar.

Fairness at work

Human resource managers also need to understand impression management in order to perform their duties fairly. Fairness is a goal to be achieved from the standpoint of ethics alone, which says that it's the right thing to do (Arvey and Renz, 1992). However, fairness is desirable for more than ethical reasons. One of these is that unfairness may serve to reduce motivation or otherwise neutralize it. Rewards that are unfairly distributed, or otherwise allocated without performance in mind, will not motivate employees (Luthans and Kreitner, 1985). Impression management is of interest to human resource managers because knowledge of how it works can help them distinguish performance from image, so that resources are more fairly allocated on substance rather than style. Also, because the suspicion or assumption of unfairness can be so harmful to the ethical climate and employee motivation, human resource managers and others making human resource decisions need to skillfully use impression management to package their decisions as being fair (Feldman and Klich, 1991). For example, Cliff is accused of playing favorites with a few of his subordinates; employees claim that the "Cliff clones" get most of the rewards in the department. When a promotion within the department opens up, Cliff recommends Jerry, an employee that the department agrees is the most qualified for the job. Although Cliff dislikes Jerry personally, he believes that he is best for the job. In order to have himself perceived as a fair decision-maker, Cliff intentionally leaks his recommendation so as to "market" himself as a fair manager.

Functionality

Impression management may be beneficial or detrimental to the organization. When impression management is beneficial, it is thought to be functional to achieving organizational goals. Impression management is beneficial when it: (1) facilitates positive interpersonal relationships and increases harmony within and outside the company; (2) accurately portrays positive persons, events, or products to those in or out of the organization; and (3) facilitates decision-making regarding persons, events, or products, and leads management and/or consumers to successful decisions. To reap these benefits, organizations may wish to train employees in good impression management techniques.

Sometimes, however, impression management is detrimental to the organization and is thought to be *dysfunctional*. We believe that the use of impression management may adversely affect the company when (1) it inhibits or obstructs positive interpersonal relationships either within or outside of the company; (2) its use fails, thereby incorrectly casting persons, events or products within the company in a negative light in the eyes of insiders or outsiders; and (3) it distorts information about persons, events, or products, and leads management and/or consumers to erroneous conclusions and/or decisions.

Human resource managers should not confuse functionality with truth. Functional strategies are those that effectively accomplish an intended objective. Impression management strategies may be functional but deceptive, or may be dysfunctional but truthful. Ultimately, managers may need to decide between making *ethical judgments* – choosing paths because they are the right and truthful thing to do – or *Machiavellian judgments* – choosing the functional courses even if they mean being deceptive or unethical.

Cues to appropriate behavior

Human resource managers need to recognize that impression management is a reciprocal and continuous process. While aware of the impression management strategies of others, human resource managers often do not recognize that their own impression management provides behavioral cues to employees as to what they consider appropriate behavior. Such cues will impact the strategies and images that employees choose to create.

Individuals will elicit cues regarding what they are expected to do, either passively or actively (Ferris and Mitchell, 1987). These cues can serve to enhance or diminish the content of an employee's performance. When cues from managers result from the manager's poor impression management, employees may fail to grasp the appropriate strategy to use. Instead, in order to alleviate a potential problem, they may choose to "go with the manager," never fully realizing that the manager may have managed his impression improperly. An employee who sees his manager shaking his head at a suggestion for restructuring the department may oppose the restructuring attempt in order to be seen as a team player. His manager, on the other hand, may not have intended to signal opposition to the restructuring, but may have shaken his head while thinking about other things.

Stakeholder management

Impression management is an important competence in dealing with external stakeholders – individuals or groups outside the organization who feel that they have an interest in the decisions the organization makes. As human resource managers realize, the processes of recruiting and interviewing, for example, are not just one-time interactions with the candidate, but are often inadvertent public relations exercises. The contact with external stakeholders offers the company the opportunity to impress these stakeholders with their competence, fairness, and community mindedness on the one hand, nor to increase the potential for lawsuits, bad publicity, and boycotts on the other. The ability to create a favorable impression on outside stakeholders is often as important to human resource managers as the managers' own employees' wishes to create favorable impressions on them. Thus, if in an interview a job candidate is given the impression that the company is treating him fairly and with respect, even if he does not get the job, his overall impression of the organization will likely be positive. On the other hand, if the job candidate is treated with contempt, verbally abused, or made to feel uncomfortable, his overall impression of the company will be negative. In either case, the overall impression that the job candidate is left with may be transmitted to the community at large.

IMPRESSION MANAGEMENT AND HRM PROCESSES

Although the human resource management (HRM) department usually has much control over the areas of recruitment, selection, placement, and training, impression management can also influence these processes. The remainder of this chapter will focus on examples of some HRM processes that have been shown to be influenced by impression management. Our perspective, based on much of the research in these areas, is that excessive impression management can, at times, act as an obstacle to organizational effectiveness. Research on the positive role of impression management in improving HRM functions is no doubt possible, but has not been done *yet*. The focus in this chapter is also more from the management position, because most of the research literature has focused on that perspective rather than on the utility of impression management to the individual employee. For example, for employee interviews there is much that can be said about which impression management tactics an interviewee *should* use. However, our vantage will be more aligned to the concerns of the human resource manager in defending against employee impression management that could negatively influence the fairness of the selection process.

Employment interviews

Hal Melbourne knew that this interview was the opportunity of a lifetime. He had the possibility of getting an executive job with one of the most prestigious banks in the country. Hal imagined what the interviewer would ask; he rehearsed what he would say and how he would say it. Hal talked to five of his closest executive friends and asked what he should wear. He even rode down to the hotel where he would be interviewed in order to become familiar with the surroundings. As Hal kept telling himself, this opportunity was too important to leave things to chance.

While we have seen that impression management phenomena occur in many social and organizational situations, the "high stakes" nature of the employment interview makes it a setting particularly ripe for impression management (Rosenfeld, in press). In a typical job interview, both the candidate (who wants to get hired) and interviewer (who wants to attract the best candidates) generally engage in a reciprocal impression management process with both attempting to manage positive impressions to achieve desired outcomes. At times, impression management in the selection interview may be deceptive. Clive Fletcher (1989) describes survey results indicating that 25 percent of respondents admitted that they had lied during a job interview.

Although the employment interview has been conceptualized as a form of cognitive information processing, and as a selection technique having legal and civil rights implications (Eder and Ferris, 1989), it can also be viewed as a type of social interaction (Liden, Martin, and Parson, 1993) where both the applicant and interviewer try to influence each other through the use of impression management. The near universality of the employment interview and the importance ascribed to it by managers have made it fertile territory for the occurrence of impression management (Rosenfeld, in press).

Both conceptual analyses and empirical studies have focused more on the impression management behaviors of applicants than on those of interviewers. Because the applicant is relatively powerless and the interviewer may be aware that much of the applicant's behavior represents style over substance, the impression management task of the applicant is far from easy. To be successful, the applicant must balance being "confident but not brash, polite but not sycophantic, lively and interested but not voluble or manic, sufficiently nervous to show an appreciation of the importance of the occasion but not visibly anxious throughout" (Fletcher 1989, p. 273). While impression management may positively influence interviewer perceptions of the applicant, its overuse might be seen as intentional manipulation and can backfire (see Chapter 2). Clive Fletcher, a pioneer in the area of selection interviews and impression management, presents a "Behind the Scenes" view of his work.

• • • •

Behind the Scenes

Clive Fletcher

I first became interested in impression management when I was training people in selection interviewing skills in the 1970s. It was clear to me as I watched them doing practice interviews that they were influenced by differing candidate self-presentation strategies. Subsequently, I talked to my own undergraduate students about their ideas on how to behave in interviews, and it became clear that they varied widely in what they thought was appropriate or effective in this rather peculiar social encounter. Some felt it best to be very open and honest, some felt it wiser to be much more guarded; some felt that you had to sell yourself in a fairly direct manner, while others did not; and so on. Looking at the extensive research literature on the interview, I was amazed to find that this, the candidate's perspective, was almost completely missing. Much of the research done up until then seemed to treat the candidate as an entirely passive element in the situation – to the extent that many studies did not have real candidates at all, and simply presented interviewers with written descriptions of the people they were assessing. So I started doing some basic research myself. Since then, there has been more work in this area, though still not a great deal.

Why would it be helpful to know more about impression management in this context? Well, first it would be useful to find out what are the determinants of impression management tactics; do they vary with experience of interviews, do they arise from candidate training, to what extent are they personality-linked? From an interviewer's perspective, more knowledge of this would help interpret and assess the implications of different candidate interview behaviors, and perhaps throw some light on whether they had any relationship to future job performance. It would also be valuable to know just how much different aspects of impression management do impact on interviewer assessments, so that some account of this could be taken in the training of interviewers; their awareness of the behaviors concerned could be raised, which would enable the interviewers to detect and evaluate the behaviors appropriately.

The need for this information is growing, as it is increasingly common for school and college graduates to be given some training in how to cope with interviews, and there are many books on the market addressing the same issue. All this serves to enhance the likelihood of impression management tactics being adopted, perhaps in a quite deliberate way. The result may be a decrease in the already rather low validity of the interview as a selection tool. One of the possible strategies organizations could adopt to offset differences in candidate impression management tactics is to specify the "rules of the interview game"; in other words, spell out to candidates what they felt was appropriate behavior in the interview, and what was expected of them. This would provide a level playing field for all, and such differences that were observed between candidates could be evaluated against that background.

● ● ● ●

As noted, research on impression management in the employment interview has typically focused on the behavior of the applicant. Von Baeyer, Sherk, and Zanna (1981) found that female job applicants tailored their nonverbal and verbal behaviors to align themselves more closely with the views of women that were held by their interviewer. When the male interviewer was known to hold views in line with the traditional female stereotype, female applicants gave more traditional responses to questions about family and relationships, spent more time on their physical appearance, and were less assertive in their verbal and nonverbal behaviors than when the interviewer held less traditional attitudes.

Baron (1989) found that impression management behaviors in interview situations can be counterproductive if overused. In his study, male and female students conducted employment interviews with a female applicant who was an experimental accomplice. The female applicant was seeking an entry-level position and she responded in a standard fashion to questions asked by the interviewers. The applicant either used a number of positive nonverbal behaviors such as smiling and leaning forward or emitted few positive nonverbal cues. She also either wore or did not wear perfume. Baron's results supported the notion that too much impression management in an employment interview can have a negative impact. Male interviewers rated the female applicant as being more intelligent and viewed her as having greater potential for success if she emitted positive nonverbals or wore perfume, but rated her lower if she used both sets of impression management behaviors. Interestingly, this effect was not found when the interviewers were female.

Gilmore and Ferris (1989a) showed that an impression management tactic, if skillfully executed, could influence interviewer perceptions more than information about the applicant's actual qualifications. Interviewers viewed a videotape in which a female applicant either engaged in impression management (e.g., complimented interviewer, smiled) or did not. She was also portrayed as being highly qualified for a customer representative job or less qualified. The results indicated that evaluations of the applicant were influenced by impression management but not applicant credentials. The applicant was perceived as doing better in the interview and was slightly more likely to be recommended for hiring when she used impression management than when she did not. However, her credentials had little impact on interviewer ratings.

An implication of the Baron (1989) and Gilmore and Ferris (1989a) studies is that not all impression management tactics work or are equally effective in employment interviews. This was demonstrated more directly by Kacmar, Delery, and Ferris (1992). They distinguished applicant impression management tactics in the employment interview as those that were *self-focused* (e.g., self-promotion) or *other-focused* (e.g., complimenting the interviewer). They found that job applicants who used impression management tactics that focused on themselves were rated higher than applicants whose impression management tactics focused on the interviewer. It may be that the other-focused tactics were ineffective because they were perceived as being ingratiating and were dismissed.

Coping with impression management in selection interviews

Given that applicants are likely to continue in their use of impression management, what should human resource managers strive to accomplish in regard to impression management in the interview?

1 *Be cognizant of fairness.* At first glance, applicant impression management tactics, such as those described in the studies reviewed above, would appear to be unfair. Arvey and Renz (1992) note that one criterion of fairness is that the processes and procedures used are objective and consistent across all applicants. Subjective, manipulative behaviors in which interviewees are able to fake "good" by distorting responses given to the interviewer are considered less fair. Given that some researchers view impression management as a form of deception with significant impact on interviewer judgment (Anderson, 1991), it appears that one could easily argue that impression management tactics are unfair. Fletcher (1992, p. 364), however, notes that while impression management occurs in employment interviews, not all of it is inherently deceptive or manipulative: "In relation to interview behavior, it may be more useful to think of it as a continuum of strategic impression management behaviors, the most extreme of which involve conscious deception." We believe that forms of impression management that involve honestly and accurately presenting and highlighting one's attributes are both fair and desirable applicant behaviors. Candidate impression management which is authentic and involves a legitimate packaging of positive traits would seem to be fair, particularly since failing to attempt to create such an image may be seen as a sign of uninterest or a lack of intelligence or social skills.

This changes the task for interviewers from elimination of impression management to the systematic creation of interview situations in which interviewees are understood to be putting their best foot forward, but where deceptive, manipulative, insincere impression management is detected, minimized, and discounted.

2 *Train interviewers to recognize various kinds of applicant impression management.* Some of the previous interview literature has viewed applicant impression management as "noise" which should be detected and discounted. But as we have noted, impression management is far more complex and not inherently "bad" or nefarious. Thus, some knowledge of the nature of the positive and negative aspects of impression management could be added to training to help interviewers recognize and defend against various impression management techniques. As Fletcher (1990, p. 747) writes, "it might be possible to sensitize interviewers to the different kinds of impression management strategies that candidates use and the effects they have, so that they can identify them more readily and take account of them in their decision-making process."

3 *View impression management as a skill, not a deficit.* There is little doubt that impression management is very common in employment interviews. Instead of maligning or discounting this behavior, Fletcher (1989) recommends using the employment interview to assess how good candidates are at impression management. Rather than viewing impression management in the employment interview as an obstacle, it might be better seen as a potential source of valuable information about an applicant's ability to do the job. Regarding impression management as a valuable skill, rather than as inherently dysfunctional, recognizes that much of organizational success depends on the ability to master "organizational politics" (Gilmore and Ferris, 1989b). The skilled use of authentic impression management displayed in an interview context might be a useful indicator that the candidate will be able to successfully utilize impression management when needed in future job settings. As Lautenschlager and Flaherty (1990, p. 313) note, "the ability to manage one's impression may be quite valuable as a variable in its own right, especially in contexts where either social influence or conformity is important, such as in sales settings."

4 *Reduce ambiguity and uncertainty of the employment interview situation.* Ambiguous uncertain environments increase the frequency of impression management behaviors. As such, the issue is how one

might reduce such ambiguity and uncertainty. Baker and Spier (1990, p. 86) suggest using more structured interview procedures, since the unstructured employment interview situation "plays into the hands of those interviewees bent on obfuscating or diverting attention from their qualifications." Fletcher (1989) advocates using board or panel interviews and assessment centers to reduce manipulative impression management by applicants. A more novel way of reducing ambiguity and uncertainty, Fletcher (1990, p. 747) suggests, is "by giving all candidates for a post a briefing on how they were expected to present themselves in the interview. This would help to establish a common set of expectations about what behavior is appropriate."

5 *Train interviewers to focus on verifiable information.* In order to increase the usefulness of interview responses, candidates should be steered toward more sincere forms of impression management. A way to encourage more sincere impression management is to increase the verifiability of the information sought. Impression management research (Schlenker, 1980) has found that individuals will act in self-enhancing ways to please significant audiences in the absence of a "reality check." However, when information exists that could repudiate an overly positive claim, individuals will present themselves in a more accurate fashion, one that is closer to what they really believe. As Schlenker (1980, p. 188) writes, "The more difficult it is for the audience to check the veracity of a self-presentation the more likely people are to self-aggrandize." Fletcher (1989, p. 275) concurs, noting that, "individuals moderate their self-assessments when they know they will be subject to subsequent external checking."

In this vein, Gilmore and Ferris (1989b) point out that an interviewer often has a great deal of information relevant to an applicant's long-term identity, usually in the form of application blank or résumé data. Furthermore, the applicant knows that the interviewer has this information and is aware that much of this information is verifiable (i.e., can be checked for accuracy). It would seem that focusing the employment interview on aspects of a candidate's competence, credibility, and long-term achievements that are closely related to material that can be verified would ultimately result in less distorting impression management.

Exit interviews and surveys

Gwen Sanders was sitting across from the human resource manager on her last day of work at Bartles Bagel Company. Gwen was leaving the organization in order to get away from the unfriendly work environment at Bartles. Gwen and her spouse agreed that the pay cut that she had to take in order to get a new job was worth it. "Less money," her husband noted, "is acceptable if there is also less stress." But when the human resource manager asked Gwen why she was leaving, Gwen looked at him, and said, "Oh, it's simple: Better pay."

The process of exit interviews and surveys (EIS) was developed as a means of gathering data from a person such as Gwen whose employment with an organization has been voluntarily or involuntarily terminated (Goodale, 1982). Because the specification of what topics should be included in EIS is not well defined, the specific issues on which an EIS focuses may vary according to long- and short-term organizational purposes and the specificity with which those goals are conceptualized.

Diagnostic purposes. Organizations use the data gathered from EIS for diagnostic and strategic reasons: determining the reasons for company turnover; helping to identify training and development needs; creating strategic planning goals; and identifying needs for change. Exiting employees are interviewed for two reasons. First, it is believed that they may have important information about what might have gone wrong and caused them to leave the organization. Relatedly, it is assumed that they may be more willing to share such information at the time of separation, since they no longer fear the repercussions of transmitting negative information.

Measurement properties. There has been little systematic research on the reliability or validity of EIS; what has been done suggests that responses within the EIS process may be tainted by response distortion. Sometimes there is little consistency between original EIS responses and responses given months later (Lefkowitz and Katz, 1969; Zarandona and Camuso, 1985). Some authors have concluded that respondents are probably not truthful at the time of separation (e.g., Giacalone and Duhon, 1991; Giacalone, Knouse, and Ashworth, 1991). Various explanations have been offered for the response distortion. For example, the exiting employee may not want to discuss uncomfortable material, might anticipate needing a letter of recommendation from management (Hinrichs, 1975), may fear retribution from management (Jablonsky, 1975), or may not want negative information to reach the new employer. Additionally, the exiting employee may perceive the questions as too personal (Drost, O'Brien, and Marsh, 1987), that there may be little to gain from the process (Garretson and Teel, 1982), or that management may bring about retribution on remaining employees based on information from the EIS process.

Employees' impression management. Impression management offers a comprehensive explanation for employees' tendencies to distort information in EIS processes: employees distort information during the EIS process so as to create or manage an image of themselves or of others in the organization. The distortion may represent an intentional attempt to act maliciously and deceptively in retaliation for perceived offenses on the part of management or fellow employees, but it is more likely an attempt to hide controversial, personal, or inside information which could endanger future options for themselves or friends left behind. The separating employee may seek to provide feedback which creates, at worst, a neutral image of himself. This attempt may be moderated by other factors. One study found that willingness to discuss EIS issues was based both on feelings toward the topic (e.g., value of compensation, salary) and the *status of the person* receiving the information (Giacalone and Duhon, 1991). Similarly, another found that feelings toward the interviewer and organization moderated the willingness to discuss issues during the EIS process (Knouse and Giacalone, 1992a). These studies by Giacalone and his colleagues are consistent with the impression management prediction that separating employees will create their impressions contextually, considering who will hear the information, the information itself, and its ultimate impact on the separating employee and those remaining (Giacalone *et al.*, 1993).

Reducing insincere impression management in EIS

What changes could be implemented so as to reduce separating employees' desire to insincerely manage impressions?

1 *Reduce the identifiability of responses.* Employees are apt to consider identifiability of their responses especially when it could have negative repercussions for them. Identifiability is associated with increased self-enhancing impression management (Giacalone and Rosenfeld, 1986), and is therefore likely to be a concern within the EIS process.

In both the practitioner and scholarly literature, the discussion of the negative impact of identifiability and the resulting lack of confidentiality have been common themes (e.g., Giacalone and Knouse, 1989; Woods and Macauley, 1987). The practitioner literature on EIS also leads us to conclude that the identifiability of responses and the subsequent lack of confidentiality may be powerful motivators of biased responding within the EIS process (Jablonsky, 1975). In fact, in an exit survey administered by the US Army, responses given under conditions of anonymity resulted in generally more critical comments about military service as compared with those given under conditions of identifiability (Giacalone *et al.*, 1993).

It would appear that, where possible, anonymity of responses should be maintained. Although this is difficult in the exit interview, it can be achieved easily in the exit survey process by not asking for identifying information (e.g., name, social security number) and/or using a third-party outside of the organization to administer the survey. In our opening example, one could easily see how Gwen would react very differently if she were not identified and/or were interviewed by an individual to whom she would not feel uncomfortable telling the truth.

2 *Change the measurement time period.* While the EIS process is generally thought of as part of the final week (or final day) procedures, this may not be the best time for organizations to request this information. Inasmuch as there is a great deal the organization still controls at this time (e.g., recommendations to new employer, final check, etc.), the employee may remain highly motivated to create the "proper" impression.

It is advantageous to the organization to engage the employee in the EIS process at a later date, when all the loose ends have been tied, and the employee is established in a new job. The organization may consider paying the employee for EIS information at a later date, where the former employee is less interested in managing a good impression and may provide unbiased responding.

3 *Eliminate data from involuntary separations.* Employees who separate involuntarily (i.e., are fired, terminated, laid off) place the information they are giving management within a very different context than those employees who quit voluntarily. While the voluntarily separating employee usually leaves with greater choice, the involuntarily separating employee typically leaves with no

choice, and may view the separation and the entire experience in a more negative context. The resultant responses may be distorted by either the desire to manage a positive impression (to reduce the implied impression of incompetence or relative lack of value to the organization), or to retaliate by saying many negative things about the organization. The latter strategy was noted by Giacalone, Knouse, and Ashworth (1991) who observed that involuntarily separating employees may be taking on negativistic roles (Weber and Cook, 1972), which may result in unduly severe appraisals of the organization. Evidence of this "screw the organization" attitude was found in involuntarily separating Army personnel. They were more negative about their military experiences than were personnel who volunteered to separate (Giacalone *et al.*, 1993).

It is common for organizations to collect data from voluntary and involuntary separations. Woods and Macauley (1987) report that 83 percent of companies surveyed gathered and used data from involuntary separations. Involuntary separations increase the potential for responses which may be highly distorted by the need to manage an impression which helps the separating employee save face. Indeed some researchers have advocated not gathering data from those who are involuntarily separated (e.g., Garrison and Ferguson, 1977; Sherwood, 1983), and found greater divergence between responses at separation and later follow-up among those involuntary separations than among voluntary separations (Lefkowitz and Katz, 1969).

It is best to deal with the responses of involuntarily separating personnel in a different way from responses gathered from voluntary separations. Information gained from involuntary separations may be of use – especially in determining what factors lead to such separations – and should be collected and critically evaluated. However, the data on involuntary separations can contaminate data collected on voluntary separations because they involve different (and more varied) impression management motivations. As such, we advocate that to minimize contamination by heightened impression management concerns, the two groups of responses be kept separately.

Labor arbitration

The arbitration of labor grievances involves the voluntary, final, and binding resolution of disputes between unions and employers by mutually acceptable third-parties (St. Antoine, 1984; Zack, 1989).

The arbitrator serves as the interpreter of that part of the collective bargaining agreement that management is allegedly violating. The expectation is that the interpretation will be done in an equitable and fair manner to both management and the *grievant* (the individual who has filed the grievance).

The objectivity of the arbitrator is particularly important, since the award he or she makes involves the appropriate interpretation of ambiguous contract language and an intention to make sense from confusing and contradictory evidence (Hill and Sinicropi, 1987; Rehmus, 1984). The arbitrator does so by reviewing the issues, the facts, the testimony, and the evidence, as well as cited arbitration decisions.

Assuming the good will of the participants, the process of arbitration is only as good as the integrity and fairness of its procedures. While research has shown that factors outside the merits of the case also impact arbitration decisions, e.g., biographical data (Heneman and Sandver, 1983) and arbitration experience (Nelson and Curry, 1981), these factors account for only a small portion of the arbitration decision.

Bob Giacalone and colleagues (Giacalone and Pollard, 1989; Giacalone, Pollard, and Brannen, 1989; Giacalone, Reiner, and Goodwin, 1992), have suggested an impression management interpretation of the labor arbitration process. They have argued that the award made by the arbitrator is subject to the impression management strategies and abilities of the grievant and his representatives.[1] Arbitrators may have their judgment influenced by impressions made; such impressions may, in fact, be made at a level beyond their conscious understanding and control.

This idea is based on findings from research on forensic studies. It has been found that the defendant's actions within the courtroom can create impressions which directly impact the jury decision. These impressions can be inadvertently drawn from actions within the process such as a refusal to testify (Shaffer and Sadowsky, 1979), or testimony which is impertinent or self-aggrandizing (Kalven and Zeisel, 1966). Similarly, impressions can be created (intentionally or unintentionally) by a defendant's explanations (e.g., via remorse, regret, or emotional conveyance) which may affect the subsequent sentence or disposition (Rumsey, 1976; Savitsky and Sim, 1974).

Arbitrators are subject to what forensic specialists call *extralegal factors*. According to Austin and Utne (1977, p. 170), an extralegal factor is one which "can be defined as information not directly bearing on the individual's guilt or innocence, nor on the nature of a convicted offender's crime or the situational context within which the offense was committed ... Extralegal factors can be either positive or negative, mitigating or incriminating, consequently they can either help or hurt a defendant." Within the arbitration context, to manage the proper impression in front of the arbitrator, the grievant needs to control the impression made, as well as the impressions extralegal factors may leave, in order to create a more favorable overall impression (of herself or of the questioned behavior). Impression management, then, can be an extralegal variable in itself (e.g., as in the use of an excuse or apology), or can be used to present extralegal variables in a way that creates the desired impression for the grievant.

The forensic literature provides ample evidence that the impressions created by an offender have a marked impact on punishment received for an offense. These impressions may involve the demeanor of the offender (Parkinson, 1979) as arrogant or humble, courteous and deferent, or able to control anxiety (Pryor and Buchanan, 1984).

In the case of arbitration, the grievant's record, either as a work record, or record of offenses, provides an extralegal factor that can be controlled by either side to give a particular impression. For example, raising the previous record of offenses (or lack thereof) can significantly impact the ultimate decisions made in the case (Kalven and Zeisel, 1966). Thus, if management's representatives raise a previous record of improper behavior on the part of the grievant, this may create an impression of the grievant as a troublemaker and may contribute to an award made against him (Hatton, Snortum, and Oskamp, 1971).

A study by Giacalone and Pollard (1989) found the degree to which arbitrators felt punishment for the grievant was appropriate was differentially influenced by the grievant's previous record and type of impression management strategy (account or apology) used. Mock arbitrators, who read of an employee infraction which led to a grievance, recommended less punishment when the grievant gave an account on the third offense as compared with an account on the first offense. When an apology was given, no significant differences between first and third offense recommendations occurred. In a later study, Giacalone, Pollard, and Eylon (1994) included information for practicing arbitrators regarding the consequences of the infraction by the grievant, as well as manipulations of impression management strategy and previous record. Results showed that all three variables independently affected the severity of the arbitrator's ruling. Thus, creating the impression that an infraction was severe, that a grievant had a history of similar infractions, as well as using a particular impression management strategy resulted in differential perceptions of the grievant and awards by an arbitrator. What was supposed to be simple "interpretation" of a contract quickly appears to become a case of wrestling with the impressions caused by extralegal variables.

Reducing excessive impression management in arbitration

The potential that impression management may bias the judgment of an arbitrator leaves HRM practitioners with the issue of how they should address these concerns. The following suggestions provide insight into addressing these problems.

1 *Require justifications based on strict contractual interpretation.* The extent to which arbitrators are capable of using extralegal factors in their awards depends largely on how much latitude they are allowed and what consequences exist for doing so. Because arbitrators are typically given considerable latitude, the likelihood of impact by impression management is high. Contractual ambiguity, along with the amount of discretion afforded the arbitrator, creates a vague situation in which either side may capitalize on the opportunity to re-define the data for the arbitrator through the use of impression management tactics. It has been found that impression management increases under ambiguous, uncertain conditions (Ferris *et al.*, 1991).

It is also important that labor arbitrators who take non-contractual factors into account when making their decisions suffer sanctions. Such sanctioning need not be formal, but may be as simple as deciding never to use an arbitrator again. Management and labor leaders need to work together on such sanctions since the biases do not necessarily always favor the grievant, but may, in many cases, favor the organization when their case is presented by company lawyers or management representatives who are skilled impression managers.

2 *Train arbitrators to recognize impression management strategies.* Recognition of impression management strategies is certainly not an expected ability of arbitrators. Still, the ability to recognize deceptive impression management, and ignore its biasing of con-

tractual interpretation remains an important factor in the equitable resolution of labor-related disputes.

Training arbitrators to recognize and discount impression management must go beyond simple recognition of tactics used by grievants and management; it must focus on a variety of biases (of which impression management is but one) that can influence decisionmakers. Training must increase the arbitrator's ability to critically evaluate contractually relevant data to discount irrelevant data, and to render decisions which focus only on contractual interpretation. Understanding the impact of impression management can lead to the implementation of techniques that minimize its influence.

Careers

> You will find it a distinct help ... if you know and look as if you know what you are doing.
> (From US Internal Revenue manual for tax auditors, quoted in Petras and Petras, 1994, p. 108)

It was his first day at work as executive vice-president, but Dick Kesler knew the questions he was asking himself all too well. It was his habit to list for himself the traits and accomplishments that he would have to have in order to get to the next level – in this case, president. Dick knew that it was not a list he could develop in a day or a week. It would require listening to what others said about the job, reading the records of his predecessors, and carefully trying to understand the environment. Eventually, Dick knew, he would find out what image they were looking to have in the president's office, and he would give it to them.

As Dick Kesler's story illustrates, a new and often effective work ethic has recently come into vogue in organizational life. This ethic stresses superficial, image-building and manipulative impression management rather than hard work, accomplishment, and performance (Riordan, 1989). Feldman and Weitz (1990) have called this new ethic a *careerist orientation to work* (see also Feldman, 1985, 1990).

This orientation is characterized by the six primary beliefs listed in Table 7.1. While these beliefs all have some impression management components, four appear to be most relevant to impression management use.

First, high caliber performance is not necessarily enough for

Table 7.1 Six central beliefs of a careerist orientation

1   Merit alone is not enough to move up the organizational ladder.
2   Social relationships provide critical assistance in career advancement.
3   The appearance of team play affords one help in career advancement.
4   Significant amounts of work cannot be assessed tangibly, either in an absolute sense or in a relative (comparative) sense.
5   An individual's long-term goals are generally not compatible with those of any one organization.
6   Career advancement sometimes requires that one use unethical behaviors.

Source: Adapted from Feldman and Klich (1991).

advancement in organizations. What is more important, is that one "appears" to be promotable, and is seen as worthy of advancement. Such appearances are founded in the effective use of impression management career strategies. According to Feldman and Klich (1991), this can be attained by using symbols of power and influence (e.g., dress, office design), generating outside offers that attest to a more absolute measure of worth, varying techniques in résumés (Knouse, Giacalone, and Pollard, 1988) and interviews, politically finessing moral dilemmas at work (Giacalone and Pollard, 1987), and creating artificial relationships at work which offer more opportunities to get ahead. Dick Kesler would probably be attempting to figure out exactly who the powerful people in the organization were and ingratiating himself with them. Dick would try to understand what power symbols he needed to have in his office, and how he should react if faced with a variety of moral dilemmas. Dick Kesler would leave nothing to chance.

Second, climbing the organization ladder requires interpersonal relationships with coworkers and supervisors that appear to be social in nature. In fact, these "social" relations are used calculatingly to ingratiate oneself with formal and informal organization gatekeepers of information in gathering inside information and job contacts to promote one's own best interest. As we have seen, the creation of a likable organizational identity provides one such political influence. Dick Kesler would no doubt make the rounds at organizational parties, maintaining friendly relations so that he could get information when he needed it.

BOX 7.1

Impression management in performance appraisal

It's not for subordinates alone

When one of the authors was young, he worked in a department store where managers would discuss the "performance appraisal (PA) blip." The PA blip was a surge in performance (be it quality or quantity) right before management engaged in the predictable yearly review. Employees would try to manage the impression of being "good workers" by engaging in higher quality or quantity performance right before PA; the objective was to get better performance appraisals from managers. The "blip" was a source of many funny stories about the various employee impression management strategies that would be used to manage the right impression.

What management did not discuss was how they used the PA to essentially manage impressions, too. Villanova and Bernardin (1989, 1991), have provided us with the other side of impression management in performance appraisal: management use of PA to create certain impressions on subordinates and superiors. PA, they argue, can provide managers (as performance raters) with the *means* to engage in social influence by manipulating PA ratings for impression management purposes. These means, consisting of inadequacies in the PA system itself (e.g., criteria used are irrelevant, rater is untrained, rater is left unaccountable for ratings), when intertwined with the rater's *motivation* to create particular impressions (e.g., when the PA has a personal impact on the rater) provide for the opportunity to use ratings as impression management tools in PA and can distort this supposedly objective process.

Let's take the example of one department manager in a clothing retail chain who insisted on selecting his own staff. When PA time came along each year he would give everyone in his department incredible appraisals, with glowing commentary on everything each person did. This created the impression

Box 7.1 continued

that he had an excellent staff which he was responsible for assembling. So what happened? In fact, the manager worked within a PA system in which the criteria were largely unverifiable: employees were evaluated on issues such as friendliness, appearance, punctuality (there were no time clocks), and enthusiasm. They were never judged on the one criterion related to their job: number of sales! Perhaps, more importantly, because the company valued highly the evaluation that staff gave the manager, the manager was placed in a position of giving good evaluations so that there would be some *reciprocal leniency* (Villanova and Bernardin, 1989) on the part of staff. PA ratings were a way of creating the impression that he supported his staff, thereby insuring that they, too, would help him maintain and enhance his position in the organization. Inadvertently, the company had created a PA process in which the ratings could be manipulated via impression management; it was the easiest way to prosper within the organization.

So how can an organization stop impression management from having a major influence on PA? Villanova and Bernardin (1991) offer eight strategies:

- Make the criteria used in PA relevant to the job: Develop and utilize criteria which are essential or important to job performance.
- Clearly define those criteria used in PA: Provide raters with a clear understanding of what the criteria mean, rather than providing terms which can be interpreted in a variety of ways.
- Provide training for raters which focuses on the appraisal process as well as on impression management: Good training which focuses on the intricacies of the rating process and offers periodic refreshers can avoid falling into impression management pitfalls.
- Increase the frequency of PA: Help the rater do his or her job by providing smaller time periods so that memory or generic impressions do not have to be relied on.
- Aggregate individual performances to a group level where

Box 7.1 continued

individual level performance is too interdependent: In some jobs, the interdependence of performance in a group does not allow for individual evaluations. This increases uncertainty and ambiguity which raises the potential for excessive impression management if individual level performance must be evaluated.

- Evaluate performance on specific dimensions and combine statistically to create an overall index of performance: Asking raters to provide overall indices of performance facilitates impression management behaviors; focusing on individual items and making a statistical judgment for aggregate data reduces the impression management impact.
- Increase the number of raters used: As the number of raters increases, more perspectives on performance are brought forth, as well as inconsistencies in the ratings resulting in part from the desire to create particular impressions.
- Hold raters accountable for their behaviors/judgments: Including accountability as part of the rating process forces raters to consider their impression management driven distortions and may help them to reconsider non-performance related criteria.

Third, the image of being a "team player" offers one career opportunities by the appearance of cooperation while still searching for more information that will strengthen one's personal image and "market value." This appearance of cooperation is important, since it seems to offer potential competitors for promotion security at a surface level, while one inwardly scrutinizes information that will aid in toppling the competition. In his attempts to get upward mobility, Dick Kesler would not only identify his competition for the presidency of the company, but would appear to cooperate with the competition so as to avoid alerting potential competitors to any threat.

Table 7.2 Impression management career strategies

Strategy	Definition	Impression management goals	Source
Altercasting	Those strategies which seek to cast another person into a role which brings about the desired response	To create an image of another which brings about one's own goals	Weinstein and Deutschberger (1963)
Disclosing obstacles	The process by which an individual reveals those obstacles, real, imagined, or fabricated, which impeded an already successful performance	The impression that the individual has overcome great hurdles in achieving success and is therefore very competent and/or motivated	Schlenker (1980)
Scapegoating	Pinning the blame for failure on an external source who is minimally or not all blameworthy	The appearance that one is not to blame for an apparent failure	Ashforth and Lee (1990)
Window-dressing	The use of physical changes in one's environment or appearance which makes a person appear more desirable	The impression of greater prestige, wealth, competence, or other socially desirable characteristics	Ornstein (1989); Riordan (1989)
Playing dumb	Giving others the impression that one is ignorant of, or unable to do, the work associated with a given job	Allows employee to help define his/her career by working only those tasks which have the greatest social desirability and career pay-off	Ashforth and Lee (1990); Becker and Martin (1995)
Depersonalizing	The avoidance of the unwanted demands of others by treating them as objects or numbers	The appearance of detachment, objectivity and professionalism which signals to others that no "personal," discretionary decisions will be made	Ashforth and Lee (1990)
Smoothing	The hiding of fluctuations in one's effort or output in performance	The appearance of a steady, productive rate of performance	Ashforth and Lee (1990)
Stalling	The overt appearance of activity while doing little or nothing	The impression is made that one is a supportive team player while actually undermining the activity	Ashforth and Lee (1990)

Buffing	The use of rigorous documentation and/or creation of documents designed to manage the impression of competence or motivation	The appearance of competence or motivation is enhanced by producing proof of work activity	Ashforth and Lee (1990); Shem (1978)
Playing safe	The evasion of those situations and decisions which may give an unfavorable impression of the employee	A preemptive attempt at minimizing or eliminating any unfavorable image	Ashforth and Lee (1990)
Misrepresenting	The avoidance of blame by manipulating information via distortion, embellishment, deception, selective presentation or withholding	To create an image of oneself that is consistent with career goals	Ashforth and Lee (1990)
Escalating commitment	The continued and enhanced commitment to a series of decisions in an attempt to make the initial decision appear to be a good one	An impression that one's decision or decision-making strategy was correct	Ashforth and Lee (1990)
Stretching	The prolonging of a given task so that one appears to be occupied	The impression given to observers is that one is busy and has little "down" time	Ashforth and Lee (1990)
Expert-citing	The use of outside high status references or people to support one's decision-making	The impression that significant people respect or otherwise value your contributions	Pfeffer (1981)
Association/disassociation	The use of symbolic association with positive events and people and disassociation from negative events and people	Impression that one is a part of good things and *apart from* negative things	Giacalone (1987); Giacalone and Knouse (1988)
Overconforming	Strict adherence to one's defined responsibilities and the associated guidelines, procedures and precedents associated with those responsibilities	Impression that one "plays by the rules" and/or that one is not to blame for problems associated with such strict adherence	Ashforth and Lee (1990); Lipsky (1980); Morgan (1987)
Passing the buck	The passing of one's responsibility for the completion of a task onto another person	A preventive strategy designed to avoid a negative impression of one's ability, especially when the task is not one that the person is particularly strong on; also, a way of having an overt career focus on those high visibility/payoff tasks	Ashforth and Lee (1990)

Finally, much of what is actually done cannot be accurately measured, nor can the person doing the work be assessed relative to others. The issue is once again one of social reality rather than of objective or physical reality. This problem can be understood in the work on performance appraisal and impression management showing that variables appraised in performance may be highly subject to impression management influences. Box 7.1 describes how the impression management motives of raters can also influence the objectivity of the performance appraisal process.

How does this careerist orientation play out in organizations? Gould and Penley (1984) investigated the role that career strategies play in organizational life. After surveying over 400 employees in a large municipality, they found that salary progression was related to the strategies of creating career opportunities (developing and seeking particular skills and experiences), extended involvement (working beyond the traditional 40-hour week), and opinion conformity and other enhancement (i.e., ingratiation). Self-nomination (i.e., self-enhancement) and networking (creating a group of contacts in and out of the organization) were also related to the salary progression of managers. Indeed, while the careerist would appear to be able to use all of these strategies, there is little doubt that creating career opportunities would appear to be the most consistent with hard work and least consistent with the careerist orientation.

Recently, Judge and Bretz (1994) gave a survey assessing career success, influence behaviors, and factors impacting career success, to a sample of past college graduates. Their findings clarify and lend further credibility to the idea that careerist impression management strategies *may* work, depending on the strategy used. Judge and Bretz found that job-focused strategies (i.e., self-promotion) negatively predicted career success, while supervisor-focused tactics (i.e., ingratiation) were positively associated with career success.

Strategies of a careerist orientation

In trying to understand the effectiveness of a careerist orientation, it is clear that our primary interest (from a management standpoint) is to gauge how careerist strategies impact the long-term career. Still, in order to truly understand this long-term impact, we must first be able to identify the basic impression management strategies that the careerist will use so that we can identify and differentiate among the strategies. Table 7.2 summarizes some impression management strategies, adapted from the sociological, organizational and psychological literatures, we think are potentially related to advancing the careerist's goals.

A few issues are worth noting regarding these strategies. First, the careerist may use other strategies that are of a more political nature in gaining whatever he might wish to gain. As such, some political tactics (such as coalition-building) will involve activities like social exchange that go beyond the attempt to control impressions. Second, the impression management strategies listed are by no means exhaustive. For example, many (if not most) of the strategies listed in Chapters 2 and 3 might also serve careerist goals and achieve similar, if not identical, ends.

We know little about whether these strategies are differentially effective at various career stages, or which of these strategies predominate in particular organizational settings. While identification of these strategies has been relatively easy, specifying when and where the strategies are used and whether they are effective is in need of investigation.

Countering careerist impression management

With the likelihood of a careerist approach becoming increasingly popular in organizations, we offer several practical suggestions for the human resource manager to address the issue:

1   *Go beyond punishment.* As we have noted previously, some theorists and researchers in the impression management literature have tended to view impression management as manipulative and consciously deceptive. Such a view of impression management might lead to more readily disciplining the impression managing employee who is viewed as being "manipulative." We would argue, however, that this approach is often short-sighted and incorrect.

    In the previous chapter, we saw that the BIDR scale suggests that there are *two* types of impression management-related phenomena – one deceitful, and the other (self-deceptive enhancement) truthful but exaggerated. It may be that the careerist is assumed to be using deceitful impression management, but may, in fact, be engaging in self-deceptive enhancement. It would be ethically questionable to discipline individuals for things they believed to be honest. Also, even if the careerist behaviors are conscious and deceitful, they may be employed as self-protective survival strategies. An employee may enter an organizational environment without a careerist orientation, but may develop such an orientation in response to an organization which rewards the careerist approach in order that he or she can survive. Dealing with the careerist orientation, therefore, must go beyond indiscriminately punishing the careerist to determining if the organizational culture fosters and rewards careerist behaviors.

2   *Use objective standards and measures.* Impression management may flourish where there is enough ambiguity in the environment that individuals may "redefine" their behaviors or the standards expected. Management may wish to use career-related measures that involve more precisely defined behaviors and outcomes, rather than measures which focus on interpretation. Management needs to establish clear goals and expectations so as to prevent the careerist from retrofitting his accomplishments and behaviors to a vaguely established series of organizational goals.

3   *Link fates.* With the increased focus upon team work and reengineering, management will need to consider evaluations which link the fates of many on a team, rather than the conventional singling out individuals for evaluation. Linking the fates of many people on a team fosters *real* cooperation in order to achieve a goal, makes self-serving impression management more difficult, and focuses more on team outputs than on perceptions of individual worker accomplishments. Under such conditions, careerists will need to either abandon the careerist ethic, or, alternatively, engage in group impression management as a team. The latter will not only be more difficult to execute, but also more difficult to conceal.

4   *Disempower dysfunctional impression management.* Because manipulative impression management has long been relegated to back-room discussion, usually among trusted friends and co-workers, its use has been limited to employees who know how to use it and choose to use it. We believe that *everyone* in the organization should know about the various techniques that impression management encompasses. Much as we have argued that interviewers and arbitrators should be made aware of these strategies, employees and managers would be well served to

know the strategies and know that others know and recognize them. Training all employees in impression management strategies levels the playing field in which everyone is at least aware of the practices. More importantly, it raises the risks for impression management usage, because recognition of the strategies is more likely to occur.

What we know and beyond

The impact of impression management on HRM decisions goes well beyond the four areas of employment interviews, exit interviews and surveys, arbitration, and careers that we have focused upon in this chapter. HRM practitioners know intuitively that impression management can influence many other organizational areas and concerns. Table 7.3 summarizes a few of these other areas.

While space limitations have prevented us from focusing on all the areas, we believe that these organizational issues and processes are susceptible to impression management attempts. Although research has been conducted to explore the impact of impression management in some of these areas, others remain to be investigated. There have been theoretical pieces written on issues such as impression management, motivation, and goal-setting (e.g., Huber, Latham, and Locke, 1989), but little work has been done in terms of actual empirical research. Still other areas have seen some preliminary research (e.g., résumés), but have done little in terms of theoretical development. A third group of areas such as organization development and employee assistance programs are potentially greatly impacted by impression management, but research and theory from an impression management standpoint has yet to appear.

Much needs to be considered about the *positive* contributions that impression management can offer the organization, and especially the human resource manager. For example, training employees to monitor their own behavior and its impact may facilitate interpersonal communication. Acknowledging and discussing the existence of impression management tactics may limit excessive use for fear of being caught. We believe that proper use of impression management may be pro-social and geared to facilitating better work relationships, increasing group cohesiveness, avoiding offending coworkers and colleagues, and creating a more pleasant organizational climate.

Table 7.3 How impression management can impact issues/processes in HRM

Issue/process	Some questions regarding the potential impact of impression management	Comments
Performance Appraisal (PA)	• Does the rater use PA to create an impression on the employee, others in the organization, or self? • How effective are IM strategies in impacting PA? • Do IM-related individual difference variables impact PA?	The impact of impression management on PA has been discussed extensively by Villanova and Bernardin (1989); Villanova and Bernardin (1991)
Letters of Recommendation (LR)	• Do differing impression management strategies impact the efficacy of the LR? • How is the LR viewed by people with different expectations of what impression management strategies should be used?	The impact of impression management on LR has been extensively discussed by Knouse (1989)
Résumés	• What impression management strategies can be used in résumés? • Are different IM strategies more or less effective, depending on the job sought? • Do high self-monitors manage the impressions of credentials more effectively?	The impact of impression management on résumés has been examined by Knouse, Giacalone, and Pollard (1988)
Cover letters	• How might cover letters be written and presented (paper type, fonts, etc.) in order to best manage the impressions sought?	The impact of impression management on cover letters has been examined by Knouse, Giacalone, and Pollard (1988)
Training	• What impact does trainer impression management ability have on training effectiveness? • How might impression management strategies be used to present training material? • What impact does impression management have on training evaluations?	No theoretical or empirical work on the impact of impression management on training has been done

Organization development	• How is impression management used to hide or mitigate resistance to change? • What role does impression management play in the diagnostic stages of organization development?	No theoretical or empirical work has been done on the impact of impression management on organization development
Motivation	• How might employee impression management concerns be used to increase employee motivation? • How might impression management be used organizationally to develop a motivation strategy which takes employee differences into account?	The impact of impression management on employee motivation has been addressed by Huber, Latham, and Locke (1989)
Employee Assistance Programs (EAPs)	• To what extent might impression management concerns prevent employees from using EAPs?	No theoretical or empirical work has been done on impression management and EAPs
Anti-social behaviors	• To what extent are the anti-social behaviors seen at work an attempt at creating a particular impression on supervisors and coworkers? • How might impression management be used to neutralize the negative aspects of anti-social behavior at work?	Some work has been done on these areas by Payne (1989) on theft, and by Giacalone and Rosenfeld (1987) and Giacalone and Knouse (1990) on employee sabotage
Leadership	• What strategies do individuals use to acquire and maintain the image of a leader? • How do individual differences in IM factors impact leadership emergence and/or effectiveness?	The impact of impression management on leadership has been addressed by Leary (1989), and has been investigated by a number of researchers (e.g., Leary and Schlenker, 1980; Leary et al., 1986)

A CONCLUDING NOTE

There is much about impression management and HRM left to determine, many parameters yet to establish regarding when and how much impression management will impact HRM decisions, and still more theoretical advances to be made. Although the research on impression management and HRM is far more advanced than the comparable organizational work on individual differences in impression management discussed in Chapter 6, we need to remember that this is a "field" still in its infancy. When considering the longer time period in which performance appraisal, recruitment, and selection models, theories, and mechanisms have been investigated, there is little doubt that the comparative development of impression management leaves it at a more basic level.

While this chapter has emphasized areas where impression management is important, there clearly are aspects of the HRM arena where impression management plays a negligible role. For example, contractually required health and medical benefits, promotions and raises based largely on collective bargaining agreements and seniority, and mandatory age-related retirements in dangerous professions (e.g., police, fire-department) are HRM activities not typically impacted by impression management factors.

However, while not all HRM-related functions are affected by impression management concerns, many core areas are. Thus, it is important for human resource managers to evaluate their decisions with a guarded eye, realizing that almost any decision they make which requires that an evaluation be made on an employee *might* be subject to the bias of a managed impression. It is critical that human resource managers discern where these biases might occur, as well as where impression management might offer refreshing and positive advantages to dated HRM processes.

NOTE

1   While the discussion in this section focuses on the impression management of the grievant, it does so because of the research which has focused on the grievant as impression manager. However, we recognize that management representatives will also manage their impressions in the process and impact the arbitrator.

8 *Current, emerging, and future directions*

THE FINAL ACT

If all the world is really a stage, let us consider this chapter our final act. Following the format of many final acts, we will revisit some key themes presented previously. In the opening chapter we showed how impression management has become a popular field of investigation in sociology, psychology, organizational behavior, management, and communication. In response to questions many students ask about impression management we offered the following conclusions based on research and theory in the field. Impression management is widespread in social and organizational life. It occurs for a variety of reasons ranging from purely selfish to the most humanitarian. The same impression management behavior can have a number of motives and will be carried out if the estimated benefits of engaging in the behavior exceed the costs. Leary and Kowalski's (1990) model describing how people monitor the impressions they are making, become motivated to impression manage and then choose a particular impression management tactic, was offered as a potential integrating framework. Our discussion showed how impression management is not inherently bad, that it is used by everyone to a greater or lesser degree, and that we manage many of our impressions automatically and without conscious awareness. Under certain conditions impression management can have influence both on the audience and on the impression manager.

In Chapter 2, ingratiation, the most common and most investigated form of acquisitive impression management, was described. Ingratiation tactics fulfill the powerful human desire to be liked by others. In Chapter 3, other acquisitive tactics used to create positive impressions were described. These included self-promotion, intimidation, exemplification, and supplication. We also reviewed indirect impression management – ways people claim identities by associating with positive and disassociating with negative things or events.

Chapters 4 and 5 summarized protective impression management tactics – those we use to repair or protect a spoiled or threatened identity. Predicaments – events which put someone's identity in a bad light – often precipitate protective impression management tactics and strategies. The tactics of excuses, justifications, disclaimers, self-handicapping and apologies are some of the direct ways individuals try to extricate themselves from predicaments that have occurred or they fear will happen. As we saw in Chapter 5, protective tactics can also be indirect, involving distancing onself from negative events.

In Chapter 6 we looked at ways differences among people in their tendencies to manage impressions can be assessed. The Self-Monitoring Scale measures differences in people's attentiveness and responsiveness to social cues. Self-monitoring is related to a person's impression management skill and to his or her success at it. The Balanced Inventory of Desirable Responding measures the inclination to impression manage others deceptively, as well as people's tendencies to deceive themselves through exaggerated positive presentations. The Self-Presentational Scale measures people's tendencies to manage positive impressions by attributing very positive characteristics to themselves and by denying negative characterizations. It has yet to be used extensively in organizations. The Measure of Ingratiatory Behaviors in Organizational Settings measures employees' tendencies to use the various forms of ingratiation with their supervisors. Use of these impression management measures in organizational settings has been relatively rare. As evidence on the reliability, validity, norms, and utility of these measures increases, we may find that impression management measures can give us clues to the causes of low employee productivity or poor managerial performance, to those positions in which skilled impression managers could be most useful, or to individuals or job groups that would benefit from training in impression management.

In Chapter 7, the importance to human resource managers of understanding impression management was examined. The possibility that the ability to impression manage may be added to the list of competencies required for many jobs was raised. That impression management plays a key role in employment interviews may have come as no surprise – the finding that impression management can outweigh job-related credentials may have. Thus, it is important that interviewers consider following a structured interview format, ask questions about experiences that the interviewee knows are verifiable, be trained to recognize impression management and remember that the interview is probably a good sample of the interviewee's impression management abilities which may be very important for success in some jobs. The potential biasing influence of impression management concerns on responses to exit interviews and surveys led to recommendations that exit interviews and surveys be conducted so that the identifiability of the exiting employee's responses can be minimized, that some time is allowed to pass after the employee's exit, and the responses of voluntary separators are distinguished from terminated employees. The possibility of impression management also heavily biasing the judgments of an arbitrator led to recommendations that arbitrators learn to recognize biasing forms of impression management and stick closely to contractual terms and avoid tangential issues that can be more easily molded to fit impression management objectives. The careerist orientation was discussed as a potentially dysfunctional form of impression management because it emphasizes appearances over competency. Studies showed that the more subtle forms of impression management used by careerists are related to career success. This led to recommendations that organizations attempt to control careerists, including using objective performance appraisal methods whenever possible, linking outcomes to cooperative rather than exclusively self-interested actions, and getting organization members to understand the dysfunctional impression management of the careerist and call it when they see it.

Some consistent themes emerged. The use of impression management requires skill. The ingratiator's dilemma illustrates what is often true about impression management – when you need it the most is when it is hardest to do effectively. Presumably this is because audiences recognize that, when the stakes are high, people may feign an identity to attain an important outcome or avoid a negative one. Throughout the chapters we offered some advice on the conditions when impression management is most likely to be effective, how delivery can increase its effectiveness, and how organizations can begin to utilize the positive effects of impression management and avoid some of its negative consequences.

More fully understanding issues of effectiveness and ways impression management can be used to foster organizational and personal goals will undoubtedly be the subject of sequels to the present text. We will suggest what those future issues and areas might be. We begin with future areas in theory and research most likely to be carried out by researchers. Then we will outline sequels that would be of greatest interest to practitioners.

SEQUELS IN IMPRESSION MANAGEMENT THEORY AND RESEARCH

As this book reveals, the field of organizational impression management is rapidly growing and is ripe for more research and application. In terms of research, answers to three key questions would greatly extend the utility of impression management: How much does impression management influence organizational functioning? How much do organizational factors influence impression management? How do impression management behaviors work together?

How much does impression management influence organizational behavior?

Organizational impression management researchers face the challenge of specifying when and how impression management influences behavior in organizations. In order to understand organizational behavior fully, the role of impression management needs to be recognized and better understood. One researcher, who has done research in both the laboratory and field is Micki Kacmar. She provides a "Behind the Scenes" look at her career, work, and ambitions for the field of organizational impression management.

• • • •

Behind the Scenes

K. Michele Kacmar

I returned to school to complete a Ph.D. at Texas A&M University in 1986. Upon arrival at A&M, each new Ph.D. student is assigned a senior Ph.D. student as a mentor. Luckily, I was assigned to Sandy Wayne. She had just finished her comprehensive examinations and was busily working on her dissertation proposal in the area of impression management. In order to complete her dissertation research she needed a confederate for her laboratory study. I eagerly volunteered. After over 100 hours in the lab repeating the same impression management cues over and over, I was hooked!

Since this first exposure to the area, I have found out that impression management can be applied to almost every area of business. For example, my research has shown the importance of impression management in interviewing, performance appraisal, job search and recruitment, and in supervisor, subordinate, and peer relationships. With respect to interviewing, I have found that individuals who are good impression managers usually are able to convince someone they are the best candidate, even when they are less qualified than other less vocal applicants. Also, interviewers do not like saying no to good impression managers because they like them.

How should organizations deal with impression management? Organizations can train interviewers to be aware of and recognize the tactics that impression managers use. Utilizing structured interviews that keep the focus of the interview on job-relevant areas and not allowing the applicant to control the topics of discussion will help select qualified candidates, and not impression managers.

• • • •

We know impression management is very common, but how much does it actually influence organizational behavior? Studies of people in organizations, and experiments simulating organizational processes (such as job interviews) described throughout this book, have shown that impression management plays a key role. However, most studies were not designed to answer the question of how *much* an influence it had. One study that did address the issue of relative influence of impression management on questionnaire responses found impression management was not so great an influence that it overwhelmed other factors (Moorman and Podsakoff, 1992). This may well be the case for much of organizational impression management – it influences behavior, but its influence is subtle, resulting in small to moderate changes or selectivity in behavior, rather than wholly altering or producing novel behaviors.

A related future issue will be a focus on those instances in which a person may be engaging in an impression management behavior that could have implications for his/her own identity, or that of his/her work group and organization. What if the individual's own self-interest conflicts with that of the work group or the organization? Understanding how these conflicts play out will become increasingly important to businesses. Mechanisms for controlling conflicting impression management objectives in the future may not be as effective as they may have been in the past. Because of the revolution in telecommunications devices such as fax machines, cellular phones and pagers, and the growing computer-linked information superhighway, individuals are able to communicate more widely and quickly. This means impression management behaviors in the near future may have a wider audience and be less controlled by typical organizational filters.

In today's workplace, there are more and more people working part-time and for multiple employers. Presumably their identification with the interests of a particular employer is reduced, meaning there is likely to be less agreement between the values of this "contingent worker" and that of the organization. This contemporary worker also depends more heavily on his own impression management efforts to find a job, so he may be taking credit for success and blaming failures on his other employers. While this may work fine for him, it does not do much for the reputation of those other companies. The future study of organizational impression management will need to address these changing employee characteristics.

How do organizational factors influence impression management?

Much of the work in impression management has been prompted by scholars noting that people's behavior is highly responsive to the social aspects of situations. Recall that throughout the text we have discussed the influence of behavior being public, the individual's feeling accountable, the goals impression management might help accomplish, the status or attitudes of the audience, and so on. Despite the many demonstrations of situational influences, we still need a richer understanding of how situations influence impression management in order to determine how impression management will operate in organizational settings. Some key situational factors in organizations are: aspects of organizational culture and policy, management behaviors, and worker relationships. How do these factors affect impression management? Does the nature of these factors increase the likelihood and impact of impression management? The three-component model developed recently by Leary and Kowalski (1990) and illustrated in Chapter 1 should help researchers exploring this question.

How do impression management behaviors work together?

Another future direction for research will be to establish how impression management behaviors work together. Some research has shown that influence attempts have different effects when used together than would be expected from knowing their individual effects (Barry and Shapiro, 1992). Recall Baron's (1989) job interview study reviewed in Chapter 7, in which he found male interviewers rated females more negatively if they wore perfume and engaged in a lot of nonverbal impression management, than if they used either impression management tactic alone. This suggests impression management can be overdone by using too many tactics or using them too vigorously.

FUTURE DIRECTIONS IN IMPRESSION MANAGEMENT APPLICATION AND PRACTICE

In this section we address four issues facing contemporary organizations that are of interest to practitioners. First, we look at improving organizational functioning through impression management training programs. Second, we consider impression management as one means of addressing the challenges of ethnic, national, gender, and age diversity. Third, the role impression management plays in business ethics will be outlined. Finally, we show how organizations can use impression management to manage the "company image."

Impression management training

We have learned that impression management behaviors are widespread in organizations. For many the next questions will be: Is it possible to modify impression management so it better suits individual and organizational purposes? Should we have impression management training programs? Should there be organizational development interventions for impression management?

The answer to each of these questions is probably "yes," but little

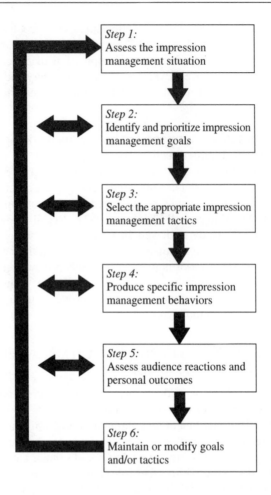

Figure 8.1 A practitioner's guide to steps in the impression management process
Source: Based on Martinko, 1991

work has been done in this area. One reason is that until recently many viewed impression management as consisting of faking and deceit (Rosenfeld and Giacalone, 1991) and organizations did not want employees learning to be expert fakers! Now with the pervasiveness and importance of impression management being increasingly recognized, it is not something that can or should be easily dismissed. Impression management can be viewed as a skill that – when developed – makes interpersonal relations in organizations more effective (Rosenfeld, Giacalone, and Riordan, 1994).

Mark Martinko (1991) offered a "practitioner's model" of the impression management process. It is summarized in Figure 8.1. This could be a useful guide for a training curriculum, with modules being developed for each step of the process.

For example, starting with Step 1, trainees could be given structured questionnaires (already existing in training/organizational literature) that would help them assess organizational climate or culture, their relationships to important audiences, and their own impression management potential. Then, goal-setting and prioritization techniques commonly found in motivational training programs could be extended and used to identify and prioritize goals for impression management. To identify appropriate impression management tactics and strategies, taxonomies of the acquisitive and protective techniques presented in Chapters 2–5 could be provided, along with information about situational and personal factors that lead to the effectiveness of the various techniques. Role-playing, behavior modeling, case-studies, and visualization exercises could be used in groups to plan and then finely tune the performance of particular impression management behaviors. Feedback could be solicited within training from group members, expert observers or trainers and used immediately to improve trainees' performance of impression management tactics. Following formal training, trainees could be asked to discuss their impression management objectives with supervisors, mentors and trusted coworkers, and solicit feedback on the effectiveness of their new impression management tactics, suggestions for improving them, and for alternative strategies that might be used. Ongoing feedback outside of training could lead to continuing focus and improvement in impression management and possibly lead to additional "advanced training" as an individual's career path evolved, or organizational circumstances changed.

Impression management and diversity

The importance of self-presentational concerns may well be culturally relative.

(Baumeister, 1982, p. 22)

The integration of the rapidly growing ethnic, national, gender, and age diversity of the workforce is seen as one of the greatest challenges facing many organizations today. We know that people are judged by the groups to which they belong. Race, nationality, gender, and age – probably because they often are indicated visually – are some of the strongest determinants of perceptions of strangers. Even ongoing relationships can be adversely affected by lack of familiarity with, or by stereotypes of, ethnic groups, nationalities, genders, and age groups. People with different backgrounds come to the workplace with divergent expectations for how they should be treated, what will be expected of them, and how they should treat others. Differences in ethnic, national, and gender backgrounds, and in age can be related to differing values relative to the types of images we respect and like in others, our own aspirations for certain images, and, consequently, our own impression management behaviors. Impression management offers the potential of helping individuals and organizations deal with the challenges posed by increasing diversity.

Until recently, there was little work linking impression management and diversity. As Gardner and Martinko's (1988) review of organizational impression management noted, "Comparatively little research has explored the relationships between actor attributes such as race, gender, and age and impression management behavior" (p. 334). To address these issues, we edited a special issue of the journal the *American Behavioral Scientist*, entitled *Impression Management and Diversity: Issues for Organizational Behavior* (Rosenfeld, Giacalone, and Riordan, 1994). Contributors to the special issue addressed impression management theory as it applied to multi-national (Giacalone and Beard, 1994; Mendenhall and Wiley, 1994), racial/ethnic/cultural (Allison and Herlocker, 1994; Crittenden and Bae, 1994; Rosenfeld, Booth-Kewley, Edwards, and Alderton, 1994) and gender issues (Kacmar and Carlson, 1994; Riordan, Gross, and Maloney, 1994; Wayne, Liden, and Sparrowe, 1994). As the articles in the special issue demonstrated, there is a good deal of potential for better understanding and for addressing the challenges of diversity through theory, research, and practice in impression management.

To illustrate, we will take up two topics we have discussed before and, using some of the articles that appeared in the special issue, show how impression management topics can address today's diversity challenges. The first topic takes the organization's perspective and deals with some innovative recommendations for training. The second focuses more sharply on a particular type of interaction in the organization – the supervisor–subordinate relationship – and offers some prospects for how ingratiation can be used to strengthen relationships and increase understanding.

Training programs that go beyond understanding

> [T]raining aging persons to be aware of the kinds of behaviors that project an "old" impression and practicing "acting young" can help them counteract the otherwise natural expectations on the part of others (and themselves) that the aging individual inevitably declines ... It is one's youthful or aged image that counts. Impression management training can help preserve the image.
>
> (Eden, 1991, p. 28)

Understanding cultural and gender differences is the basis for many current diversity training programs: their purpose is to sensitize people to noticing and respecting others' values, and to understanding how subtle aspects of verbal and nonverbal communication can lead to misunderstandings. Sensitivity, respect, and knowledge are very important. However, this approach to training has been faulted for emphasizing differences leading to discomfort and avoidance and reinforcing passivity (e.g., thinking not doing).

The next phase of diversity training must go beyond merely understanding differences to developing skills to more effectively manage interactions and communications so organization members can work together. Mark Martinko's (1991) model of impression management training could be applied to diversity training as well. Special focus would be placed on assessing the situation as individuals with diverse backgrounds do not always share the same perceptions of situations (Riordan, 1993). Additionally, careful attention would have to be paid to the feedback and outcome processes because we do not yet know a lot about how impression management operates in environments characterized by diversity (Gardner and Martinko, 1988).

There are many instances of the same impression management behavior having different effects depending on the demographic characteristics of the perceiver and/or performer. This serves to caution us that recommendations about impression management may depend on the cultural background of the impression manager and the audience. Michael Bond is someone who has had a good deal of personal and professional experience with impression management and cultural diversity. He shares some of these experiences in a "Behind the Scenes" profile.

• • • •

Behind the Scenes

Michael Harris Bond

> An actor creates an illusion in order to discover reality.
>
> Sir Alec Guiness

I accept the premise that, "One cannot not communicate." If this premise about our lives together is true, then three possible consequences would seem to follow: one may remain unaware of this fact of life, one may choose to ignore it and live life "naturally," or one may take charge of the power that is ours to communicate – what we wish about ourselves to others.

But what shall we communicate? In organizations it seems that we would be well advised to communicate what is necessary for us to survive, indeed prosper. Given that we are mutually interdependent for our security, those communications must signal some commitment to our colleagues and to the organization itself. As the twentieth century gives way to the twenty-first, these commitments will be toward people and institutions that are more ethnically, linguistically, and culturally diverse than has been the case before.

Many people would like to communicate an open, welcoming stance toward this diversity. Their reasons may be personal, social, or political, but they must all answer the question, "How?" How does one manifest competence, concern, enthusiasm, integrity, steadiness, and happiness to people of different backgrounds? How does one escape the prison of the stereotypes into which they will cast us? How can we maintain the harmony of the organization while still honoring the various backgrounds of those people who enliven it?

These are new and testing questions in a post-colonial world. I am a Baha'i committed to the process of forging a unity across cultural lines in practical ways. The world of work is the testing ground for this enterprise, as it is here that people are most likely to cross cultural lines. My experience in consulting for Hong Kong organizations suggests that we need new knowledge, new skills and new resolve to produce synergy out of this diversity.

All this newness makes us self-conscious. Many people feel they must deliberately stage-manage their behavior across ethnic lines to enhance organizational life. And indeed we must, at least until we become as unselfconsciously fluent in our behavior across ethnic lines as we are with people similar to us. The learning sequence is: unconscious incompetence. After all, our own culture is simply a system of habits and skills we have acquired over our lifespan; we need the same process of plodding acquisition to become bi-cultural, tri-cultural, multi-cultural. So, we become as children again in order to live more effectively as adults.

Personally, I have had to undergo this same struggle. Hong Kong Chinese culture is very different from my Canadian culture of origin. It socializes its members to different values, beliefs, interpersonal styles, and ideal personalities. Compromising, turning a blind eye, giving the benefit of the doubt, discovering sources of delight, communicating mindfully and, yes, carefully managing impressions, have all been required of me to survive and prosper in this organization people call the Chinese University of Hong Kong. What I have learned, I teach to others. In the process I have come to respect my Canadian heritage and appreciate the Hong Kong Chinese people.

> Cultivate the way yourself and your virtue will be genuine
> Cultivate it in the realm and the realm will flourish.
>
> Lao-tzu, *Tao-te ching*

• • • •

Some attempts have been made to understand these demographic and cultural differences. Micki Kacmar and Dawn Carlson (1994) theorize that in the job interview process men and women tend to use self- and other-promotional tactics at different rates. Self-promotional tactics focus on the applicant's own qualities and credentials whereas other-promotional tactics include things like complimenting the company and asking questions about the interviewer. They contend that women may benefit in the job search process from the use of subtle other-focused tactics, and additional training in the use of self-focused tactics. Along the same line, Sandy Wayne, Robert Liden, and Raymond Sparrowe (1994) outlined how gender may be related to the development of leader–member exchanges, i.e., the relationship between an employee and his or her boss. High-quality leader–member exchanges have been shown to be related to important organizational outcomes like personal influence, access to information and opportunities for professional development. Thus, for someone wanting to have a successful career in an organization, the quality of leader–member exchanges he or she establishes could be critical. For females, to counteract some of the potential negative effects of gender on the quality of a relationship with a male supervisor, they will need to be active impression managers, skillfully using acquisitive impression management tactics. We suspect many of the recommendations for females working with male bosses might well apply to any individual working in a situation in which the "organizational power structure" is composed primarily of individuals of different gender, ethnicity, nationality, or age.

The two articles summarized above point to how difficult male–female interactions among individuals raised in the same country can be. Imagine how confused things can get when the diversity in assumptions, perceptions, impression management styles, and life experiences is even greater! Take the situation of an individual working for a company owned and operated in another country with a very different culture. Studies of different cultures have shown substantial differences among them in people's reactions to impression management strategies and their preferences for certain identities. In a series of studies, Crittenden and Bae (1994) had individuals in four Asian cultures evaluate scenarios describing how a fictitious person explained his or her successes and failures. Not surprisingly, the cultures differed markedly in their evaluations of an individual who, for example, took a great deal of credit for his success and blamed his failures on factors external to himself. They found, contrary to what many assume, that individuals in some collectivist cultures do not automatically devalue individuals who take credit for their successes. Across the Asian cultures they studied, individuals who gave self-enhancing explanations were seen as smarter and as having higher achievement; those making more modest attributions were seen as having a greater sense of social responsibility but as being less productive. Thus, it seems that acquisitive impression management is needed even in collectivist cultures. However, self-enhancing impression management tactics are risky. This would be especially true if the culture is not well understood by the prospective impression manager.

Take a basic dilemma faced by all employees regardless of their locale – how to get credit for their successes while avoiding blame for failures. Giacalone and Beard (1994) proposed models that outline where and how culturally based attributions lead to functional or dysfunctional outcomes. Together, the models strongly recommend new cross-cultural training programs in both culturally bound attributions and impression management strategies.

Impression management skill-building offers a promising framework for improving cross-cultural training. It has been suggested that individuals who are perceptive and willing to actively manage impressions will be the ones who will be most successful managing identities that help them to be effective working in a foreign culture (Mendenhall and Wiley, 1994). Impression management training could teach specific techniques, how they operate within a particular culture, and how to read feedback from those who hold key organizational positions.

Impression management training is likely to provide the additional benefit of helping people to feel more confident and in control of their interactions. This would make them more willing to engage in the necessary trial-and-error learning of cross-cultural impression management so they more quickly become effective (Mendenhall and Wiley, 1994). The confidence to practice may well be a powerful side-effect of any impression management training program. Impression management is a skill that requires much practice to perfect.

A possible future avenue for impression management training is teaching trainees how to redefine situations so they can be more effective. Allison and Herlocker (1994) suggest two ways this could be done in the area of diversity training: (1) develop *superordinate goals* that everyone is working toward, and (2) have an outside group everyone is working against. Impression management can play a key role in these actions. For example, Rich, a new manager viewed as an "affirmative action hire" could emphasize in interactions with his department, their long-range departmental goals and his commitment to them, and try to elicit similar claims from them. He could also carefully manage the identity of being a hostile, aggressive manager toward another department which his department is competing with. In this way he can become a member of the *in-group*, and facilitate the types of departmental relationships that will help him be effective.

BOX 8.1

Stereotypes, ingratiation, and diversity

Interpersonal understanding is often negatively affected by stereotypes of race, ethnicity, nationality, or gender. Stereotypes can lead to false assumptions about individuals especially since the nature of most stereotypes is negative – more negative at least than the characteristics attributed to one's own group. We explain our own behaviors and those of our *in-group* more favorably than we do the actions of *out-group* members (Allison and Herlocker, 1994).

Cognitive social psychologists have found that stereotyping is an often inevitable by-product of the universal human tendencies to categorize, simplify, and group social stimuli. Stereotyping typically involves using a primary category like race, nationality, gender, or age. This occurs quickly and can have a restricting influence on the range of characteristics attributed to individuals: they are believed to have the stereotypical characteristics and not other characteristics, especially those that would be inconsistent with the stereotype.

We believe that as organizations grow increasingly diverse and multi-national, the impression management tactic of ingratiation may be crucial to members of racial/ethnic minority groups, women, immigrants, and expatriates who often need to please majority group members in positions of greater social power. As we suggested in Chapter 2, by generating liking and feelings of good will, ingratiation may counteract cognitive tendencies to stigmatize, stereotype, and devalue people who are different. Thus, ingratiation may provide a possible "antidote" to the constricting nature of stereotyping and *out-group stigmatization*. By achieving his or her goal – increasing liking and attraction – the successful ingratiator becomes familiar, activates norms of reciprocity, and goes from an unpopular "outsider" to a liked "insider."

Because of their lower social power in many organizations, we believe that members of diverse groups may be more likely to use ingratiation – the impression management tactic of

Box 8.1 continued

> choice of the powerless. In doing so, minority group members and women may face a dual-edged sword. On the one hand, the relatively lower social power of women and minorities in organizational settings results in their frequent use of ingratiation. It is precisely this lack of social power, however, that may hinder the effectiveness of these influence attempts – a case of the ingratiator's dilemma meeting the diverse workforce!

As organizations grow increasingly diverse and multi-national, the impression management tactic of ingratiation may be especially crucial to members of racial/ethnic minority groups, women, immigrants, and expatriates who often need to please majority group members in positions of greater social power. Box 8.1 explores this emerging diversity–ingratiation relationship.

On a final note, an interesting aspect of diversity and impression management is the degree to which the increased use of the term "diversity" is itself an attempt to project a more positive, inclusive, "warm and fuzzy" image rather than the negative, divisive connotations associated with terms such as "affirmative action" and "equal opportunity." According to Jenkins and Carr (1991–1992, p. 8), "The concept [of diversity] sometimes is treated or seized upon as the latest buzzword in organizational management. It even appears to be embraced by a few who wish to avoid dealing with 'affirmative action.'" We have also noticed that the language used to describe diversity initiatives in organizations often has a reverent tone. In addition to "celebrating" diversity, organizations should, "embrace diversity" (Kennedy and Everest, 1991, p. 50), "value diversity" (Broadnax, 1991–1992, p. 10) or make it something to be "nurtured" (Dominquez, 1991–1992, p. 16). Thus, it appears that "more and more employers view diversity as good business as well as good public relations" (Williams, 1992, p. A1).

Impression management and business ethics

Anecdotal and popular press evidence confirms that the process of impression management and business ethics are interrelated. But as

Knouse and Giacalone (1992b) have noted, there are few scientific inquiries on the role that impression management may play in business ethics. Although a few articles discussing the issues of impression management and ethics at work can be found in the literature (Giacalone and Payne, in press; Moberg, 1989; Payne and Giacalone, 1990), the role that impression management plays in business ethics has not been systematically studied. However, with the growing concern business has developed for ethical behavior, the role impression management may play in creating or thwarting the maintenance of an ethical work environment would appear to be of growing future interest.

The literature that does exist would lead us to conclude that future investigations of the roles impression management might play in business ethics should be focused in two different directions. On one hand, the focus could be on ethically evaluating the use of impression management at work, and focusing on its appropriateness, fairness, and moral repercussions. Conversely, the focus might also be on the effectiveness of using impression management tactics to reduce ethical infractions and corporate wrongdoing.

The ethics of impression management

A typical concern that arises whenever impression management is discussed regards the ethics of using impression management. This concern has arisen in discussing the ethics of using impression management at work, especially in those cases where individuals use it for the sake of internal political gain (Cavanagh, Moberg, and Velasquez, 1981; Velasquez, Moberg, and Cavanagh, 1983).

What constitutes ethically acceptable impression management at work? While the answers to this question have been primarily in the form of philosophical guidelines, the implicit assumption has been that impression management is intentional – that it is knowingly used by individuals as a political means to an end. From this approach, what constitutes ethical use of impression management has tended to focus more on traditional utilitarian concerns, justice, and rights. What has not been addressed, however, is that not all impression management is done with the intent to deceive others. Entirely different questions emerge about the ethics of impression management use if one considers that some impression management behaviors could actually be self-deceptive enhancement (see Chapter 6). These questions would focus not on the repercussions of the behaviors themselves, but on whether ethical responsibility can be attributed to those who deceived others unintentionally, and how intent could be established. Essentially, much more future discussion and scientific inquiry must be done in order to assess the ethical implications of impression management use at work.

Making wrong look right (or not too bad)

What happens when an individual worker, or an organization as a whole, is accused or found guilty of behaviors which are unethical or dangerous? The impression management literature would indicate that the individuals or the company representatives would attempt to make themselves appear more favorably by using protective tactics such as excuses and justifications. The ability to create a less negative impression of an unethical act may allow an employee to moderate the perception of that act, and thereby impact the degree of punishment that management doles out. In such cases, the employee's use of impression management is an attempt to provide some disciplinary relief which will lessen long-term financial or political repercussions (Payne and Giacalone,1990).

Recent work has looked at how individuals and organizations use impression management to get others to redefine unethical behavior to make it appear more positive. Giacalone and Payne (in press) reported that impression management behaviors, in the service of lessening the appearance of unethical behavior, can be found in simple press reports. They provided a series of actual examples in which organizations used denials, disassociation, scapegoating, accounts, and apologies as means of recasting their questionable behaviors. In his book on corporate doublespeak, Lutz (1989) provides a good example of such an impression management attempt by National Airlines. Because one of the company's airplanes crashed while attempting to land in Pensacola, Florida, in 1978, National received an after-tax insurance benefit of $1.7 million. While National had to account for this money in its annual report, it did not want to do so by discussing a topic as uncomfortable as an airline crash. Instead, the report contained a footnote which attributed the income to "the involuntary conversion of a 727" (p. 4). What the company was trying to do was manage the impression of being profitable without appearing to be a dangerous airline.

Little has been done to investigate whether this type of impression management is effective in helping to overcome perceptions that an employee or organization is unethical. In a study using management and non-management employees of an American bank, the effectiveness of accounts was affected by the perceived severity of the manager's deceptive tactics in an interview situation (Giacalone and Pollard, 1990). In another study, using a similar sample and vignette methodology, the acceptability of the accounts a manager used was also related to the perceived severity of the manager's breach of confidentiality (Giacalone and Pollard, 1987). While these two studies provide interesting findings, they are but initial investigations into how impression management might impact the perception of unethical acts. Given the growing pressure from the public for greater organizational accountability, and the intertwined ethical concerns of the companies themselves, the role that impression management plays in business ethics is likely to expand further.

How do organizations manage their images?

This text has focused largely on how individuals manage impressions of themselves. But impression management can also involve managing the impressions of organizations. An area ripe for future work is understanding how individuals and groups manage images of organizations (Ginzel, Kramer, and Sutton, 1993).

One example involves the impression management strategies of two international radical social groups studied by Elsbach and Sutton (1992). Earth First! is associated with using confrontational tactics as a means of protecting wilderness areas and the wildlife that live there. Driving spikes into trees in an old growth forest is one of the approaches attributed to them. The other group studied, ACT UP (AIDS Coalition to Unleash Power), targets governmental agencies and businesses that it feels obstruct or slow medical treatment for individuals with AIDS. ACT UP is associated with confrontational tactics like having members lie under the wheels of targeted drug company trucks to prevent them from moving freely. By employing an impression management perspective, Elsbach and Sutton were able to find similarities in how these two organizations maintained a positive public image, even though members of their organizations were involved in actions of which the public did not approve.

Following an incident like those described above, the organizations would respond in very rational terms and in a manner consistent with how mainstream organizations are expected to respond to such charges. In this way the organization was perceived as being more credible because it responded as more reputable organizations were expected to respond. They would also claim individuals who committed the acts were merely fringe elements acting on their own, without any direction from the organization. By these claims, the organizations also distanced themselves from the perpetrators.

After credibility was established, and the organizations dis-associated themselves, they impression managed by using protective followed by acquisitive impression management tactics. The organizations justified the actions by citing the greater wrongs being committed by the targeted groups (i.e., destroying the forests and slowing the treatment of individuals with AIDS). Entitlements and enhancements were then used, focusing on the potential positive consequences of the actions and how their organizations had been responsible for "what little" progress that had been made on these issues.

Can these same impression management techniques be seen in more mainstream organizations? Elsbach and Sutton (1992) have speculated that mainstream organizations adopt a strategy similar to that of radical social groups. In the early 1990s the book *Satanic Verses* was pulled from the shelves of Walden Book Stores in the United States. After its author, Salman Rushdie, was the target of death threats for supposedly insulting the Muslim religion, book-stores were afraid of being targets of violence themselves. Because some perceived this as unwarranted censorship, Walden Books' action was called into question. In responding to criticism, Walden Books denied they had stopped selling the book, claimed that it was just temporarily sold out, that they had removed the book because of concerns for employee safety, and that in fact the employees deserved a lot of credit for working despite bomb threats. This sequence of accounts is a good example of how organizations often offer a series of accounts, not all of which are consistent with each other, to manage their corporate image.

Gail Russ (1991) has looked at the ways organizations and organizational members manage the image of the company through company annual reports, letters to stockholders, press releases and similar written archival materials. Using these materials, Russ analyzed how companies manage stakeholders' impressions of the company and key figures within it. She points out, for instance, that organizational leaders do not just give the financial figures that are required by law, but spend a great deal of effort and resources to present a positive picture of the company. Expensive brochures with glossy paper and attractive graphics are common. Events affecting the company are interpreted in ways that will lead the organization to be perceived in positive ways, such as attributing failure to external causes (e.g., "the inability of Congress and the Administration to act"; quoted in Rush, 1991). Self-promotion and enhancement are common (e.g., "everyone is a hero in our company"; quoted in Rush, 1991, p. 234).

Linda Ginzel and her colleagues have looked at how top leadership in organizations manages the identity of the company at times when the company's image is threatened (Ginzel, Kramer, and Sutton, 1993). They too argue that the process is much like the protective impression management process used by individuals (see Chapters 4 and 5). In situations where a company's image is threatened, the leadership engages in a damage-control process, relying heavily on accounts (e.g., excuses, justification, apologies, denials) much as individuals do. Their analysis emphasizes the iterative nature of accounts by organizations in crisis. Often company leadership will test and then offer a sequence of accounts – sometimes quite different in form and content – until it finds an account or set of accounts important audiences will accept as satisfactory explanations for events. "The cycle of interlocked behavior continues until organizational actors and their audiences have reduced, or eliminated, perceived equivocality regarding the event. As audience members become satisfied, the salience of the predicament decreases ... In such cases, top management and their organizational audiences have achieved a 'settlement' regarding the final interpretation to be placed on the event" (Ginzel, Kramer, and Sutton, 1993, pp. 246–247).

As our understanding of how the impressions of organizations are managed increases it will be interesting to contrast the management of individual identities with the management of organizational identities/images. Organizations may have a more difficult time impression managing because they are likely to have more audiences to please and those audiences may have very different interests (e.g., competitors versus stockholders) that may also be very political (Pfeffer, 1981). It is not uncommon for additional predicaments to arise for companies as they attempt to satisfy different audiences. Because companies are abstract entities (not people with feelings, families, coauthors, etc.) audiences may feel more free to doubt and harshly criticize companies in public. This may require organizations to be more active impression managers.

It also may be why many large organizations have individuals on staff who are trained in impression management and have responsibility for maintaining the company's image. While helpful most of the time, having professional public relations staff may lead management to ignore implications of their own actions for public relations because they think someone else will handle that (Ginzel, Kramer, and Sutton, 1993).

A CONCLUDING NOTE

Because this is the first book in the new field of organizational impression management, we suspect it has raised as many questions as it has answered. That is as it should be. The chapters in this book characterize the basic nature of impression management and how it is applied in organizations. They illustrate how impression management is measured and review much of the research to date on organizational impression management. Our projections throughout the text on how impression management can be used by individuals working in organizations, and by organizations themselves, are the areas where we and others working in the field have the most questions. We suspect that it is in these areas that your questions will lie too. We hope they will be addressed in future efforts.

Fifteen years ago when the three authors of this text first met, the concept of organizational impression management existed only as a very rough plot line (with a strong fantasy component!). Even though we were studying impression management in the highly controlled social psychology laboratory, few had thought to apply impression management to organizations. If someone had told us then we would write an entire book on this topic we (and our "beloved" professors!) would have laughed in disbelief. Now that we have finished, we hope you have found our effort to be plausible and that the basic message of our work comes through clearly: Impression management is a pervasive process – integral to functioning and success in today's organizations.

— Appendix
Impression management methodologies

Although many people assume that impression management can be studied through simple observation or by using common sense, researchers depend on more systematic techniques called *methodologies*. These methodologies are the formalized conditions a researcher establishes under which he or she observes or measures behavior. Methodologies employed by impression management researchers reflect the journey of the field through the behavioral and organizational sciences. By looking at studies grouped by methodological approaches, we can capture a sense of how the field of impression management has progressed and evolved.

OBSERVATIONAL STUDIES

Goffman and other symbolic interactionists studied impression management through the use of *observational studies*. These involve the researcher observing many and varied interactions, looking for patterns, and then summarizing the patterns in a narrative. Goffman and others working at the time used observational studies to learn about impression management processes in career progress (Becker and Strauss, 1956), being labeled as "crazy" (Rosenhan, 1973), acting "sick" (Braginsky, Braginsky, and Ring, 1969), interactions between practitioner and client (Kuhn, 1962), street life (Whyte, 1943), families (Goffman, 1962) and even in the career of funeral director (Habenstein, 1962)!

A weakness in this approach is that observational studies tend to be less objective and conclusions drawn using this approach are not as open to verification and replication by others. Recent observational studies in organizational contexts, however, tend to be more structured and scientific in their collection and analysis of data. A study by Gardner and Martinko (1988), for example, had observers record school administrators' verbal statements which observers then related to the characteristics of the audience hearing the statements. One conclusion the researchers reached was that administrators engaged in more impression management when they were addressing their supervisors than when they were addressing other types of audiences.

EXPERIMENTS

When psychologists began studying impression management they used a methodology popular in psychology – the *laboratory experiment*. With this method, the researcher sets up a highly controlled situation in a laboratory in which an *independent variable* is manipulated and another variable – the *dependent variable* – is observed and measured. Usually there are at least two conditions: an *experimental condition* which includes the independent variable, and a *control condition* which does not. If the dependent variable changes when the independent variable is present, it is assumed to be the result of the independent variable.

Sandy Wayne and Gerald Ferris (1990) provide a good example of a laboratory experiment that has organizational relevance. In their study using undergraduate students, a "supervisor" (the actual subject) interacted with a "subordinate" (who was a confederate of the experimenter) as they processed mail orders for a catalogue marketing firm. As they worked, the confederate engaged in different types of impression management (e.g., giving compliments; doing favors for the supervisor) or no impression management (a control condition). Thus, the type of impression management was an independent variable. At the end of the work session, the researcher gave the supervisor information that indicated that the subordinate had had high, average, or low performance. This was the second independent variable. Supervisor subjects were then asked to evaluate the subordinate. The findings of this study indicated that impression management worked: subordinates who used it were seen as significantly more productive than those who did not, even when their real performance was the same.

Three of the most common independent variable manipulations used in impression management experiments are: changing the audience characteristics, having a behavior occur publicly or privately, and having participants use a simulated lie-detector called the bogus pipeline.

Changing the audience characteristics

As we discussed in Chapter 2, Edward E. Jones was one of the most influential of all impression management theorists. Many of Jones' laboratory studies manipulated audience characteristics to determine their impact on impression management behaviors. He, his students, and colleagues, demonstrated under a variety of conditions that people would change their behavior based on what they had been told about an audience and/or the target of their impression management (Jones, 1964). For example, when research participants role-playing a job interview thought the interviewer liked domineering people, they acted in more domineering ways than participants who had been told the interviewer liked passive people or those not told anything about the interviewer's preferences (cited in Jones, 1964).

Public–private manipulations

Public conditions are those where individuals feel they are identifiable and that someone may be watching their behavior. Private conditions are those in which people feel more anonymous – they do not feel they can be identified or associated with their actions. Presumably, in an experimental setting that differs in no other way, if research participants under public (but not those under private) conditions perform a behavior, the behavior is assumed to be a form of impression management since it occurs only when there is an audience for which to manage an identity. If a behavior occurs whether or not an audience is present, it is assumed to result from something other than just impression management – being the result of the person's personality, or deeply held core convictions for example.

Take an experiment by Forsyth, Riess, and Schlenker (1977) in which research participants spent 20 minutes doing a really boring task (no, it wasn't reading this Appendix!). They were then asked to evaluate the task on a questionnaire they either signed (public) or did not sign (private). As you might expect, their ratings were more positive when they knew they could be identified, presumably because they were concerned about the impression they were making. While this effect was obtained with college students, you can imagine how much putting names on company surveys – especially those dealing with sensitive information – could influence employees' responses. This has led some to recommend guaranteeing anonymity and confidentiality as standard policy on organizational surveys – especially those that contain sensitive topics (Rosenfeld, Booth-Kewley, and Edwards, 1993).

The bogus pipeline

The bogus pipeline (BPL) is an elaborate piece of electronic equipment represented to laboratory research participants as being a powerful lie-detector (Jones and Sigall, 1971; see Roese and Jamieson, 1993 for a review). Although it doesn't really work, the BPL has been used as a means of measuring the influence of impression management on various behaviors such as reactions to success and failure (Rosenfeld, 1990). The reasoning is that people will be more truthful and less likely to engage in deceptive impression management when they believe their "real" feelings can be detected by a machine. In an experiment one student in a pair of students role-playing workers received much more pay than the other student even though his work was the same (Rivera, 1976). The students who were asked on a questionnaire how satisfied they were with the money they received, did not say they were pleased. However, the students who were hooked up to the BPL, "admitted" they were pleased. Presumably, students were afraid they would appear "greedy" if they acknowledged they were pleased to receive a large payment at the other student's expense, so they managed a more positive identity in their response to the questionnaire. Students hooked up to the BPL did not do this for fear their real feelings would be detected.

While the BPL produced many interesting findings in social psychological studies, it is not likely to be used in organizations. The BPL was used in these social psychology experiments in ways analogous to how some companies have used lie-detectors with their employees. However, claims for the polygraph's ability to weed out liars from truthtellers have been overstated and its use in many organizations has been severely limited (see Bashore and Rapp, 1993; Steinbrook, 1992; Saxe, 1991). Thus, even if the BPL really did live up to its lie-detecting potential, it would likely meet with stiff resistance both as a research and practical tool in organizational settings.

FIELD STUDIES

A common research strategy used to study organizational impression management is the *field study*. In a field study, relationships among naturally occurring organizational characteristics, personal variables, and various behaviors are explored. For example, Wayne and Ferris (1990) gave employees at two banks a questionnaire asking them the extent to which they had engaged in a given behavior over the previous three months. They also asked employees' supervisors to rate them. They found that employees who used supervisor-focused impression management were rated more positively by their supervisors than employees who used impression management that was either self-focused or job-focused.

A comparison of this field study with the experimental study by Wayne and Ferris discussed earlier shows the relative advantages of each approach. The experiment used undergraduate students acting as subordinates, whereas the field study used actual employees in the work setting. Thus, findings of field studies may be more generalizable to people working in organizations. However, there are two common features of field studies that limit conclusions drawn from them. First, the researcher cannot always be sure that employee groups being compared have employees who were randomly assigned to these groups. Without random assignment, it may be that the groups differ even before the study begins. In the Wayne and Ferris field study, groups were defined by what impression management strategies employers *said* they used. Second, the researcher in a field study has less control over the introduction of the independent variable and the measurement of the dependent variable than in an experiment. Again, taking this study, two questionnaires were filled out and their results correlated. The researcher only knows these variables are related, not necessarily that new variables (impression management strategies) actually cause the other (supervisor evaluations). Despite these shortcomings, field methodologies are very valuable to the organizational researcher because they deal with work-related and organization-related variables that are often difficult to simulate or otherwise study in the laboratory.

SCENARIO STUDIES

A problem that occurs when studying impression management is that it can be impractical or unethical to manipulate or find naturally occurring instances of certain variables (e.g., fraud, sabotage, aggression). To get around this, impression management researchers sometimes choose to conduct *scenario studies*. One kind of scenario study has research participants read about other people in a situation and give their reactions. In one study, research participants read scenarios of a fictitious US Senator who had accepted a bribe or solicited the services of a prostitute (Riordan, Marlin, and Kellogg, 1983). The scenario included the Senator's explanation for his actions: either an excuse or a justification (see Chapter 4). To find out how people evaluate actions in the light of excuses and justifications, research participants answered questions about what they thought about the Senator and his action. One interesting finding of this study was that Senators who excused their actions by claiming some temporary debilitating condition (e.g., drunkenness) were seen in a more positive light than Senators who tried to minimize the gravity of their action (e.g., claiming the action was carried out for reputable reasons and was not really what it seemed). Many scenario studies have a similar focus – how do audiences react to impression management tactics? The disadvantage of this approach is that the researcher cannot be sure that people react to scenarios the same way they would if they were really in the situation.

INDIVIDUAL DIFFERENCE MEASURES

Since people differ in the degree to which they use impression management, the type of impression management behaviors they engage in, and how good they are at it, another way to study impression management is by focusing on these differences in impression management styles (see Chapter 6). In a typical individual difference study, participants take a test that measures how much or how little of an impression management-related trait such as self-monitoring (Snyder, 1974), need for approval (Crowne and Marlowe, 1964), or fear of negative evaluation (Leary, 1983a; Watson and Friend, 1969) they have. They are then placed in an experimental setting that should affect people who are either high or low in that trait more than others, or their scores on the test measuring the trait are correlated with their behavior in the experiment. In one study, research participants worked on a boring task with a group leader who clearly appreciated hard work or did not (Watson and Friend, 1969). Participants with a high fear of negative evaluation worked harder than other participants. Another example is a study which showed that bank employees who scored high on tests measuring their tendencies to impression manage and to deceive others were more effective in influencing their supervisors than were other types of employees (Deluga, 1991).

RESPONSE BIAS

Some studies have been generated by researchers concerned that responses to organizational questionnaires are contaminated by too much impression management. If people manage their impressions by answering questionnaires so that they "look good," how can researchers know if their questionnaire results reflect anything about the topic they want to be studying? This is especially a problem if people are asked sensitive questions about things such as drug and alcohol use, organizational theft, and sexual harassment (Hosseini and Armacost, 1993).

To address this issue Moorman and Podsakoff (1992) used a powerful statistical technique called *meta-analysis* in which the findings from many related studies are analyzed simultaneously so that general conclusions can be drawn about the topic of interest. The two researchers looked at the results of 33 studies and found that managing a socially desirable identity was a significant factor on many questionnaires, meaning that respondents were trying to manage a positive impression with their questionnaire responses by distorting them somewhat. However, the authors were able to show that the questionnaires were also measuring real differences among people in, for example, job satisfaction, a sense of personal control, role conflict and role ambiguity, and not just people's attempts to look good.

A CONTEMPORARY APPROACH: STUDYING IMPRESSION MANAGEMENT IN ITS OWN RIGHT

Today, impression management is studied in its own right, not just as an after-the-fact reinterpretation of experimental or questionnaire responses as was popular among social psychologists during the 1970s (Rosenfeld and Giacalone, 1991). A great variety of methodologies and findings have emerged: people's motivation to impression manage is heightened by including incentives for the management of particular impressions or by leading respondents to anticipate or create a negative identity for themselves (Ashford and Northcraft, 1992; Daubman, Heatherington, and Ahn, 1992). Other studies look at what identities subjects try to construct as a function of their personalities and values, the identities they desire, or role constraints inherent in the situation (Kumar and Beyerlein, 1991; Leary, 1992). Studies are even now looking at the consequences of impression management for audiences as well as for the impression manager (Abdolmohammadi and Shanteau, 1992; Jones, Brenner, and Knight, 1990).

Given the recent increase in citations in the psychological, organizational, and sociological literatures, it is clear that research specifically designed to investigate impression management is growing dramatically. Years ago, when it was difficult to publish articles about impression management in the professional literature, the present authors used to joke that we wished there was a *Journal of Impression Management* that would accept our work. Now, as the field continues to expand so rapidly, this pipedream of the late 1970s may soon become a reality of the 1990s.

— Bibliography

Abdolmohammadi, M. J., and Shanteau, J. (1992). Personal attributes of expert auditors. *Organizational Behavior and Human Decision Processes*, 53, 158–172.

Abrams, G. (1991, June 14). All smiles: The Dale Carnegie brand of optimism is still winning friends and influencing people. *Los Angeles Times*, pp. E1, E16–E17.

Albas, D. and Albas, C. (1988). Aces and bombers: The post-exam impression management strategies of students. *Symbolic Interaction*, 11, 289–302.

Allen, R. W., Madison, D. L., Porter, L. W., Renwick, P. A., and Mayes, B. T. (1979). Organization politics: Tactics and characteristics of the actors. *California Management Review*, 22, 77–83.

Allison, S. T., and Herlocker, C. E. (1994). Constructing impressions in demographically diverse organizational settings: A group categorization analysis. *American Behavioral Scientist*, 37, 637–652.

Anderson, N. R. (1991). Decision making in the graduate selection interview: An experimental investigation. *Human Relations*, 44, 403–417.

Anderson, L. R., and Tolson, J. (1989). Group members' self-monitoring as a possible neutralizer of leadership. *Small Group Behavior*, 20, 24–36.

Anti-Scud Duds (1993, November 29). *Newsweek*, p. 7.

Arkin, R. (1981). Self-presentation styles. In J. T. Tedeschi (Ed.), *Impression management and social psychological research*. New York: Academic Press, pp. 311–333.

Arkin, R. M., and Baumgardner, A. H. (1985). Self-handicapping. In J. H. Harvey, W. Ickes, and R. F. Kidd (Eds), *New directions in attributional research*. Hillsdale, N.J.: Lawrence Erlbaum Associates (Vol. 3), pp. 169–202.

Arkin, R. M., and Shepperd, J. A. (1989). Self-presentation styles in organizations. In R. A. Giacalone and P. Rosenfeld (Eds), *Impression management in the organization*. Hillsdale, N.J.: Lawrence Erlbaum Associates, pp. 125–139.

Arkin, R. M., and Shepperd, J. A. (1990). Strategic self-presentation: An overview. In M. J. Cody and M. L. McLaughlin (Eds), *The psychology of tactical communication*. Clevedon, UK: Multilingual Matters Ltd, pp. 175–193.

Arvey, R. D., and Renz, G. L. (1992). Fairness in the selection of employees. *Journal of Business Ethics*, 11, 331–340.

Ashford, S. J., and Northcraft, G. B. (1992). Conveying more (or less) than we realize: The role of impression management in feedback-seeking. *Organizational Behavior and Human Decision Processes*, 53, 310–334.

Ashforth, B. E., and Lee, R. T. (1990). Defensive behavior in organizations: A preliminary model. *Human Relations*, 43, 621–648.

Austin, W., and Utne, M. K. (1977). Sentencing: Discretion and justice in judicial decision-making. In B. D. Sales (Ed.), *Psychology in the legal process*. New York: Spectrum, pp. 163–194.

Ave, C. (1994, June 5). It's time to tell your best–worst boss tale. *San Diego Union Tribune*, p. D-12.

Baker, H. G., and Spier, M. S. (1990). The employment interview: Guaranteed improvement in reliability. *Public Personnel Management*, 19, 85–90.

Barker, K. A. (1992). Changing assumptions and contingent solutions. The cost and benefits of women working full- and part-time. *Sex Roles*, 28, 47–71.

Baron, R. A. (1986). Self-presentation in job interviews: When there can be "too much of a good thing." *Journal of Applied Psychology*, 16, 16–28.

Baron, R. A. (1989). Impression management by applicants during employment interviews: The "too much of a good thing" effect. In R. W. Eder and G. R. Ferris (Eds), *The employment interview: Theory, research, practice*. Newbury Park, Calif.: Sage Publications, pp. 204–215.

Baron, R. A. (1990). Countering the effects of destructive criticism: The relative efficacy of four interventions. *Journal of Applied Psychology*, 75, 235–245.

Barry, B., and Shapiro, D. L. (1992). Influence tactics in combination: The interactive effects of soft versus hard tactics and rational exchange. *Journal of Applied Social Psychology*, 22, 13, 1429–1441.

Bashore, T. R., and Rapp, P. E. (1993). Are there alternatives to traditional polygraph procedures? *Psychological Bulletin*, 113, 3–22.

Baumeister, R. F. (1982). A self-presentational view of social phenomena. *Psychological Bulletin*, 91, 3–26.

Baumeister, R. F. (Ed.) (1986). *Public self and private self*. New York: Springer-Verlag.

Baumeister, R. F. (1989). Motives and costs of self-presentation in organizations. In R. A. Giacalone and P. Rosenfeld (Eds), *Impression management in the organization*. Hillsdale, N.J.: Lawrence Erlbaum Associates, pp. 57–85.

Baumeister, R. F., and Hutton, R. F. (1987). Self-presentation theory: Self-construction and audience pleasing. In B. Mullen and George R. Goethals (Eds), *Theories of group behavior*. New York: Springer-Verlag, pp. 71–87.

Baumeister, R. F. and Jones, E. E. (1978). When self-presentation is constrained by the target's knowledge: Consistency and compensation. *Journal of Personality and Social Psychology*, 36, 608–618.

Baumeister, R. F., Kahn, J., and Tice, D. M. (1990). Obesity as a self-handicapping strategy: Personality, selective attribution of problems, and weight loss. *Journal of Social Psychology*, 130, 121–123.

Becker, H. S., and Strauss, A. (1956). Careers, personality and adult socialization. *American Journal of Sociology*, 62, 253–263.

Becker, T. E. and Martin, S. L. (1995). Trying to look bad at work: Methods and motives for managing poor impressions in organizations. *Academy of Management Journal*, 38, 174–199.

Beeman, D. R., and Sharkey, T. W. (1987). The use and abuse of corporate politics. *Business Horizons*, March–April, 26–30.

Berglas, S., and Jones, E. E. (1978). Drug choice as a self-handicapping strategy in response to noncontingent success. *Journal of Personality and Social Psychology*, 36, 405–417.

Bernstein, D. A. (1993). Excuses, excuses. *APS Observer*, 6, 4.

Bies, R. J., Shapiro, D. L., and Cummings, L. L. (1988). Causal accounts and managing organizational conflict: Is it enough to say it's not my fault? *Communication Research*, 15, 381–399.

Bies, R. S., and Sitkin, S. B. (1992). Explanation as legitimation: Excuse-making in organizations. In M. L. McLaughlin, M. J. Cody, and S. J. Read (Eds), *Explaining one's self to others: Reason-giving in a social context*. Hillsdale, N.J.: Lawrence Erlbaum Associates, pp. 183–198.

Bleifuss, J. (1994, March 20). New angles from the spin doctors. *NY Times*, p. F-13.

Bohra, K. A., and Pandey, J. (1984). Ingratiation toward strangers, friends, and bosses. *Journal of Social Psychology*, 124, 217–222.

Booth-Kewley, S., Edwards, J. E., and Rosenfeld, P. (1992). Impression management, social desirability, and computer administration of attitude questionnaires: Does the computer make a difference? *Journal of Applied Psychology*, 77, 562–566.

Booth-Kewley, S., Rosenfeld, P., and Edwards, J. E. (1992). Impression management and self-deceptive enhancement among Hispanic and non-Hispanic White Navy recruits. *Journal of Social Psychology*, 132, 323–329.

Braaten, D. O., Cody, M. J., and DeTienne, K. B. (1993). Account episodes in organizations: Remedial work and impression management. *Management Communication Quarterly*, 6, 219–250.

Braginsky, B. M., Braginsky, D. D., and Ring, K. (1969). *Methods of madness: The mental hospital as last resort*. New York: Holt.

Broadnax, W. D. (Winter 1991–1992). From civil rights to valuing diversity. *The Bureaucrat*, 20, 9–13.

Butcher, L. (1989). *Accidental millionaire: The rise and fall of Steve Jobs*. New York: Paragon House.

Byrne, D. (1971). *The attraction paradigm*. New York: Academic Press.

Cain, R. (1994). Managing impressions of an AIDS service organization:

Into the mainstream or out of the closet? *Qualitative Sociology*, 17, 43–61.

Caldwell, D. F., and O'Reilly, C. A. (1982). Boundary spanning and individual performance: The impact of self-monitoring. *Journal of Applied Psychology*, 67, 124–127.

Carnegie, D. (1936). *How to win friends and influence people*. New York: Simon & Schuster.

Carnegie, D. (1973). *How to win friends and influence people*. New York: Pocket Books.

Cascio, W. F. (1975). Accuracy of verifiable biographical information blank responses. *Journal of Applied Psychology*, 60, 767–769.

Cavanagh, G. F., Moberg, D. J., and Valasquez, M. (1981). The ethics of organizational politics. *Academy of Management Review*, 6, 363–374.

Christie, R., and Geis, F. (1970). *Studies in Machiavellianism*. New York: Academic Press.

Cialdini, R. B. (1989). Indirect tactics of image management: Beyond basking. In R. A. Giacalone and P. Rosenfeld (Eds), *Impression management in the organization*. Hillsdale, N.J.: Lawrence Erlbaum Associates, pp. 45–56.

Cialdini, R. B. (1993). *Influence: The psychology of persuasion*. New York: William Morrow and Company, Inc.

Cialdini, R. B., Borden, R. J., Thorne, A., Walker, M. R., Freeman, S., and Sloan, L. R. (1976). Basking in reflected glory: Three (football) field studies. *Journal of Personality and Social Psychology*, 34, 366–375.

Cialdini, R. B., and De Nicolas, M. E. (1989). Self-presentation by association. *Journal of Personality and Social Psychology*, 57, 626–631.

Cialdini, R. B., Finch, J. F., and De Nicolas, M. E. (1990). Strategic self-presentation: The indirect route. In M. J. Cody and M. L. McLaughlin (Eds), *The psychology of tactical communication*. Clevedon, UK: Multilingual Matters Ltd, pp. 194–206.

Cialdini, R. B., and Richardson, K. D. (1980). Two indirect tactics of impression management: Basking and blasting. *Journal of Personality and Social Psychology*, 39, 406–415.

Clary, E. G., and Shaffer, D. R. (1980). Effects of evidence withholding and defendant's prior record on juridic decisions. *Journal of Psychology*, 112, 237–245.

Cobb, A. T. (1986). Political diagnosis: Applications in organizational development. *Academy of Management Review*, 11, 482–496.

Cooley, C. H. (1964). *Human nature and the social order*. New York: Schocken Books.

Cooper, J., and Jones, E. E. (1969). Opinion divergence as a strategy to avoid being miscast. *Journal of Personality and Social Psychology*, 13, 23–40.

Craig, D., and Rosato, D. (1994, April 1). Portfolio managers spark market's volatility. *USA Today*, p. B-1.

Crant, J. M., and Bateman, T. S. (1993). Assignment of credit and blame for performance outcomes. *Academy of Management Journal*, 36, 7–27.

Crawford, K. S., Thomas, E. D., and Funk, J. J. (1980). Pygmalion at sea: Improving the work effectiveness of low performers. *Journal of Applied Behavioral Science*, 16, 482–505.

Crittenden, K. S., and Bae, H. (1994). Self-effacement and social responsibility: Attribution as impression management in Asian cultures. *American Behavioral Scientist*, 37, 653–671.

Crowne, D. P. (1979). *The experimental study of personality*. Hillsdale, N.J.: Lawrence Erlbaum Associates.

Crowne, D. P., and Marlowe, D. (1960). A new scale of social desirability independent of psychopathology. *Journal of Consulting and Clinical Psychology*, 24, 349–354.

Crowne, D. P., and Marlowe, D. (1964). *The approval motive*. New York: Wiley.

Daubman, K. A., Heatherington, L., and Ahn, A. (1992). Gender and the self-presentation of academic achievement. *Sex Roles*, 27, 187–204.

DeGree, C. E., and Snyder, C. R. (1985). Adler's psychology (of use) today: Personal history of traumatic life events as a self-handicapping strategy. *Journal of Personality and Social Psychology*, 48,1512–1519.

Deluga, R. J. (1991). The relationship of upward-influencing behavior with subordinate impression management characteristics. *Journal of Applied Social Psychology*, 21, 1145–1160.

Deluga, R. J., and Perry, J. T. (1994). The role of subordinate performance and ingratiation in leader–member exchanges. *Group and Organization Management*, 19, 67–86.

DePaulo, B. M. (1992). Nonverbal behavior and self-presentation. *Psychological Bulletin*, 111, 203–243.

Dobbins, G. H., Long, W. S., Dedrick, E. J., and Clemons, T. C. (1990). The role of self-monitoring and gender on leader emergence: A laboratory and field study. *Journal of Management*, 16, 609–618.

Dominquez, C. M. (Winter 1991–1992). The challenge of Workforce 2000. *The Bureaucrat*, 20, 15–18.

Drost, D. A., O'Brien, F. P., and Marsh, S. (1987). Exit interviews: Master the possibilities. *Personnel Administrator*, 32, 104–110.

Du Pont de Nemours and Company (1952). *Du Pont, the autobiography of an American enterprise*. Wilmington, Del.: E.I. Du Pont de Nemours & Company.

Eden, D. (1991). Applying impression management to create productive self-fulfilling prophecy at work. In R. A. Giacalone and P. Rosenfeld (Eds), *Applied impression management: How image-making affects managerial decisions*. Newbury Park, Calif.: Sage Publications, pp. 13–40.

Eder, R. W., and Ferris, G. R. (Eds) (1989). *The employment interview: Theory, research, practice*. Newbury Park, Calif.: Sage Publications.

Elsbach, K. D., and Sutton, R. I. (1992). Acquiring organizational legitimacy through illegitimate actions: A marriage of institutional and impression management theories. *Academy of Management Review*, 35, 699–738.

Fehr, B., Samsom, D., and Paulhus, D. L. (1992). The construct of

Machiavellianism: Twenty years later. In C. D. Spielberger and J. N. Butcher (Eds), *Advances in personality assessment* (Vol. 9). Hillsdale, N.J.: Lawrence Erlbaum.

Feldman, D. C. (1985). The new careerism: Origins, tenets, and consequences. *Industrial–Organizational Psychologist*, 22, 39–44.

Feldman, D. C. (1988). *Managing careers in organizations*. Glenview, Ill.: Scott, Foresman.

Feldman, D. C. (1990). Risky business: The recruitment, selection, and socialization of new managers in the twenty-first century. *Journal of Organizational Change Management*, 2, 16–29.

Feldman, D. C., and Klich, N. (1991). Impression management and career strategies. In R. A. Giacalone and P. Rosenfeld (Eds), *Applied impression management: How image-making affects managerial decisions*. Newbury Park, Calif.: Sage Publications, pp. 67–80.

Feldman, D. C., and Weitz, B. A. (1990). From the invisible hand to the glad hand: Understanding the antecedents and consequences of a careerist orientation to work. Unpublished manuscript.

Ferrari, J. R. (1991). A preference for favorable public impression by procrastinators: Selecting among cognitive and social tasks. *Personality and Individual Differences*, 12, 1233–1237.

Ferrari, J. R. (1992). Procrastinators and perfect behavior: An exploratory factor analysis of self-presentation, self-awareness, and self-handicapping components. *Journal of Research in Personality*, 26, 75–84.

Ferris, G. R., King, T. R., Judge, T. A., and Kacmar, K. M. (1991). The management of shared meaning in organizations: Opportunism in the reflection of attitudes, beliefs, and values. In R. A. Giacalone and P. Rosenfeld (Eds), *Applied impression management: How image-making affects managerial decisions*. Newbury Park, Calif.: Sage Publications, pp. 41–66.

Ferris, G. R., and Mitchell, T. R. (1987). The components of social influence and their importance for human resources research. In K. M. Rowland and G. R. Ferris (Eds), *Research in personnel and human resources management*. Greenwich, Conn.: JAI Press, pp. 103–128.

Ferris, G. R., Russ, G. S., and Fandt, P. M. (1989). Politics in organizations. In R. A. Giacalone and P. Rosenfeld (Eds), *Impression management in the organization*. Hillsdale, N.J.: Lawrence Erlbaum Associates, pp. 143–170.

Finch, J. F., and Cialdini, R. B. (1989). Another indirect tactic of (self-) image management: Boosting. *Personality and Social Psychology Bulletin*, 15, 222–232.

Fletcher, C. (1989). Impression management in the selection interview. In R. A. Giacalone and P. Rosenfeld (Eds), *Impression management in the organization*. Hillsdale, N.J.: Lawrence Erlbaum Associates, pp. 269–281.

Fletcher, C. (1990). The relationship between candidate personality, self-presentation strategies, and interviewer assessments in selection interviews: An empirical study. *Human Relations*, 43, 739–749.

Fletcher, C. (1992). Ethical issues in the selection interview. *Journal of Business Ethics*, 11, 362–367.

"For California cow, one caricature too many" (1993, December 12). *New York Times*, p. A-12.

Forsyth, D. R., Riess, M., and Schlenker, B. R. (1977). Impression management concerns governing reactions to a faulty decision. *Representative Research in Social Psychology*, 8, 12–22.

Freiberg, P. (1991, March). Black men may act cool to advertise masculinity. *APA Monitor*, 22, 30.

Furnham, A. (1992). *Personality at work: The role of individual differences in the workplace*. London: Routledge.

Gabrenya, W. K., and Arkin, R. M. (1980). Factor structure and factor correlates of the self-monitoring scale. *Personality and Social Psychology Bulletin*, 6, 13–22.

Gardner, W. L., and Martinko, M. J. (1988). Impression management in organizations. *Journal of Management*, 14, 321–328.

Garland, H., and Beard, J. F. (1979). The relationship between self-monitoring and leader emergence across two task situations. *Journal of Applied Psychology*, 64, 72–76.

Garretson, P., and Teel, K. S. (1982). The exit interview: Effective tool or meaningless gesture? *Personnel*, 4, 70–77.

Garrison, L., and Ferguson, J. (1977). Separation interviews. *Personnel Journal*, 56, 438–442.

Geier, T., and Hawkins, D. (1993, December 20). Outlook: Eye on the '90s. *U.S. News & World Report*, p. 12.

Giacalone, R. A. (1985). On slipping when you thought you had put your best foot forward: Self-promotion, self-destruction, and entitlements. *Group and Organization Studies*, 10, 61–80.

Giacalone, R. A. (1987). Management, sex, and symbolic association/disassociation following success and failure. *Basic and Applied Social Psychology*, 1&2, 45–56.

Giacalone, R. A. (1988). The effects of administrative accounts and gender on the perception of leadership. *Group and Organization Studies*, 13, 195–207.

Giacalone, R. A. (1989). Image control: The strategies of impression management. *Personnel*, May, 52–55.

Giacalone, R. A., and Beard, J. W. (1994). Impression management, diversity and international management. *American Behavioral Scientist*, 37, 621–636.

Giacalone, R. A., and Duhon, D. (1991). Assessing intended employee behavior in exit interviews. *Journal of Psychology: Interdisciplinary and Applied*, 125, 83–90.

Giacalone, R. A., Elig, T. W., Ginexi, E. M., and Bright, A. J. (1993). The impact of identification and type of separation on measures of satisfaction and missing data in the exit survey process. Unpublished manuscript, University of Richmond, Richmond, Va.

Giacalone, R. A., and Falvo, R. (1985, August). Self-presentation, self-monitoring, and organizational commitment. Paper presented at the

93rd Annual Meeting of the American Psychological Association, Los Angeles, Calif.

Giacolone, R. A., and Knouse, S. B. (1988). Males' attitudes toward women and symbolic association/disassociation with female managers. *Basic and Applied Social Psychology*, 9, 289–300.

Giacalone, R. A., and Knouse, S. B. (1989). Farewell to fruitless exit interviews. *Personnel*, 66, 60–62.

Giacalone, R. A., and Knouse, S. B. (1990). Justifying wrongful employee behavior: The role of personality in organizational sabotage. *Journal of Business Ethics*, 9, 55–61.

Giacalone, R. A., Knouse, S. B., and Ashworth, D. N. (1991). Impression management and exit interview distortion. In R. A. Giacalone and P. Rosenfeld (Eds), *Applied impression management: How image-making affects managerial decisions*. Newbury Park, Calif.: Sage Publications, pp. 97–107.

Giacalone, R. A., and Payne, S. L. (in press). Punishment for employee ethical infractions: Impression management effects in historical context. *Journal of Business Ethics*.

Giacalone, R. A., and Pollard, H. G. (1987). The efficacy of accounts for a breach of confidentiality by management. *Journal of Business Ethics*, 6, 19–23.

Giacalone, R. A., and Pollard, H. G. (1989). Comparative effectiveness of impression management tactics on the recommendation of grievant punishment: An exploratory investigation. *Forensic Reports*, 2, 147–160.

Giacalone, R. A., and Pollard, H. G. (1990). Acceptance of managerial accounts for unethical supervisory behavior. *Journal of Social Psychology*, 130, 103–111.

Giacalone, R. A., Pollard, H. G., and Brannen, D. (1989). The role of forensic factors and grievant impression management on labor arbitration decisions. In R. A. Giacalone and P. Rosenfeld (Eds), *Impression management in the organization*. Hillsdale, N.J.: Lawrence Erlbaum Associates, pp. 315–326.

Giacalone, R. A., Pollard, H. G., and Eylon, D. (1994). Beyond contractual interpretation: Bias in arbitrators' case perceptions and recommendation of awards. Unpublished manuscript, University of Richmond, Richmond, Va.

Giacalone, R. A., Reiner, M. L., and Goodwin, J. (1992). Ethical concerns in grievance arbitration. *Journal of Business Ethics*, 11, 267–272.

Giacalone, R. A., and Riordan, C. A. (1990). Effect of self-presentation on perceptions and recognition in an organization. *Journal of Psychology*, 124, 25–38.

Giacalone, R. A., and Rosenfeld, P. (1984). The effect of perceived planning and propriety on the effectiveness of leadership accounts. *Social Behavior and Personality*, 12, 217–224.

Giacalone, R. A., and Rosenfeld, P. (1986). Self-presentation and self-promotion in an organizational setting. *Journal of Social Psychology*, 126, 321–326.

Giacalone, R. A., and Rosenfeld, P. (1987). Justification and procedures for implementing institutional review boards in organizations. *Journal of Business Ethics*, 6, 5–17.

Giacalone, R. A., and Rosenfeld, P. (Eds) (1989). *Impression management in the organization.* Hillsdale, N.J.: Lawrence Erlbaum Associates.

Giacalone, R. A., and Rosenfeld, P. (Eds) (1991). *Applied impression management: How image-making affects managerial decisions.* Newbury Park, Calif.: Sage Publications.

Gilbert, D. T., and Jones, E. E. (1986). Exemplification: The self-presentation of moral character. *Journal of Personality*, 54, 593–615.

Gilmore, D. C., and Ferris, G. R. (1989a). The effects of applicant impression management tactics on interviewer judgments. *Journal of Management*, 15, 557–564.

Gilmore, D. C., and Ferris, G. R. (1989b). The politics of the employment interview. In R. W. Eder and G. R. Ferris (Eds), *The employment interview: Theory, research, practice.* Newbury Park, Calif.: Sage Publications, pp. 195–203.

Ginzel, L. E. (1994). The impact of biased inquiry strategies on performance judgments. *Organizational Behavior and Human Decision Processes*, 57, 1–19.

Ginzel, L. E., Kramer, R. M., and Sutton, R. I. (1993). Organizational impression management as a reciprocal influence process: The neglected role of organizational audience. *Research in Organizational Behavior*, 15, 227–266.

Godfrey, D. K., Jones, E. E., and Lord, C. G. (1986). Self-promotion is not ingratiating. *Journal of Personality and Social Psychology*, 50, 106–115.

Goffman, E. (1959). *The presentation of self in everyday life.* Garden City, N.Y.: Doubleday Anchor.

Goffman, E. (1962). On cooling out the mark: Some aspects of adaptation to failure. In A. M. Rose (Ed.), *Human behavior and social processes: An interactionist approach.* Boston: Houghton Mifflin Company, pp. 482–505.

Goffman, E. (1971). *Relations in public.* New York: Harper & Row.

Goldstein, I. L. (1971). The application blank: How honest are the responses? *Journal of Applied Personality*, 55, 491–492.

Good, L. R., and Good, K. C. (1973). An objective measure of the motive to avoid appearing incompetent. *Psychological Reports*, 32, 1075–1077.

Goodale, J. G. (1982). *The fine art of interviewing.* Englewood Cliffs, N.J.: Prentice-Hall.

Goodwin, C., and Ross, I. (1992). Consumer responses to service failures: Influence of procedural and interactional fairness perceptions. *Journal of Business Research*, 25, 149–163.

Gordon, L. V., and Stapleton, E. S. (1956). Fakability of a forced-choice personality test under realistic high school employment conditions. *Journal of Applied Psychology*, 40, 258–262.

Gould, S., and Penley, L. E. (1984). Career strategies and salary progression: A study of their relationships in a municipal bureaucracy. *Organizational Behavior and Human Performance*, 34, 244–265.

Gouldner, A. W. (1960). The norm of reciprocity: A preliminary statement. *American Sociological Review*, 25, 161–178.

Gove, W. R., Hughes, M., and Geerkin, M. R. (1980). Playing dumb: A form of impression management with undesirable side effects. *Social Psychology Quarterly*, 43, 89–102.

Greenberg, J. (1990). Employee theft as a reaction to underpayment inequity: The hidden cost of pay cuts. *Journal of Applied Psychology*, 75, 561–568.

Greenberg, J., Bies, R. J., and Eskew, D. E. (1991). Establishing fairness in the eye of the beholder: Managing impressions of organizational justice. In R. A. Giacalone and P. Rosenfeld (Eds), *Applied impression management: How image-making affects managerial decisions.* Newbury Park, Calif.: Sage Publications, pp. 111–132.

Habenstein, R. W. (1962). Sociology of occupations: The case of the American funeral director. In A. M. Rose (Ed.), *Human behavior and social processes: An interactionist approach.* Boston: Houghton Mifflin Company, pp. 225–246.

Halle, L. J. (1965). *The society of man.* New York: Harper & Row.

Hamashige, H. (1994, October 29). Club's ongoing success speaks volumes. *Los Angeles Times*, pp. A1, A16, A18.

Hatton, D. E., Snortum, J. R., and Oskamp, S. (1971). The effects of biasing information and dogmatism upon witness testimony. *Psychonomic Science*, 23, 425–427.

Hedges, S. J., Walsh, K. T., and Headden, S. (1994, Jan 17). The Whitewater files. *U.S. News and World Report*, p. 43.

Henderson, M., and Hewstone, M. (1984). Prison inmates' explanations for interpersonal violence: Accounts and attributions. *Journal of Consulting and Clinical Psychology*, 52, 789–794.

Hendricks, M., and Brickman, P. (1974). Effects of status and knowledgeability of audience on self-presentation. *Sociometry*, 37, 440–449.

Heneman, H. G., III, and Sandver, M. G. (1983). Arbitrators' backgrounds and behavior. *Journal of Labor Research*, 4, 115.

Hewitt, J. P., and Hall, P. M. (1973). Social problems, problematic situations, and quasi-theories. *American Sociological Review*, 38, 367–374.

Hewitt, J., and Stokes, R. (1975). Disclaimers. *American Sociological Review*, 40, 1–11.

Hewstone, M., and Brown, R. (Eds) (1986). *Contact and conflict in intergroup encounters.* Oxford/New York: Basil Blackwell.

Hiestand, M. (1991, January 15). Even reputations can be insured. *USA Today*, p. C2.

Hill, M. F., Jr., and Sinicropi, A. V. (1987). *Evidence in arbitration.* BNA Books, Arbitration Series.

Hinkin, T. R., and Schriesheim, C. A. (1989). Development and application of new scales to measure the French and Raven (1959) bases of social power. *Journal of Applied Psychology*, 74, 561–567.

Hinrichs, J. H. (1975). Measurement of reasons for resignation of professionals: Questionnaire versus company and consultant exit interviews. *Journal of Applied Psychology*, 60, 530–532.

Hollander, E. P. (1958). Conformity, status, and idiosyncrasy credit. *Psychological Review*, 65, 117–127.

Holtgraves, T. (1992). The linguistic realization of face management: Implications for language production and comprehension, person perception, and cross-cultural communication. *Social Psychology Quarterly*, 55, 141–159.

Hosseini, J. C., and Armacost, R. L. (1993). Gathering sensitive data in organizations. In P. Rosenfeld, J. E. Edwards and M. D. Thomas (Eds), *Improving organizational surveys: New directions, methods and applications*. Newbury Park, Calif.: Sage Publications, pp. 29–50.

Hu, D. H. (1944). The Chinese concepts of face. *American Anthropologist*, 46, 45–64.

Huber, V., Latham, G., and Locke, E. (1989). The management of impressions through goal setting. In R. A. Giacalone and P. Rosenfeld (Eds), *Impression management in the organization*. Hillsdale, N.J.: Lawrence Erlbaum Associates, pp. 203–218.

Iacocca, L. (1984). *Iacocca: An autobiography*. Toronto: Bantam Books.

Ickes, W., Reidhead, S., and Patterson, M. (1986). Machiavellianism and self-monitoring: As different as "me" and "you." *Social Cognition*, 4, 58–74.

Jablonsky, W. A. (1975). How useful are exit interviews? *Supervisory Management*, 20(5), 8–14.

James, W. (1890). *Principles of psychology*. New York: Holt.

Jellison, J. M., and Gentry, K. W. (1978). A self-presentation interpretation of the seeking of social approval. *Personality and Social Psychology Bulletin*, 4, 227–230.

Jenkins, H. G., and Carr, J. R. (Winter 1991–1992). Valuing differences and managing diversity: Introduction to the forum. *The Bureaucrat*, 20, 8–9.

Johnson, D. (1987, Dec. 13). At 75, Carnegie's message lives on. *NY Times*, p. A28.

Jones, E. E. (1964). *Ingratiation: A social psychological analysis*. New York: Appleton-Century-Crofts.

Jones, E. E. (1990). *Interpersonal perception*. W. H. Freeman and Company: New York.

Jones, E. E., Brenner, K. J., and Knight, J. S. (1990). When failure elevates self-esteem. *Personality and Social Psychology Bulletin*, 16, 209–220.

Jones, E. E., Gergen, K. J., Gumpert, P., and Thibaut, J. W. (1965). Some conditions affecting the use of ingratiation to influence performance evaluation. *Journal of Personality and Social Psychology*, 1, 613–625.

Jones, E. E., Jones, R. G., and Gergen, K. J. (1963). Some conditions affecting the evaluation of a conformist. *Journal of Personality*, 31, 270–288.

Jones, E. E., and Pittman, T. S. (1982). Toward a general theory of strategic self-presentation. In J. Suls (Ed.), *Psychological perspectives on the self* (Vol. 1). Hillsdale, N.J.: Lawrence Erlbaum Associates, pp. 231–262.

Jones, E. E., and Rhodewalt, F. (1982). *The self-handicapping scale*. Unpublished scale, Princeton University.

Jones, E. E., and Sigall, H. (1971). The bogus pipeline. A new paradigm for measuring affect and attitudes. *Psychological Bulletin*, 76, 349–364.

Jones, E. E., and Wortman, C. B. (1973). *Ingratiation: An attributional approach*. Morristown, N.J.: General Learning Press.

Judge, T. A., and Bretz, R. D. (1994). Political influence behavior and career success. *Journal of Management*, 20, 43–65.

Jung, J. (1987). Anticipatory excuses in relation to expected versus actual task performance. *Journal of Psychology*, 121, 413–421.

Kacmar, K. M., and Carlson, D. S. (1994). Using impression management in women's job search processes. *American Behavioral Scientist*, 37, 682–696.

Kacmar, K., Delery, J. E., and Ferris, G. R. (1992). Differential effectiveness of applicant impression management tactics on employment interview decisions. *Journal of Applied Social Psychology*, 22, 1250–1272.

Kalab, K. A. (1987). Student vocabularies of motive: Accounts for absence. *Symbolic Interaction*, 10, 71–83.

Kalven, H., and Zeisel, H. (1966). *The American jury*. Chicago: University of Chicago Press.

Kennedy, J., and Everest, A. (1991, September) Put diversity in context. *Personnel Journal*, 70, 50–54.

Kipnis, D., and Vanderveer, R. (1971). Ingratiation and the use of power. *Journal of Personality and Social Psychology*, 17, 280–286.

Knapp, M. L., Stafford, L., and Daly, J. A. (1986). Regrettable messages: Things people wish they hadn't said. *Journal of Communication*, 36, 40–59.

Knouse, S. B. (1989). Impression management and the letter of recommendation. In R. A. Giacalone and P. Rosenfeld (Eds), *Impression management in the organization*. Hillsdale, N.J.: Lawrence Erlbaum Associates, pp. 283–296.

Knouse, S. B., and Giacalone, R. A. (1992a). Discussion willingness in the exit interview. *Canadian Journal of Administrative Sciences*, 9, 24–29.

Knouse, S. B., and Giacalone, R. A. (1992b). Ethical decision-making in business: Behavioral issues and concerns. *Journal of Business Ethics*, 11, 369–372.

Knouse, S. B., Giacalone, R. A., and Pollard, H. G. (1988). Impression management in the résumé and its cover letter. *Journal of Business and Psychology*, 3, 242–249.

Knouse, S. B., Rosenfeld, P., and Culbertson, A. L. (Eds) (1992). *Hispanics in the workplace*. Newbury Park, Calif.: Sage Publications.

Korda, M. (1975). *Power: How to get it, how to use it*. New York: Ballantine.

Kuhn, M. H. (1964). The interview and the professional relationship. In A. M. Rose (Ed.), *Human behavior and social processes: An interactionist approach*. Boston: Houghton Mifflin Company, pp. 193–297.

Kumar, K., and Beyerlein, M. (1991). Construction and validation of an instrument for measuring ingratiatory behaviors in organizational settings. *Journal of Applied Psychology*, 76, 619–627.

Larwood, L. (1991). Start with a rational group of people ... Gender effects of impression management in organizations. In R. A. Giacalone and P. Rosenfeld (Eds), *Applied impression management: How image-making affects managerial decisions.* Newbury Park, Calif.: Sage Publications, pp. 177–194.

Latham, V. M. (1985, May). The role of personality in the job search process. Paper presented at the annual meetings of the Midwestern Psychological Association, Chicago, Ill.

Lautenschlager, G. J., and Flaherty, V. L. (1990). Computer administration of questions: More desirable or more social desirability? *Journal of Applied Psychology,* 75, 310–314.

Lay, C. H., Knish, S., and Zanatta, R. (1992). Self-handicappers and procrastinators: A comparison of their practice behavior prior to an evaluation. *Journal of Research in Personality,* 26, 242–257.

Lazare, A. (1995). Go ahead, say you're sorry. *Psychology Today,* Jan/Feb, 40–43, 76, 78.

Leary, M. R. (1983a). A brief version of the fear of negative evaluation scale. *Personality and Social Psychology Bulletin,* 9, 371–376.

Leary, M. R. (1983b). Social anxiousness: The construct and its measurement. *Journal of Personality Assessment,* 47, 66–75.

Leary, M. R. (1989). Self-presentational processes in leadership emergence and effectiveness. In R. A. Giacalone and P. Rosenfeld (Eds), *Impression management in the organization.* Hillsdale, N.J.: Lawrence Erlbaum Associates, pp. 363–374.

Leary, M. R. (1992). Self-presentational processes in exercise and sport. *Journal of Sport and Exercise Psychology,* 14, 339–351.

Leary, M. R. (1993). The interplay of private self processes and interpersonal factors in self-presentation. In J. Suls (Ed.), *Psychological perspectives on the self: The self in social perspective* (Vol. 4). Hillsdale, N.J.: Lawrence Erlbaum Associates, pp. 127–155.

Leary, M. R., and Kowalski, R. M. (1990). Impression management: A literature review and two component model. *Psychological Bulletin,* 107, 34–47.

Leary, M. R., and Kowalski, R. M. (1993). The interaction anxiousness scale: Construct and criterion-related validity. *Journal of Personality Assessment,* 61, 136–146.

Leary, M. R., Robertson, R. B., Barnes, B. D., and Miller, R. S. (1986). Self-presentation of small group leaders as a function of role requirements and leadership orientation. *Journal of Personality and Social Psychology,* 51, 742–748.

Leary, M. R., and Schlenker, B. R. (1980). Self-presentation in a task-oriented leadership situation. *Representative Research in Social Psychology,* 11, 152–159.

Lefkowitz, J., and Katz, M. L. (1969). Validity of exit interviews. *Personnel Psychology,* 22, 445–455.

Levinson, D. J. (1978). *The seasons of a man's life.* New York: Ballantine.

Liden, R. C., Martin, C. L., and Parson, C. K. (1993). Interviewer and applicant behaviors in employment interviews. *Academy of Management Journal,* 36, 372–386.

Liden, R. C., and Mitchell, T. R. (1988). Ingratiatory behaviors in organizational settings. *Academy of Management Review*, 13, 572–587.

Lipsky, M. (1980). *Street-level bureaucracy: Dilemmas of the individual in public services*. New York: Russell Sage Foundation.

Luthans, F., and Kreitner, R. (1985). *Organizational behavior modification and beyond*. Glenview, Ill.: Scott, Foresman.

Lutz, W. (1989). *Doublespeak*. New York: Harper/Perennial.

McCall, M. W., Lombardo, M. M., and Morrison, A. M. (1988). *The lessons of experience*. Lexington, Mass.: Lexington.

McCroskey, J. C. (1992). Reliability and validity of the willingness to communicate scale. *Communication Quarterly*, 40, 16–25.

McGraw, K. M. (1991). Managing blame: An experimental test of the effects of political accounts. *American Political Science Review*, 85, 1133–1157.

Maddux, J. E., Norton, L. W., and Leary, M. R. (1988). Cognitive components of social anxiety: An investigation of the integration of self-presentation theory and self-efficacy theory. *Journal of Social and Clinical Psychology*, 6, 180–190.

Martinko, M. J. (1991). Future directions: Toward a model for applying impression management strategies in the workplace. In R. A. Giacalone and P. Rosenfeld (Eds), *Applied impression management: How image-making affects managerial decisions*. Newbury Park, Calif.: Sage Publications, pp. 259–277.

Mayes, B. T., and Allen, R. W. (1977). Toward a definition of organizational politics. *Academy of Management Review*, 2, 672–678.

Mendenhall, M. E., and Wiley, C. (1994). Strangers in a strange land: The relationship between expatriate adjustment and impression management. *American Behavioral Scientist*, 37, 605–620.

Merton, R. K. (1948). The self-fulfilling prophecy. *Antioch Review*, 8, 193–210.

Miller, A., Smith, V. E., and Mabry, M. (1992, November 23). Shooting the messenger?: How Food Lion handled a damaging TV exposé. *Newsweek*, p. 51.

Millham, J., and Jacobson, L. I. (1978). The need for approval. In H. London and J. E. Exner (Eds), *Dimension of personality*. New York: Wiley, pp. 365–390.

Mills, C. W. (1940). Situation identities and vocabularies of motive. *American Sociological Review*, 5, 904–915.

Moberg, D. J. (1989). The ethics of impression management. In R. A. Giacalone and P. Rosenfeld (Eds), *Impression management in the organization*. Hillsdale, N.J.: Lawrence Erlbaum, pp. 171–187.

Molloy, J. T. (1978). *Dress for Success*. New York: Warner.

Moorman, R. H., and Podsakoff, P. M. (1992). A meta-analytic review and empirical test of the potential of confounding effects of social desirability response sets in organizational behavior research. *Journal of Occupational and Organizational Psychology*, 65, 131–149.

Morgan, D. F. (1987). Varieties of administrative abuse: Some reflections on ethics and discretion. *Administration & Society*, 19, 267–284.

Nelson, N. E., and Curry, E. M., Jr., (1981). Arbitrator characteristics and arbitral decisions. *Industrial Relations*, 20, 316.

O'Brien, G. (1993). Sucking up: Today getting ahead is a rearguard action. *Playboy*, 40, pp. 144, 146.

Odom, M. (1993, August 12). Kissing up really works on boss. *San Diego Union-Tribune*, p. E-12.

Ornstein, S. (1989). Impression management through office design. In R. A. Giacalone and P. Rosenfeld (Eds), *Impression management in the organization.* Hillsdale, N.J.: Lawrence Erlbaum Associates, pp. 411–426.

Overstreet, J. (1994, Oct 17), How to be a better negotiator. *USA Today*, p. 2B.

Pandey, J., and Kakkar, S. (1982). Supervisor's affect: Attraction and positive evaluation as a function of other-enhancement. *Psychological Reports*, 50, 479–486.

Pandey, J., and Rastogi, R. (1979). Machiavellianism and ingratiation. *Journal of Social Psychology*, 108, 221–225.

Pandey, J., and Singh, P. (1987). Effects of Machiavellianism, other-enhancement, and power-position on affect, power-feeling, and evaluation of the ingratiator. *Journal of Psychology*, 12, 287–300.

Parkinson, M. G. (1979, July). Language behavior and courtroom success. Paper presented at the Annual Meeting of the British Psychological Society, Bristol.

Paulhus, D. L. (1984). Two-component models of social desirable responding. *Journal of Personality and Social Psychology*, 46, 598–609.

Paulhus, D. L. (1988). Assessing self-deception and impression management in self-reports: The Balanced Inventory of Desirable Responding. Unpublished manual. University of British Columbia, Vancouver, Canada.

Paulhus, D. L. (1991). Measurement and control of response bias. In J. P. Robinson, P. R. Shaver, and L. S. Wrightsman (Eds), *Measurement of personality and social psychological attitudes.* San Diego: Academic Press, pp. 17–59.

Paulhus, D. L., Graf, P., and VanSelst, M. (1989). Attentional load increases the possibility of self-presentation. *Social Cognition*, 7, 389–400.

Payne, S. L. (1989). Self-presentational tactics and employee theft. In R. A. Giacalone and P. Rosenfeld (Eds), *Impression management in the organization.* Hillsdale, N.J.: Lawrence Erlbaum Associates, pp. 397–408.

Payne, S. L., and Giacalone, R. A. (1990). Social psychological approaches to the perception of ethical dilemmas. *Human Relations*, 43, 649–665.

Peters, T. J., and Waterman, R. H. (1982). *In search of excellence: Lessons from America's best run companies.* New York: Harper & Row.

Petras, R., and Petras, K. (1994). *The 776 even stupider things ever said.* New York: HarperCollins.

Pettigrew, A. (1973). *The politics of organizational decision-making.* London: Tavistock.

Pfeffer, J. (1981). *Power in organizations.* Boston: Pitman.

Pinker, S. (1994, September 25). Is there a gene for compassion? *New York Times Book Review*, pp. 3, 34.

Pryor, B., and Buchanan, R. W. (1984). The effects of a defendant's demeanor on juror perceptions of credibility and guilt. *Journal of Communication*, 24, 92–99.

Rafaeli, A., and Pratt, M. G. (1993). Tailored meanings: On the meaning and impact of organizational dress. *Academy of Management Review*, 18, 32–55.

Raia, A. (1985). Power, politics, and the human resource professional. *Human Resource Planning*, 4, 200–205.

Ralston, D. A. (1985). Employee ingratiation: The role of management. *Academy of Management Review*, 10, 477–487.

Ralston, D. A., and Elsass, P. M. (1989). Ingratiation and impression management in the organization. In R. A. Giacalone and P. Rosenfeld (Eds), *Impression management in the organization*. Hillsdale, N.J.: Lawrence Erlbaum Associates, pp. 235–249.

Ray, M. C., and Simons, R. L. (1987). Convicted murderers' accounts of their crimes: A study of homicide in small communities. *Symbolic Interaction*, 10, 57–70.

Rehmus, C. M. (1984). *Writing the Opinion*. Ithaca, N.Y.: ILR Press.

Rhodewalt, F., Saltzman, A. T., and Wittmer, J. (1984). Self-handicapping among competitive athletes: The role of practice in self-esteem protection. *Basic and Applied Social Psychology*, 5, 197–210.

Riess, M., and Rosenfeld, P. (1980). Seating preferences as nonverbal communication: A self-presentational analysis. *Journal of Applied Communications Research*, 8, 22–30.

Ringer, R. J. (1976). *Winning through intimidation*. Greenwich, Conn.: Fawcett.

Riordan, C. A. (1989). Images of corporate success. In R. A. Giacalone and P. Rosenfeld (Eds), *Impression management in the organization*. Hillsdale, N.J.: Lawrence Erlbaum Associates, pp. 87–104.

Riordan, C. A. (1993). A study of campus climate: Methodology and results. In J. Q. Adams and J. R. Welsch (Eds), *Multicultural education: Strategies for implementation in colleges and universities*. Macomb, Ill.: Illinois Staff and Curriculum Developers Association, pp. 113–124.

Riordan, C. A., Gross, T., and Maloney, C. C. (1994). Self-monitoring, gender and the personal consequences of impression management. *American Behavioral Scientist*, 37, 715–725.

Riordan, C. A., James, M. K., and Runzi, M. J. (1989). Explaining failures at work: An accounter's dilemma. *The Journal of General Psychology*, 116(2), 197–205.

Riordan, C. A., Marlin, N. A., and Kellogg, J. T. (1983). The effectiveness of accounts following transgression. *Social Psychology Quarterly*, 46, 213–219.

Rivera, A. N. (1976). Public versus private reactions to positive inequity. *Journal of Personality and Social Psychology*, 34, 895–900.

Roese, N. J., and Jamieson, D. W. (1993). Twenty years of bogus pipeline research: A critical review and meta-analysis. *Psychological Bulletin,* 113, 363–375.

Rosenfeld, P. (1990). Self-esteem and impression management explanations for self-serving biases. *Journal of Social Psychology,* 130, 495–500.

Rosenfeld, P. (in press). Impression management, fairness and the employment interview. *Journal of Business Ethics.*

Rosenfeld, P., Booth-Kewley, S., and Edwards, J. E. (1993). Computer-administered surveys in organizational settings: Alternative, advantages, applications. *American Behavioral Scientist,* 36, 485–511.

Rosenfeld, P., Booth-Kewley, S., Edwards, J. E., and Alderton, D. L (1994). Linking diversity and impression management: A study of Hispanic, Black and White Navy Recruits. *American Behavioral Scientist,* 37, 672–681.

Rosenfeld, P., Booth-Kewley, S., Edwards, J. E., and Thomas, M. D. (in press). Responses on computer surveys: Impression management, social desirability, and the Big Brother syndrome. *Computers in Human Behavior.*

Rosenfeld, P., Edwards, J. E., and Thomas, M. D. (Eds) (1993). *Improving organizational surveys: New directions, methods and applications.* Newbury Park, Calif.: Sage Publications.

Rosenfeld, P., and Garrison, M. (1991). *Instructor's resource manual to accompany "Psychology Today"* (7th edition). New York: McGraw-Hill.

Rosenfeld, P., and Giacalone, R. A. (1991). From extreme to mainstream: Applied impression management in organizations. In R. A. Giacalone and P. Rosenfeld (Eds), *Applied impression management: How image-making affects managerial decisions.* Newbury Park, Calif.: Sage Publications, pp. 3–12.

Rosenfeld, P., Giacalone, R., and Bond, M. (1983). The cross-cultural efficacy of entitlements in American and Hong Kong Chinese students. In J. B. Deregowski, S. Dziurawiec, and R. C. Annis (Eds), *Explications in cross-cultural psychology.* Lisse: Swets & Zeitlinger, pp. 266–269.

Rosenfeld, P., Giacalone, R. A., and Riordan, C. A. (1994). Impression management theory and diversity: Lessons for organizational behavior. *American Behavioral Scientist,* 37, 601–604.

Rosenfeld, P., Giacalone, R. A., and Riordan, C. A. (1995). Impression management. In N. Nicholson (Ed.), *Blackwell dictionary of organizational behavior.* Oxford, UK: Blackwell Publishers.

Rosenthal, R., and Jacobson, L. (1968). *Pygmalion in the classroom.* New York: Holt, Rinehart & Winston, Inc.

Rosenhan, D. L. (1973). On being sane in insane places. *Science,* 179, 250–258.

Ross, C. E., and Mirowsky, J. (1984). Socially desirable response and acquiescence in a cross-cultural survey of mental health. *Journal of Health and Social Behavior,* 25, 189–197.

Roth, D. L., Harris, R. N., and Snyder, C. R. (1988). An individual differences measure of attributive and repudiative tactics of favorable self-presentation. *Journal of Social and Clinical Psychology*, 6, 159–170.

Roth, D. L., Snyder, C. R., and Pace, L. M. (1986). Dimensions of favorable self-presentation. *Journal of Personality and Social Psychology*, 51, 867–874.

Rumsey, M. (1976). Effects of defendant background and remorse on sentencing judgments. *Journal of Applied Social Psychology*, 6, 247–259.

Russ, G. S. (1991). Symbolic communication and image management in organizations. In R. A. Giacalone and P. Rosenfeld (Eds), *Applied impression management: How image-making affects managerial decisions*. Newbury Park: Sage Publications, pp. 219–240.

Savitsky, J., and Sim, M. (1974). Trading emotions: Equity theory of reward and punishment. *Journal of Communication*, 24, 140–147.

Saxe, C. (1991). Science and the CQT Polygraph: A theoretical critique. *Integrative Physiological and Behavioral Science*, 26, 223–231.

Schlenker, B. R. (1975). Self-presentation: Managing the impression of consistency when reality interferes with self-enhancement. *Journal of Personality and Social Psychology*, 32, 1030–1037.

Schlenker, B. R. (1980). *Impression management: The self-concept, social identity, and interpersonal relations*. Monterey, Calif.: Brooks/Cole.

Schlenker, B. R., and Darby, B. W. (1981). The use of apologies in social predicaments. *Social Psychology Quarterly*, 44, 271–278.

Schlenker, B. R., and Leary, M. R. (1982). Social anxiety and self-presentation: A conceptualization and model. *Psychological Bulletin*, 92, 641–669.

Schlenker, B. R., and Weigold, M. F. (1992). Interpersonal processes involving impression regulation and management. *Annual Review of Psychology*, 43, 133–168.

Schmit, J., and Jones, D. (1994, September 12). How USAir coped with the crash. *USA Today*, pp. B1–B2.

Schonbach, P., and Kleibaumhuter, P. (1990). Severity of reproach and defensiveness of accounts. In M. J. Cody and M. L. McLaughlin (Eds), *The psychology of tactical communication*. Clevedon, UK: Multilingual Matters Ltd, pp. 229–243.

Schriesheim, C. A., and Hinkin, T. R. (1990). Influence tactics used by subordinates: A theoretical and empirical analysis and refinement of the Kipnis, Schmidt, and Wilkinson subscales. *Journal of Applied Psychology*, 75, 246–257.

Scott, M. B., and Lyman, S. M. (1968). Accounts. *American Sociological Review*, 33, 46–62.

Scully, D., and Marolla, J. (1984). Convicted rapists' vocabulary of motive: Excuses and justifications. *Social Problems*, 31, 530–544.

"Serial killer" (1994, March 30). *USA Today*, p. 3A.

Shaffer, D. R., and Sadowsky, C. (1979). Effects of withheld evidence on juridic decisions, II: Locus of withholding strategy. *Personality and Social Psychology Bulletin*, 5, 40–43.

Shapiro, L. (1994, Oct 10). Sexual desk jockeying. *Newsweek*, p. 59.

Shem, S. (1978). *The house of God*. New York: Dell.

Sherwood, A. (1983). Exit interviews: Don't just say goodbye. *Personnel Journal*, 62, 744–750.

Smith, A., and Davidson, J., Jr. (1983). Personality and situational variables in the evaluation screening process. Unpublished manuscript, Boston University and University of Utah.

Smith, D. S., and Strube, M. J. (1991). Self-protective tendencies as moderators of self-handicapping impressions. *Basic and Applied Social Psychology*, 12, 63–80.

Smith, T. W., Snyder, C. R., and Perkins, S. C. (1983). The self-serving function of hypochondriacal complaints: Physical symptoms as self-handicapping strategies. *Journal of Personality and Social Psychology*, 44, 787–797.

Snyder, C. R., Higgins, R. L., and Stucky, R. J. (1983). *Excuses: Masquerades in search of grace*. New York: Wiley.

Snyder, C. R., Lassegard, M., and Ford, C. E. (1986). Distancing after group success and failure: Basking in reflected glory and cutting off reflected failure. *Journal of Personality and Social Psychology*, 51, 382–388.

Snyder, M. (1974). Self-monitoring of expressive behavior. *Journal of Personality and Social Psychology*, 30, 526–537.

Snyder, M. (1987). *Public appearances, private realities: The psychology of self-monitoring*. New York: W.H. Freeman.

Snyder, M., Berscheid, E., and Matwychuk, A. (1988). Orientations toward personnel selection: Differential reliance on appearance and personality. *Journal of Personality and Social Psychology*, 54, 972–979.

Snyder, M., and Copeland, J. (1989). Self-monitoring processes in organizational settings. In R. A. Giacalone and P. Rosenfeld (Eds), *Impression management in the organization*. Hillsdale, N.J.: Lawrence Erlbaum Associates, pp. 7–19.

Snyder, M., and Gangstead, S. (1982). Choosing social situations: Two investigations of self-monitoring processes. *Journal of Personality and Social Psychology*, 43, 123–125.

Spector, P. E. (1975). Relationships of organizational frustration with reported behavioral reactions of employees. *Journal of Applied Psychology*, 60, 635–637.

St. Antoine, T. J. (1984). *Arbitration and the law*. Ithaca, N.Y.: ILR Press.

Steinbrook, R. (1992). The polygraph: A flawed diagnostic method. *New England Journal of Medicine*, 327, 122–123.

Stephens, M. (1992, August 23). To thine own selves be true. *Los Angeles Times Magazine*, pp. 40–42, 60–62.

Stokes, R., and Hewitt, J. P. (1976). Aligning actions. *American Sociological Review*, 41, 838–849.

Strube, M. J. (1986). An analysis of the self-handicapping scale. *Basic and Applied Social Psychology*, 7, 211–224.

Sykes, G., and Matza, D. (1957). Techniques of neutralization: A theory of delinquency. *American Journal of Sociology*, 22, 664–670.

Szwajkowski, E. (1992). Accounting for organizational misconduct. *Journal of Business Ethics*, 11, 401–411.

Tennen, H., and Affleck, G. (1991). Blaming others for threatening events. *Psychological Bulletin*, 108, 209–232.

Tetlock, P. E., and Manstead, A. S. R. (1985). Impression management versus intrapsychic explanations in social psychology: A useful dichotomy? *Psychological Review*, 92, 59–77.

Tice, D. M., and Baumeister, R. F. (1990). Self-esteem, self-handicapping, and self-presentation: The strategy of inadequate practice. *Journal of Personality*, 58, 443–464.

Tuohy, W. (1993, December 19). BBC to air Mao documentary over China's objections. *Los Angeles Times*, p. A-4.

Ungar, S. (1981). The effects of others' expectations on the fabrication of opinions. *The Journal of Social Psychology*, 114, 173–185.

Velasquez, M., Moberg, D. J., and Cavanaugh, G. F. (1983, autumn). Organizational statesmanship and dirty politics: Ethical guidelines for the organizational politician. *Organizational Dynamics*, 65–80.

Villanova, P., and Bernardin, H. J. (1989). Impression management in the context of performance appraisal. In R. A. Giacalone and P. Rosenfeld (Eds), *Impression management in the organization*. Hillsdale, N.J.: Lawrence Erlbaum Associates, pp. 299–314.

Villanova, P., and Bernardin, H. J. (1991). Performance appraisal: The means, motive and opportunity to manage impressions. In R. A. Giacalone and P. Rosenfeld (Eds), *Applied impression management*. Newbury Park, Calif.: Sage, pp. 81–96.

Von Baeyer, C. L., Sherk, D. L., and Zanna, M. P. (1981). Impression management in the job interview. *Personality and Social Psychology Bulletin*, 7, 45–51.

Watson, O., and Friend, R. (1969). Measurement of social evaluative anxiety. *Journal of Consulting and Clinical Psychology*, 33, 448–457.

Watt, J. D. (1993). The impact of the frequency of ingratiation on the performance evaluation of bank personnel. *The Journal of Psychology*, 127, 171–177.

Wayne, S. J., and Ferris, G. R. (1990). Influence tactics, affect and exchange quality in supervisor–subordinate interactions: A laboratory experiment and field study. *Journal of Applied Psychology*, 75, 487–499.

Wayne, S. J. and Liden, R. C. (1995). Effects of impression management on performance rating: A longitudinal study. *Academy of Management Journal*, 38, 232–260.

Wayne, S. J., Liden, R. C., and Sparrowe, R. T. (1994). Developing leader member exchanges: The influence of gender and ingratiation. *American Behavioral Scientist*, 37, 697–714.

Weatherly, K., and Beach, L. R. (1994). Making the right impression. *Contemporary Psychology*, 39, 416–417.

Weber, S. J., and Cook, T. D. (1972). Subject effects in laboratory research: An examination of subject roles, demand characteristics, and valid inference. *Psychological Bulletin*, 77, 273–295.

Weiner, B., Amirkhan, J., Folkes, V. S., and Verette, J. A. (1987). An attributional analysis of excuse giving: Studies of naive theory of emotion. *Journal of Personality and Social Psychology*, 52, 316–324.

Weinstein, E. A., and Deutschberger, P. (1963). Some dimensions of altercasting. *Sociometry*, 26, 454–466.

Wexler, M. N. (1986). Impression management and the new competence. *Et cetera*, 20, 247–258.

Whrenberg, S. (1980). The exit interview: Why bother? *Supervising Management*, 5, 20–25.

Whyte, W. F. (1943). *Street corner society*. Chicago: The University of Chicago Press.

Williams, L. (1992, December 15). Companies capitalizing on worker diversity. *New York Times*, pp. A1, D20.

Wood, R. E., and Mitchell, T. E. (1981). Manager behavior in a social context: The impact of impression management on attributions and disciplinary actions. *Organizational Behavior and Human Performance*, 28, 356–378.

Woods, R. H., and Macauley, J. F. (1987). Exit interviews: How to turn a file filler into a management tool. *Cornell Hotel and Restaurant Administration Quarterly*, 28, 39–46.

Wortman, C. B., and Linsenmeier, J. A. W. (1977). Interpersonal attraction and techniques of ingratiation in organizational settings. In B. M. Staw and G. R. Salancik (Eds), *New directions in organizational behavior*. Chicago, Ill.: St Clair Press, pp. 133–178.

Wright, J. P. (1979). *On a clear day you can see General Motors*. New York: Avon.

Yandell, B. (1979). Those who protest too much are seen as guilty. *Personality and Social Psychology Bulletin*, 5, 44–47.

Zack, A.M. (1989). *Grievance arbitration*. Boston: Lexington Books.

Zarandona, J. L., and Camuso, M. A. (1985). A study of exit interviews: Does the last word count? *Personnel*, 62, 47–48.

Zerbe, W. J., and Paulhus, D. L. (1987). Socially desirable responding in organizational behavior: A reconception. *Academy of Management Review*, 12, 250–264.

Index